Small States, Smart Solutions

Small States, Smart Solutions

*Improving Connectivity and Increasing the
Effectiveness of Public Services*

Edgardo M. Favaro, Editor

THE WORLD BANK
Washington, DC

© 2008 The International Bank for Reconstruction and Development / The World Bank

1818 H Street, NW
Washington, DC 20433
Telephone 202-473-1000
Internet www.worldbank.org
E-mail feedback@worldbank.org

1 2 3 4 :: 11 10 09 08

This volume is a product of the staff of the International Bank for Reconstruction and Development / The World Bank. The findings, interpretations, and conclusions expressed in this volume do not necessarily reflect the views of the Executive Directors of The World Bank or the governments they represent.

The World Bank does not guarantee the accuracy of the data included in this work. The boundaries, colors, denominations, and other information shown on any map in this work do not imply any judgment on the part of The World Bank concerning the legal status of any territory or the endorsement or acceptance of such boundaries.

ISBN: 978-0-8213-7460-3
eISBN: 978-0-8213-7461-0
DOI: 10.1596/978-0-8213-7460-3

Cover artwork: *Abstraction*, Tamiz Etemadi. ©World Bank Art Program.

Library of Congress Cataloging-in-Publication Data has been applied for.

Contents

Figures

Tables

Boxes

Foreword

Small states face special hurdles in achieving development gains. These geographic disadvantages are well recognized. What is new and different is that there are valuable experiences concerning the ways and means of overcoming these impediments in certain areas. That is the focus of this volume.

This book is the result of a partnership between the World Bank and the Australian Agency for International Development (AusAID). It follows the path initiated by the Commonwealth Secretariat—World Bank Task Force on Small States a decade ago, which advocated the study of the distinctive development problems of small states.

The book examines how some small states use international trade and telecommunications technology to source services such as justice, banking supervision, public utilities regulation, high quality medicine, and education. Sourcing these services internationally is in sharp contrast with the reality of other countries where most of these services are nontradeable.

Studying this is of critical importance to small states. Forty-eight out of 185 members of the World Bank are small states, defined as countries with population below 2 million. High quality public services are an important aspect of development, but high-quality services are expensive to produce, especially when there are indivisibilities in production and capacity limitations.

Sourcing some public goods internationally fosters the bridging of domestic capacity limitations and accessing high quality services. But how do small states outsource the provision of these services? The case studies illustrate the historical context in which the outsourcing of public services has developed, the type of services that are more likely to be outsourced, and the complexity of the contractual structure required to govern the relationship between the service provider and the country client.

The most common model of outsourcing found is to a regional organization. The creation and operation of a regional body is facilitated when countries share a common culture, history, and language. Success is more difficult to achieve when a common historical background does not exist. Other forms of outsourcing—for instance to other countries, when there are special historical ties, or to international organizations—may also be viable.

The outsourcing of some public service provision is an attractive proposition for larger countries as well, especially for fragile states where institutions are weak. The international outsourcing of some services provision has been greatly facilitated by worldwide improvements in telecommunications technology. But sharing in these improvements requires investments in infrastructure and organization to create the necessary interfaces with the rest of the world.

There is some understanding of which public goods and institutions are important to development, but less understanding of how these institutions are built over time and what agenda is to be followed when these institutions are fledging or weak. An important development challenge is to identify shortcuts so that today's low- and middle-income countries do not have to undergo the same slow developing process taken by high-income countries to develop high-quality institutions. The case study methodology may contribute to this effort by reporting what states actually do to address their development problems, and how the institutions and policies they implement work over time.

It is hoped that this collection of country experiences will provide practical inspiration to small states seeking to convert both to global markets, to one another in specific regional circumstances, and will enable their governments to improve the lives of their citizenry.

Danny Leipziger
Vice President and Head
Poverty Reduction and Economic Management Network
The World Bank

Preface

The case studies collected in this volume arise from a project on small states—their economic growth, and their integration into the world economy—that was sponsored by the Australian Agency for International Development (AusAID) and the World Bank.

The case studies focus on specific attempts made by a number of small states to overcome the handicaps of their size and isolation and take advantage of growing opportunities for integration with their neighbors and with the rest of the world. Two policy issues have been of prime importance in that effort: how to reduce the costs and increase the effectiveness of public goods and services, and how to improve, and reduce the costs of, connectivity with the rest of the world.

The Introduction to this volume (chapter 1) outlines the recurrent issues and the main findings of the studies. The cases in section I focus on multicountry provision of regulatory services, and those in section II examine regulatory and organizational innovations aimed at improving connectivity. An appendix summarizes the principal findings from four in-depth regional studies on economic growth in small states in Africa, the Caribbean, Europe, and the Pacific that were produced to support the case studies.

The methodology used in the studies is closer to that of the business history literature (Chandler 1962) than to the tradition of modeling and econometric testing of hypotheses that dominates the economics literature.

The analytical framework is simple and is importantly influenced by the work of Karl R. Popper (Popper 1999). Policy and institutional reforms are seen as the result of an iterative problem-solving process: (a) identifying the initial problem and describing what policy options were available at the time of the reform; (b) identifying the main actors in the reform process and describing their role; (c) describing the institutional design and governance structure of the new institution or policy; (d) reporting on the implementation of the reform; and (e) reporting on changes to the original policy design introduced in response to new challenges (new iterations in the problem-solving process).

The case studies are based on interviews with government officers and citizens who have direct experience relevant to the design and development of agencies, institutions, or policies that address the problems involved.

A case study methodology has two advantages. First, case histories shed light on the factors that influence institutional design and on the development of institutions in small states—a clear plus when there is not much theory on which to base hypotheses and little data available for testing the hypotheses rigorously. Second, the method documents the transition from one institutional setting to another and helps identify problems that arise during the implementation of an institutional reform; this information is clearly valuable for policy makers.

A risk of the case study method is that inferences may be entirely driven by the selection of cases and that the lessons derived may be of limited applicability. To reduce this risk, more than one case was examined, generally, for each of the topics. Thus, section I, on outsourcing and cooperative provision of public services, examines the Eastern Caribbean Central Bank, the central banks of West and Central Africa, and the Eastern Caribbean Supreme Court. Similarly, section II, on information and communications technology (ICT) regulation and access, surveys Samoa telecommunications deregulation, the Eastern Caribbean Telecommunications Authority, the University of the South Pacific, and e-government in Cape Verde.

Additional research using the analytical framework and methodology devised for these studies would be extremely useful for enlarging the empirical base on institutional and policy reform issues in small states. Four promising areas can be identified:

- Failed initiatives—unsuccessful experiences with outsourcing public services to a multilateral organization, or ineffective reforms in the information and communications area.
- How small states use international cooperation to reduce the per-unit costs of physical infrastructure. (For example, the design of a road or a port serving more than one country can be improved through cooperation among the parties involved.)
- How small states cope with domestic limits on risk diversification.
- How market size and fixed costs influence the administrative costs of different tax and budgetary systems. Most public sector specialists recognize than decentralized budget execution encourages efficiency more that does centralized budget execution, but they seldom consider the costs associated with the transition from one system to the other and with the operation of a decentralized system. The case study on Samoa's budget reform in chapter 9 illustrates these difficulties.

Acknowledgments

I would like to thank Danny Leipziger, vice president and head of network, Poverty Reduction and Economic Management (PREM), at the World Bank, whose idea it was to undertake this study; Vikram Nehru, then director of the Economic Policy and Debt Department of the World Bank, who asked me to lead the task; Stephen Howes, then chief economist of the Australian Aid Agency (AUSAID), who enthusiastically supported the project and AUSAID who contributed to its financing.

Many of the ideas in the book were developed at the time I was lead economist in the Caribbean Department of the World Bank and then as member of the Commonwealth-World Bank Task Force on Small States. Orsalia Kalantzopoulos, then my boss at the Bank, first got me interested in the problems of small states and showed me ways in which institutions like the World Bank could best serve their needs.

The peer reviewers of this project, Orsalia Kalantzopoulos, K. Dwight Venner, and L. Alan Winters, were generous with their time and supportive of the project. In addition to providing ideas, Orsalia also suggested the title of this book.

I would like to thank:

- The management of the Eastern Caribbean Central Bank, the Central Bank of West Africa and the Central Bank of Central Africa, the Eastern Caribbean Supreme Court, the Eastern Caribbean Telecommunications Authority, the Operational Information Society Nucleus (NOSI) in Cape Verde, the University of the South Pacific, and the Ministry of Finance of Samoa. Without their support and candidness, writing the case studies would have been impossible;
- The authors of the papers—Christian Brachet, Dennis Byron, Maria Dakolias, Geoff Dixon, Ron Duncan, Naomi Halewood, James McMasters, Samia Melhem, Carlo M. Rossotto, David Peretz, Frits Van Beck, and Brian Winter—for their efforts to respect deadlines;
- Colleagues that have contributed with comments at different stages of the project: J.Adams, C.Anstey, N.Chamlou, A.Choksi, H.Codippily, P.Dongier, C.Eigen-Zucchi, S.Howes, O.Karazapan, A.Marcincin, A.Meltzer, D.Morrow, C. Mousset, T.O'Brien, D.Papageorgiou, N.Roberts, C.Sepulveda, G. Shepherd, P.T. Spiller, R.Stern, E.Vidal, and R.Zagha;
- Philippa Shepherd, an outstanding editor, who transformed a set of papers written in different styles into a presentable manuscript;
- The manager of PRMED, Carlos Primo Braga, for his support to complete this project;
- My counterparts at the World Bank's Office of the Publisher, Mark Ingebretsen and Stephen McGroarty, who guided me through the final stages of production of the book;
- Maria Abundo and Nancy Pinto who provided advice on budget issues; and
- My assistant, Debbie L. Sturgess, who handled contracts, seminar logistics, and the preparation of several manuscripts. She is dependable, efficient, and good-humored.

CHAPTER 1

Introduction

Edgardo Favaro and David Peretz

Studies of small states generally make the point that these countries face huge challenges of size and isolation, but they rarely go on to report what small states have done to overcome such limitations.[1]

This study takes a different tack. It focuses on two policy areas: (a) the use of outsourcing of government functions as a means of reducing the costs and improving the quality of some public goods and services, and (b) policies, institutions, and regulations designed to harness the power of information and telecommunications technology (ICT) to reduce the costs and improve the quality of connectivity with the rest of the world.

The problems underlying these policies are important. Small states spend 3.7 percentage points more of their gross domestic product (GDP) on producing public goods and services than do larger states (see table 1.1). The gap mainly reflects the higher costs of producing public goods, originating from indivisibilities in production and the small size of the domestic market (Alesina and Wacziarg 1998). For instance, the cost of operating a telecommunications regulator is probably much the same

Edgardo Favaro is a Lead Economist at the World Bank. David Peretz is a consultant to the World Bank.

Table 1.1. Ratio of Government Consumption and of Telecommunications to GDP in Small States and in Larger States

Ratio	Small states	Larger states
Government consumption/GDP	19.4	15.7
Telecom revenue/GDP	4.5	3.5

Source: World Bank (2007); ITU (2007).

for Samoa, with 200,000 inhabitants, as for a country with a population several times larger; the per unit cost of regulatory services is therefore much higher in Samoa than in a larger state. The public services cost differential has an adverse impact on per capita income through its effect on overall productivity and, indirectly, on incentives to accumulate physical and human capital. If the provision of public services could be organized in a way that reduces costs by 5 percent, there could be a nontrivial saving of 1 percent of per capita income.

Similarly, small states spend 1 percentage point of GDP more than do larger states on telephone services, principally because of noncompetitive monopoly market structures. The cost of these monopolies, in terms of forgone consumption and slower introduction of new goods and new production technologies, is enormous, especially for small, isolated states that could take advantage of lower communications costs to offset high transportation costs (Goolsbee 2006). High telecommunication costs are especially damaging for isolated small states. (On the impact of distance on small states' incomes, see Winters and Martins [2004].)

The case studies in chapters 2 through 9 describe what certain small states have done to deal with these issues and how countries have addressed specific problems in their particular contexts. (See the section "The Organization of This Book," later in this chapter.)

Characteristics of Small States

Most of the world's small states are very young, having achieved independence in the past 50 years. Of the 47 countries listed in box 1.1, 41 became independent after 1961, and 27 did so after 1970.[2] Political independence meant that services formerly provided through colonial institutions had to be supplied by fledgling national institutions. Several cases studied in this book illustrate the problems involved in this transition.

There have always been questions about the implications of a small domestic market for small states' incomes and growth. A small domestic market limits capacity to exploit economies of scale and diversify risk.

Box 1.1

A Roster of Small States

Listed in the table are the 48 small states that are members of the World Bank. (As defined here, small states are sovereign countries with populations of less than 2 million.) Most of these states are located in three regions: Africa, East Asia and the Pacific, and Latin America and the Caribbean. Thirty-one are islands. Several small states, including the Cook Islands, Nauru, Niue, and Tuvalu, are not members of the World Bank.

Small States among World Bank Members

Africa	East Asia and the Pacific	Latin America and the Caribbean	Europe, Middle East, and South Asia
Botswana	Brunei	Antigua and Barbuda	Bahrain
Cape Verde	Fiji	Bahamas, The	Bhutan
Comoros	Kiribati	Barbados	Cyprus
Djibouti	Marshall Islands	Belize	Estonia
Equatorial	Micronesia,	Dominica	Iceland
Guinea	Federated	Grenada	Luxembourg
Gabon	States of	Guyana	Maldives
Gambia, The	Palau	St. Kitts and Nevis	Malta
Guinea-Bissau	Samoa	St. Lucia	Montenegro
Lesotho	Solomon Islands	St. Vincent and	Qatar
Mauritius	Timor-Leste	the Grenadines	San Marino
Namibia	Tonga	Suriname	
São Tomé and	Vanuatu	Trinidad and Tobago	
Príncipe			
Seychelles			
Swaziland			

Source: Prepared by World Bank staff.

It implies, other things being equal, high per unit costs of production, especially in activities where fixed costs are significant (Kuznetz 1960); low capacity to adapt to shocks in international demand for exports; and low capacity to diversify risk within the economy. A small domestic market also usually implies specialization in production and exports, highly volatile rates of growth of GDP and consumption (Favaro 2005), and high shares of government consumption in GDP. Alesina and Wacziarg (1998) explain the high share of government consumption in GDP as an indicator of the high cost of production of public goods and services (see also Rodrik 1998).

This insight is further developed in Commonwealth Secretariat and World Bank (2000) and in Briguglio, Persaud, and Stern (2005).

Yet small states as a group do not have low incomes, nor are their growth rates lower, on average, than those of other countries (Favaro 2005). There are reasons (compensating factors) why this is so: the expansion of world trade; endowments of human and physical resources; the proximity of some small states to the main world markets; and the policies, institutions, and regulations some small states have adopted to facilitate integration into world markets.

The expansion of world trade has reduced the importance of domestic market size for development. Small states have actively used this channel, leading to a share of trade in GDP that is higher than in larger states (even after controlling for population size) (see table 1.2).

Other factors—a relative abundance of highly qualified human resources, as in Cyprus and Luxembourg; endowments of natural resources, as in Bahrain and Qatar; or a location close to important markets, as in Luxembourg and Slovenia—have helped offset the disadvantages of a small domestic market. But good policies, institutions, and regulations are needed to successfully exploit international trade opportunities, natural resources, or location. For instance, over the past three decades Lesotho and Mauritius effectively used industrial policy and trade preferences to facilitate the development of their manufacturing industries and to increase exports. Iceland's investments in port and marine infrastructure encouraged the development of its marine business. The Maldives' investments in infrastructure promoted the expansion of tourism. And in The Bahamas, Barbados, and Luxembourg, appropriate laws, institutions,

Table 1.2. Selected Indicators: Small States and Large States, 1986–2005

Country group	Fiscal burden (government consumption and expenditure as % of GDP)	Trade share (sum of exports and imports of goods and services as % of GDP)	Remittances (workers' remittances and compensation as % of GDP)
Small states (median)	19.8	114.4	3.0
Large states (median)	15.3	64.6	1.0

Source: Authors, World Bank (forthcoming).

and political and economic stability made possible the development of international financial centers.

The characteristics of small states outlined here are pertinent to the issues that are the focus of the case studies: policy and institutional reforms in the provision of public goods and services, and regulatory and technical innovations to improve connectivity.

Improving the Quality and Reducing the Cost of Public Services

Small market size affects the domestic production of many private goods and services, but such goods can often be imported. Public goods and services such as security, justice, and regulation of economic activity are another matter. Nevertheless, several small states (and larger states, as well) have pursued outsourcing in some guise, especially through cooperation with other countries.

Outsourcing and Transnational Cooperation

International outsourcing of intermediate goods and services by private firms has attracted increasing attention in recent years. The development of this type of commerce has been greatly facilitated by parallel improvements in the quality and reduction in the costs of telecommunications. Outsourcing of government functions, usually to regional organizations, has not received comparable attention.

Yet all states—not just small ones—have long used varieties of outsourcing to reduce some public sector costs. Many countries, in essence, outsource their defense through international treaties. The International Development Association (IDA) of the World Bank is an example of how developed countries have outsourced part of their budgets for international cooperation. Several countries around the world outsource monetary policy to other countries through fixed exchange rate systems or formal currency boards; examples are the Eastern Caribbean Central Bank, the South African Monetary Union, and the CFA franc zones in Central and West Africa. Countries may also outsource aspects of their legal systems by allowing appeals to, for example, the European Court of Justice or the United Kingdom Privy Council.

The international outsourcing of government functions presents unique challenges. For instance, an arm's-length relationship between the service provider and the client government augments the risk that the actions taken by the supplier may not represent the interests of the client government. (This risk is, in general, reduced when governments produce all public goods and services in-house.)

Several of the case studies illustrate what is perhaps the most common form of outsourcing: creating regional bodies to handle certain functions that would otherwise be carried out by individual states. Small states have been pioneers in this movement, as is seen in the three cases presented in part 1. These studies report on the origins and operations of selected regional bodies, the circumstances that led to the decision to outsource, the mechanisms used to align the incentives of the service provider with those of the government client, the evolution of the agreements over time, and the results achieved. They suggest that this type of cooperation works best in the following circumstances:

- *Historical or cultural ties already exist between the cooperating states.* A tradition of cooperation in central banking, justice, and civil aviation regulation existed among countries in the Eastern Caribbean region in the colonial era, and this tradition made it easier to develop formal mechanisms for cooperation after the countries became independent. Similarly, most of the countries that formed the central banks in Central and West Africa—the Banque des Etats de l'Afrique Centrale (BEAC) and the Banque Centrale des Etats de l'Afrique de l'Ouest (BCEAO)—were part of a colonial system that favored cooperation in central banking. By contrast, with the exception of the University of the South Pacific, cooperation has been less frequent among the island states of the Pacific, with their quite different cultures, languages, and colonial experiences.

- *What is outsourced is an advisory rather than an executive function.* In the Eastern Caribbean and in West and Central Africa, countries have delegated traditional functions of central banks, including supervision of the banking sector, to regional bodies. Governments in the Eastern Caribbean outsource regulation of telecommunications and civil aviation matters to regional institutions. In the Eastern Caribbean and in the Pacific, states cooperate in the provision of tertiary education. Outsourcing advisory functions, as distinguished from executive functions, raises less political resistance, as governments maintain their right to accept or reject the recommendations of the regional bodies. Understandably, governments are reluctant to delegate decisions that have budgetary implications.

- *The function requires technical expertise that is in short supply in the region.* Engineers with experience in telecommunications regulation are scarce in the Eastern Caribbean, and so pooling resources in a regional body, the Eastern Caribbean Telecommunications Authority (ECTEL), makes it easier to build up a center of knowledge for the subregion. Similarly, the support that countries in the Caribbean and the South Pacific have given to regional universities has widened access to tertiary education.

- *The service provider is subject to clear rules, and member countries abide by those rules.* The Eastern Caribbean Central Bank (ECCB) was set up as a central bank, but it retained some currency board characteristics and has in fact generally followed quasi–currency board practices. To insulate it from pressures to expand credit, its statutes place strict limits on the amounts of credit it can extend to individual member governments through a variety of prescribed instruments (van Beek et al. 2000). By contrast, the statutes of the Central and West African central banks were not equally effective in controlling expansion of credit to the development banks or the liberal use of rediscount mechanisms. The consequent excessive credit growth contributed to balance of payments crises in the 1980s.

- *Legislation and regulation among member countries are consistent.* Disharmony in the underlying banking legislation and regulations would greatly reduce the benefits from centralizing the regulatory function. A uniform legislative framework has been crucial for the efficient operation of the multicountry regulatory solution in the Eastern Caribbean. In Africa, in the aftermath of the 1980s financial crisis, countries embarked on a regional effort to harmonize their legal and regulatory frameworks for conduct of business.

- *There is a power imbalance between individual small states and regulated entities that a regional structure can help correct.* Cooperation among Eastern Caribbean countries was critical in the deregulation of telecommunications in the subregion and the opening of the market to competition.

The case studies also illustrate a number of other points:

- *The authority of multicountry institutions is much less dependent on formal political autonomy than might be expected.* It is usually argued that the autonomy of institutions such as the central bank, the supreme court, or regulatory offices is essential to their functioning. But in the cases studied, the regional bodies have been able to build considerable authority on the basis of technical reputation rather than formal autonomy.

- *Regional bodies that initially had mainly advisory roles can develop into de facto executive bodies if cooperation between countries is working well.* For instance, although the ECCB has no power to grant or cancel a bank license or to enforce sanctions on banks not in compliance with current rules, its advice is extremely influential in policy decisions by member countries.

- *An independent source of revenue reduces budget interference and helps build a high-quality civil service.* Central bank seigniorage, in the cases of the ECCB, the BEAC, and the BCEAO, and fees from managing the communications spectrum, as with ECTEL, limit day-to-day interference in budget management and help create a highly qualified cadre of civil servants. (Absence of an independent source of revenue, however, is not always a deterrent to the prestige and effectiveness of an institution, as is shown by the experience of the Eastern Caribbean Supreme Court, the ECSC.)[3]

- *Governance rules may contribute to the stability of the policies of a regional body.* An example is the ECCB, where the requirement of unanimity among board members on major policy decisions has helped ensure the stability of its policies. In the case of the BEAC and the BCEAO in Central and West Africa, governance rules did have a stabilizing effect, but loopholes in the rules were instrumental in undermining stability during the 1980s.

- *Rules anchoring some regional body decisions to a third party with recognized prestige may strengthen fledgling institutions.* For instance, the role of the U.K. Privy Council as a final appellate court for the ECSC, and the position of the French treasury as lender of last resort for the central banks in Central and West Africa, may have helped keep the regional institutions stable, especially in their early years.

Outsourcing and transnational cooperation have had a number of beneficial effects:

- *They have facilitated access to higher-quality services than countries could have afforded otherwise.* There is general consensus in both the Eastern

Caribbean and in West and Central Africa that sustaining a high-quality cadre of civil servants in each country in isolation would have been prohibitively expensive.

- *They have contributed to stability of policies.*[4] It is plausible that outsourcing monetary policy and banking supervision may have had a positive impact on the productivity of the economies of Eastern Caribbean.

- *They have encouraged experiments elsewhere.* For instance, the ECCB, the ECSC, and the Eastern Caribbean Civil Aviation Authority were forerunners of ECTEL.[5] The creation of Central and West African central banks was followed, after 1981, by an effort to harmonize legislation through such initiatives as the Organization for the Harmonization of Business Law in Africa (OHADA) and by other developments in regionalization such as the West Africa Telecommunications Regulators Assembly (WATRA).[6]

Careful Design of Government Processes and Regulation

International outsourcing is not always the least expensive means of overcoming small size and capacity limitation, nor is it always feasible. For the members of the Organization of Eastern Caribbean States (OECS), which had a tradition of cooperation, the creation of a multicountry telecommunications regulator was not surprising. For Samoa, however, outsourcing telecommunications regulatory advice to a regional body is not as yet a viable option.

Several case studies point to alternative ways of organizing service provision and designing regulation that can reduce government costs and increase effectiveness:

- Cape Verde, in developing a comprehensive reform of its communications and service delivery systems, opted for in-house provision of services rather than outsourcing. Faced with a weak domestic private ICT sector, and cognizant of the importance of ensuring the cooperation of civil servants and government departments with the reform, the government created an in-house agency responsible for the design and implementation of the e-government plan. The agency is financed by a budget line, but it is not subject to civil service salary limitations or work conditions, permitting flexibility in personnel and program management decisions. Initially, the implementation unit centralized all available technical skills; later it deployed them in support of other ministries and agencies. The plan has been very effective in developing domestic capacity and spreading the use of modern ICT in the central government and in some municipalities.

- The case study on budget reform in Samoa illustrates how a small country can circumvent its limited buying power by tapping into systems designed for small administrative entities in larger states. Samoa found that it could adapt leading-edge business processes used in municipal governments to support decentralized budget execution—despite the differences between national and municipal governments in funding sources and in the range of services provided. To this end, it used a well-designed tender process that performed the dual role of simultaneously identifying solutions while procuring the appropriate system.

- The studies on telecommunications in Samoa and in the Eastern Caribbean illustrate the importance of keeping regulation simple to reduce overall costs. The drafting of regulations requires sophisticated engineering, economics, and legal skills that are scarce in most small states. Moreover, enforcement of these regulations implies high costs to the government and the consumer. Given this constraint it is less costly to rely on market mechanisms (when possible) than on sophisticated control processes. For instance, the regulatory office may employ a sophisticated cost system to assess interconnection costs with existing infrastructure, or it may authorize new investment in transmission towers when and if disputes arise regarding interconnection service charges. These matters are particularly important in Samoa, which has a national regulatory agency that is responsible for overseeing the application of the new competitive regulatory framework for telecommunications.

Improving Connectivity

ICT is important for every country in the world, but arguably more so for small, isolated states. Today, ICT makes it feasible for an engineering student in Vanuatu to access notes posted online in the Massachussett's Institute of Technology (MIT) Open Courseware or for a doctor in Praia, Cape Verde, to consult with a colleague in Coimbra, Portugal, to sharpen a clinical diagnosis.[7] Ten years ago this would have been impossible; the only way to access such knowledge would have been by mail or through expensive and time-consuming travel. Similarly, high-quality, low-cost ICT makes it possible to provide many forms of international services (for instance, call centers) from small, remote locations in a way that would not previously have been feasible.

ICT may thus be used to offset in part the problems posed by geography. Unfortunately, many small states have telecommunication regulations that hinder competition, impose high costs, and impede access to low-cost, high-quality international communications. The direct cost, in terms of consumption loss, attributable to these uncompetitive market structures is high, and the indirect cost, from discouraging activities that use telecommunications services as an input in production, is likely to be even higher. Introducing competition in telecommunications is one of the policy reforms with the highest payoffs for small states.

The costs of access to information technology through the Internet have fallen steeply in recent years.[8] Access, however, requires investments in infrastructure, regulation, and organization to build the necessary interfaces between local organizations and those located abroad.

Improving connectivity in small states poses unique challenges (see ITU 2007). For instance, setting up a telecommunications regulatory office in St. Kitts and Nevis or in the Solomon Islands, where telecommunications engineers are scarce or nonexistent, is a very different proposition from doing so in South Africa. This difficulty is what led St. Kitts and Nevis and five other countries in the Caribbean to create a regional telecommunications advisory body, ECTEL, in 2003. In Cape Verde the weakness of the private ICT sector led the government to set up a government-run agency responsible for implementing the e-government action plan. This strategy was successful in Cape Verde—but it would probably have been absurd in Brazil. Both in St. Kitts and Nevis and in Cape Verde, small market size and limited capacity called for institutional and organizational solutions that would not have made sense in larger states.

Opening the Telecommunications Market to Competition

The revolution in telecommunications technology of the past three decades holds considerable potential for reducing the cost of connectivity for small states. In both large and small states the key to accessing the benefits offered by new technology has been to open the domestic market to competition. This step has been arduous for many small states that were locked into sole-provider contractual arrangements which had to be renegotiated and radically modified.

- Countries in the Eastern Caribbean took a common stand that facilitated reform of the telecommunications regulatory framework and unlocked competition. Competition, in turn, dramatically reduced connectivity costs and broadened the range of services available.

- In Samoa, opening the market to competition took six years of arduous negotiations. As of 2007, the domestic market in mobile phone services is open, but uncompetitive restrictions still pose an obstacle to reducing the cost of international telephone services. The move from monopoly to competition in mobile phone services has brought rapid improvement in the quality and quantity of services.

- The experiences of the University of the South Pacific and of Cape Verde's e-government show how initiatives that might have substantially improved connectivity can be harmed by uncompetitive domestic market structures. The introduction of ICT in Cape Verde has already had tangible results: all government databases are interconnected; the government has in place a modern information management system that facilitates preparation of the budget and control of its execution; and the efficiency of information systems in the tax revenue agency, customs, and some municipalities has improved remarkably. But e-government services have not yet reached the people of Cape Verde. The main obstacle has been high telephone and broadband rates—the result of a private monopoly in telecommunications. Similarly, telecommunications monopolies in the South Pacific have posed a major impediment to extending the benefits of distance learning programs to a wider audience.

Using ICT to Improve Quality of Services

The case study on the University of the South Pacific illustrates how an immense force for economic development can be unleashed by improving communications in scattered regions like the Pacific islands in order to share knowledge, educate future managers, and even handle disruptions from natural and other disasters. The reach of the programs offered by the university could be enhanced by deregulation of the telephone markets in countries in the region.

Assistance from Multilateral and Bilateral Institutions

International and bilateral development agencies have supported the creation and development of the institutions, agencies, and policies described in the case studies. Collaboration between governments and development agencies works best when the following conditions are met:

- *The government's reform program has a clear direction from the outset, and the development agency assists in developing and implementing the program.* Good examples are the IDA technical assistance loans in support of telecommunications reform in Samoa and the Eastern Caribbean and in support of public sector reform in Cape Verde.
- *The development agency accommodates to the circuitous path of reform while keeping in view the main objectives,* as in the cases of ECTEL and Samoa telecommunications. For instance, in the Samoa telecommunications deregulation, the World Bank accommodated the internal political discussion and the delays generated by lack of consensus among several agencies while holding a steady course with respect to reform.
- *The development agency has the staying capacity to provide technical assistance to the country during the typically long time that it takes for a reform to mature.* Examples are the recognized roles of the International Monetary Fund (IMF) in the creation and development of the ECCB, the BEAC, and the BCEAO and of the World Bank in the cases of Samoa and ECTEL.
- *The development agency possesses instruments adapted to the needs of the countries.* For instance, a loan in support of a regional body requires processing of several loans, to each of the countries that are members of the agency. A World Bank instrument adapted to this need was used effectively to support ECTEL.
- *The country sets a clear agenda and has appropriate processes for absorbing aid.* Cape Verde, for example, has been a pioneer in designing an agenda that supports its ICT program and in channeling bilateral and multilateral aid to finance implementation of the agenda, allowing for minimum departures.

The Organization of This Book

Below are brief summaries of the case studies discussed in chapters 2 through 9, grouped by the two main issues discussed—regional approaches to public service provision, and initiatives designed to take the fullest advantage of ICT. The appendix to this volume provides additional information on the current state of small states in the world economy, as well as an overview of four in-depth regional analyses of economic growth in small countries that were undertaken as background for this study: Domeland and Sander (2007); Duncan and Nakagawa (2006); Kida (2006); and Thomas and Pang (2006).

Regional Solutions

Chapter 2, "Banking Supervision in OECS Member Countries," relates how in 1983—in response to the development challenge posed by the need to replace colonial with national government institutions—the OECS countries founded the ECCB and vested it with responsibility for banking supervision in the region. The decision to pool resources and supervise banks in the subregion through a multicountry agency had clear advantages on grounds of exploiting economies of scale. But the creation of the ECCB did not mean that each national government relinquished its banking jurisdiction entirely to the multicountry central bank. In fact, member governments retained authority over the licensing of new banks, the enforcement of the law, and imposition of sanctions.

The intrinsic tension built in by the overlapping jurisdictions of the national governments and the ECCB resembles that between state and national governments in federally organized states. Over the past 30 years this tension has been wisely managed through sensible rules—in particular, the enactment of a uniform legal framework for bank operations in the region, which has been critical to the efficiency of the multicountry regulatory body. The adoption of procedures and rules that preclude interference with the daily management of central bank operations while ensuring that the bank fully represents the interests of the shareholders, and a management strategy that favors cooperation over confrontation, have helped reduce the number of conflicts and expedite their resolution.

Today Eastern Caribbean countries are faced with a new challenge: the emergence of a vast system of unregulated nonbank financial intermediaries. In contrast to the strategy followed 30 years ago, the governments of the region have decided to create regulatory units in each country rather than establish a regional regulatory body. This is not necessarily a step backward. The absence of unified regulation of nonbank financial activities across countries in the region would be a serious obstacle to realization of the benefits of pooling national resources in a single multistate body, and the weakness of a political consensus for committing budget resources in support of a regional body make that option unrealistic at present.

Chapter 3, "Banking Supervision in CFA Franc Countries," describes the origins and evolution of the central banks of West and Central Africa (the BCEAO and the BEAC); the initial arrangement that created the two CFA franc zones; the governance rules and the changes in governance introduced in the 1970s; the evolution of the financial systems of member countries; the allocation of central bank credit across member countries; and the way domestic credit expansion eventually undermined financial stability.

The establishment of regional bank supervision mechanisms, with a single supervisory authority in each of the two zones was principally the product of the crises that beset the banking systems of the zones starting in the late 1980s. These crises both contributed to and fed on the broader economic and financial imbalances that led to the devaluation of the CFA franc on January 12, 1994, the subsequent tightening of fiscal policies, and extensive restructuring in the banking sector. Somewhat paradoxically, the impetus toward regional cooperation also followed from the realization of the inconsistency between national supervision mechanisms and the lender-of-last-resort responsibilities vested in regional central banks (and, ultimately, in the French treasury). There was some institutional logic, therefore, to adopting regional supervision mechanisms.

These regional arrangements have certainly led to important savings of financial and human resources, compared with the largely nation-based systems that prevailed until 1990. But their main claims to success have been the improvements in corporate governance in an industry where it had been severely lacking, the professionalization of the supervision function, and the depoliticization of a process that had had much to do with the eruption of the banking crises of the 1980s.

The discussion in chapter 4, "The Regional Court Systems in the Organization of Eastern Caribbean States and the Caribbean," begins with a history of the Eastern Caribbean Supreme Court—a pioneering example of outsourcing by individual sovereign countries of the provision of justice to a regional court. The ECSC, established 40 years ago as a step in the transition from colonialism to independence, offered a feasible federal mechanism for resolving disputes within the group of small islands, a solution to the problem of the scarce resources of small states, and a way to meet the need for independent institutions to take over responsibility from the colonial courts. The final appellate function was, in turn, outsourced by the group of countries as a whole to the Judicial Committee of the Privy Council in London. The functioning of the ECSC required the design of a governance structure to manage the relationship between the court and sovereign member countries, the appointment of judges, and so on.

With the formation of the Caribbean Community (CARICOM) Single Market and Economy under the Revised Treaty of Chaguaramas in 2001, the court systems faced new challenges and opportunities. The parties to the treaty considered it important to have a specialized court for the interpretation and application of its provisions. Thus, the Caribbean Court of Justice (CCJ) was created. It has two jurisdictions: it interprets and applies the treaty, and it is seen as eventually replacing the Judicial Committee of the Privy Council in London as a final appellate court for hearing appeals from the parties.

The creation of the CCJ ushers in a new stage in the development of regional legal cooperation and the independence of small states. Its functioning will require the creation of a new governance structure to direct the management of the court and its relationship with member countries. As a regional court, the CCJ is able to draw on the 40 years of experience with the ECSC and on the experiences of the short-lived but very prestigious Federal Supreme Court during the four years of existence of the West Indies Federation.

ICT Regulation and Outsourcing

The case study reported in chapter 5, "Telecommunications Regulation in the Eastern Caribbean," describes the transition from monopoly to competition in telecommunications in that region. The central narrative concerns the creation and early life of the ECTEL, which in 2000 became the world's first multicountry regulatory telecommunications agency.

Until 2000, Cable & Wireless (C&W) was the sole provider of telecommunications services for most countries in the Eastern Caribbean. The colonial authorities had oversight over the company, but in practice C&W was self-regulated. With the coming of independence, the OECS countries had to create a regulatory office. Meanwhile, dramatic improvements were taking place in technology worldwide, but OECS countries were deriving little benefit from them. A consensus gradually emerged in the region that the telecommunications monopoly stood in the way of enjoying of those benefits.

Two watershed events triggered deregulation. First, a second company operating in Dominica, Marpin Telecommunications, successfully challenged C&W's monopoly in the courts. Second, a confrontation between C&W and the government of St. Lucia about the renewal of the company's exclusivity license led to a joint response by five governments in the region, which essentially made it known that if C&W left St. Lucia, it would have to leave all the other states as well. The successful outcome of the formation of a united front on this issue convinced the five governments that they had strength in numbers and that a new telecommunications regulator should be formed to reflect this fact.

ECTEL was conceived as a regional advisory body rather than as an independent authority vested with executive power. The clear intention was to design a new regulatory entity that would break up a monopoly, foster competition, and then regulate the sector. The challenge was to figure out exactly how to structure such an organization.

The positive effects of deregulation were immediate: the number of mobile phone subscribers in ECTEL countries rose steeply, suggesting that the institutional and market structure in the sector before the creation of ECTEL had led to significant pent-up demand for telephone services. The competition for the mobile telephone market was the primary engine of a precipitous decline in fees for international calls.

This story raises questions relevant beyond the Caribbean islands and outside the realm of the telecommunications industry. How are regional organizations formed? How much sovereignty must countries delegate when cooperating with others? And, finally, what is the future of regional organizations?

Chapter 6, "E-Government in Cape Verde," describes an ambitious and far-reaching program to apply ICT systematically in government operations. This effort has been led by the Operational Information Society Nucleus (NOSI), a project implementation unit with a unique internal structure and culture akin to a Silicon Valley start-up that operates under the prime minister's office.

Between 2000 and 2007 NOSI set up a network linking 3,000 computers in the public sector; it designed and implemented an integrated financial management system to provide budget information in real time; it set up a national identification database unifying information from several public registries; and it developed domestic capacity to design software applications adapted to the needs of Cape Verde's public sector.

Some of the results are visible to the average citizen. The use of ICT has increased transparency, enhanced tax collection, and reduced opportunities for fraud and corruption. Many more benefits are yet to materialize as the various units in the public sector learn to exploit the information generated by the new systems and as competition in telecommunications allows more people to access e-services.

Although in-house provision and informality facilitated the emergence of the e-government program, outsourcing the provision of some services may be more appropriate in the future. In anticipation of this eventuality, NOSI is studying how to ensure a smooth transition from its current structure into, possibly, several private and mixed spin-offs and an ICT regulator.

The issues raised in the Cape Verde experience have wide application for small states that are considering harnessing ICT in the interests of reform. These concerns include the role of the government in developing the ICT sector, the links between development of the sector and the cost of telecommunications, the pros and cons of developing an incipient ICT sector in a small isolated state, and the challenges ICT poses to the reform of the state.

Chapter 7, "Impact of ICT on University Education in Small Island States: The Case of the University of the South Pacific," recounts how the University of the South Pacific has transformed its delivery systems for teaching and learning in the past decade. The study shows how advances in communications technology could be exploited to meet the complex challenges of delivering tertiary education to students dispersed among thousands of small islands in the Pacific Ocean. It traces the history of the foundation of the university by 12 island nations and examines the university's development, via communications technology, of distance learning to overcome the obstacles posed by isolation, the small size of dispersed campuses, and the natural hazards of the physical environment.

Developing a regional university to serve 12 tiny countries spread out over the vast Pacific Ocean was a monumental task. At present, over half of the university's more than 20,000 students are distance students, learning with the assistance of such modern telecommunications media as audioconferencing, videoconferencing, and the Internet, as well as paper-based materials.

The case study describes how the university tapped into the initial stages of the development of satellite-based communication, how it has struggled to find the financing necessary to improve its crucial communications facility, and how it has coped with the extremely high telecommunications charges and the regulatory obstacles resulting from monopolized telecommunications facilities in the member countries. As the study shows, uncompetitive domestic market structures have been a major impediment to extending the benefits from distance learning programs to a wider audience.

Chapter 8, "From Monopoly to Competition: Reform of Samoa's Telecommunications Sector," illustrates the winding path of government decision making on reform, the cost of delays, and the peculiarities of regulating telecommunications in a small state.

In 1997 the government of Samoa awarded a 10-year monopoly on mobile phone services to a joint venture by the government and Telecom New Zealand. The decision brought cellular phones to Samoa, but the quantity and quality of the service were always poor.

Growing discontent with the quality of mobile phone services built a consensus about the need to change course and open up the telecommunications market to competition. But the views of government agencies on the telecommunications sector were not always in concert, and it was eight years before a new telecommunications regulatory act was enacted, in 2005. The accumulated cost of the delay in opening the telecommunications market to competition was high—about 4–5 percent of GDP.

Twelve months after the opening of the market to competition, results are visible. Even so, challenges remain: barriers to competition in international communications and to the expansion of broadband technology persist, and the privatization of the state-owned telephone company is still pending. Moreover, establishing and financing a regulatory office in a country the size of Samoa is expensive. Pooling resources and setting up a regional regulatory body such as ECTEL may be an option in the future but is not feasible today.

Chapter 9, "Exploiting Tender Processes for Budget Reform in Small Countries: The Case of Samoa," tells how a software crisis forced a small country to overhaul its budget system in an innovative way.

Samoa introduced performance-based budget preparation in 1995, but for almost a decade thereafter, the benefits of the reform were blocked by the obstinate persistence of a highly centralized system of budget execution. This centralized control might have continued indefinitely had not the Australian company supporting the budget software unexpectedly announced that it would stop doing so in a year's time. The government of Samoa turned this misfortune into an opportunity to introduce a more decentralized budget system, consistent with real performance budgeting, through ingenious use of the tender process for procuring new software.

A central problem for decentralization had been how to devolve enough financial flexibility to line ministries for an output-based system to work effectively, without loss of financial control. Samoa used the tender process to identify and tap into available technologies that could be tailored to the cost constraints and low transaction volumes of a small country, while reconciling the needs for devolved responsibility and for high standards of financial control. The government combined a broad, nonprescriptive approach to the supply side of the tender process—giving potential suppliers with large-country knowledge maximum scope to identify small-country solutions—with a high level of specificity on the demand side, in the form of a well-thought-out and very detailed set of user requirements. Highly prescriptive user requirements, together with flexibility about possible solutions, helped identify options not readily apparent from the vantage point of a small country.

The solution eventually adopted was based on the applicability to Samoa's national ministries of leading-edge business processes used in municipal governments in larger states. Adopting and adapting existing solutions allowed Samoa to avoid unaffordable development costs and achieve its desired level of functionality.

Conclusions and Future Work

Many small states face large challenges in reducing the costs and increasing the effectiveness of public services. And, improving connectivity and reducing telecommunication costs are critical to future economic development. Many of the case studies in this volume illustrate the power of regional approaches in tackling both issues, the circumstances in which such approaches are most likely to be successful, and the role that external support can play. They also show how, with good cooperation, a pooling of advisory functions can develop into a de facto pooling of executive functions and how continued cooperation is required between countries to make such arrangements work. Other case studies show what can be achieved on a purely national basis.

Several case studies underline the important role of multilateral agencies such as the World Bank and the IMF in supporting the reforms. Bilateral agencies have also provided critical assistance. The contributions of these agencies have been most effective when (a) the government reform plan had, from its inception, a clear direction; (b) the agencies adapted to the circuitous path of reforms while holding a steady course toward the final objectives; and (c) the development institutions had the staying power to continue providing advice in spite of prolonged delays.

The case studies cover a wide range of operational subjects and underscore the various ways and circumstances in which small states can benefit from a wider sharing of their own experiences and from a greater recognition of the collective expertise they embody. The studies highlight the potential value added once the international Small States Network for Economic Development becomes fully functional in 2008. Among the functions of the network are "to act as a clearing house to share expertise and technologies specific to small states," providing countries with "just-in-time services on specific policy and institutional development" and involving the utilization of expertise from small states, and to "promote appropriate training opportunities utilizing the considerable experience and expertise available in small states" (World Bank 2006a; see also World Bank 2006b).

Development is problem solving, and the case studies illustrate that addressing a problem is not the same as solving it. In most cases the initial development solutions are partial and imperfect. Over time, new problems arise (sometimes generated by the initial policy or institutional reform), and they have to be addressed sequentially and by adapting agencies, institutions, and regulations accordingly.

The development solutions reported in these case histories may not be directly applicable or effective in different circumstances, but their analysis will help inform and discipline the debate on related problems in other countries. The studies may also be useful in drawing attention to the long maturation time needed for reform and to pitfalls to be avoided in assessing the outcomes of policy reform.

Notes

1. Small states are defined here as sovereign countries with populations below 2 million inhabitants; all others are defined as larger states. The population threshold selected is somewhat arbitrary and is posited only to facilitate presentation of stylized facts (see Michaely and Papageorgiou 1998).

2. Alesina, Spolaore, and Wacziarg (2000, 2005) argue that the surge in the number of sovereign countries in the past five decades was facilitated by the expansion of world trade.

3. The ECSC is a superior court of record for the Organization of Eastern Caribbean States (OECS).

4. Guyana, Belize, and Trinidad and Tobago did not adhere to the ECCB and have had more volatile monetary and exchange rate policies than the ECCB. Barbados, however, also opted for central bank independence and has been a bulwark of macroeconomic stability. It has been argued that the CFA franc arrangements were not effective in preventing the credit expansion that ultimately undermined exchange rate policy in the CFA zone. As in any other

assessment, what is relevant (in this case, for assessing the contribution of the monetary arrangements) is comparison with a realistic benchmark.

5. The Eastern Caribbean Civil Aviation Authority was another early experience of multicountry regulation.

6. OHADA, which was created by international treaty in October 1993, groups all members of the CFA zones. Its stated objective is to overcome the juridical and judicial insecurity which exists in its member states; see http://www. ohada.org/. WATRA was set up to coordinate telecommunications policy and regulations in the region; see http://www.watra.org/.

7. For the MIT Open Courseware, see http://ocw.mit.edu/index.html.

8. At the heart of the digital technology revolution is "Moore's Law," which predicts the doubling of the density of semiconductor chips every 18 to 24 months.

References

Alesina, Alberto, and Romain Wacziarg. 1998. "Openness, Country Size, and the Government." *Journal of Public Economics* 69 (3, September): 305–21.

Alesina, Alberto, Enrico Spolaore, and Romain Wacziarg. 2000. "Economic Integration and Political Disintegration." *American Economic Review* 90 (5, December): 1276–96.

———. 2005. "Trade, Growth, and the Size of Countries." In *Handbook of Economic Growth*, ed. P. Aghion and S. Durlauf. Amsterdam: North Holland.

Briguglio, Lino, Bishnodat Persaud, and Richard Stern. 2005. *Toward an Outward-Oriented Development Strategy for Small States: Issues, Opportunities, and Resilience Building*. Washington, DC: World Bank.

Chandler, Alfred. 1962. *Strategy and Structure: Chapters in the History of the Industrial Enterprise*. Cambridge, MA: MIT Press.

Commonwealth Secretariat and World Bank. 2000. "Small States: Meeting Challenges in the Global Economy." Excerpt from the Final Communiqué of the Development Committee held in Washington, DC, on April 17, 2000, Commonwealth Secretariat/World Bank Task Force on Small States, Washington, DC.

Domeland, Dorte, and Frederico Gil Sander. 2007. "Growth in African Small States." Working paper. World Bank, Washington, DC.

Duncan, Ron, and Haruo Nakagawa. 2006. "Obstacles to Economic Growth in Six Pacific Island Countries." Working paper. World Bank, Washington, DC.

Easterly, William, and Aart Kraay. 2000. "Small States, Small Problems? Income, Growth, and Volatility in Small States." *World Development* 28 (11): 2013–27.

Goolsbee, Austan. 2006. "The Value of Broadband and the Deadweight Loss of Taxing New Technology." *Contributions to Economic Analysis & Policy* 5 (1). http://faculty.chicagogsb.edu/austan.goolsbee/research/broadb.pdf.

ITU (International Telecommunications Union). 2007. *World Telecommunications Indicators.* http://www.itu.int/ITU-D/ict/publications/world/world.html.

Kida, Mizuho. 2006. "Caribbean Small States: Growth Diagnostics." Working paper. World Bank, Washington, DC.

Kuznetz, Simon. 1960. "Economic Growth of Small Nations." In *The Economic Consequences of the Size of Nations,* ed. E. A. G. Robinson. Proceedings of a conference held by the International Economic Association. London: Macmillan.

Michaely, Michael, and Demetris Papageorgiou. 1998. "Small Economies, Trade Liberalization, Trade Preferences, and Growth." *Iberoamericana: Nordic Journal of Latin American and Caribbean Studies* 28 (1–2): 121–59. Stockholm University, Institute of Latin American Studies.

Popper, Karl R. 1999. *All Life is Problem Solving.* London: Routledge.

Rodrik, Dani. 1998. "Why Do More Open Countries Have Bigger Governments?" *Journal of Political Economy* 106 (5, October): 997–1032.

Thomas, Mark Roland, and Gaobo Pang. 2006. "Lessons from Europe for Economic Policy in Small States." Working paper. World Bank, Washington, DC.

van Beek, Frits, José Roberto Rosales, Mayra Zermeño, Ruby Randall, and Jorge Shepherd. 2000. "The Eastern Caribbean Currency Union: Performance, Progress, and Policy Issues." Occasional Paper 195, International Monetary Fund, Washington, DC.

Winters, L. Alan, and Pedro M. G. Martins. 2004. "When Comparative Advantage Is Not Enough: Business Costs in Small Remote Economies." *World Trade Review* 3 (3): 347–83.

World Bank. 2006a. "Statute of the Small States Network for Economic Development." World Bank, Washington, DC. http://siteresources.worldbank.org/PROJECTS/Resources/SSNEDstatutereviewedapproved.pdf.

———. 2006b. "Small States, Big Strides, One Network." World Bank, Washington, DC. http://go.worldbank.org/3HMKZCTK50.

———. 2007. *World Development Indicators.* Washington, DC: World Bank.

———. Forthcoming. *World Development Indicators.* Washington, DC: World Bank.

PART 1

Case Studies on Regional Solutions

The following chapters describe regional bodies in the Eastern Caribbean and Central and West Africa created to handle government functions (banking supervision, central banking matters, and justice) that would otherwise be handled by individual states.

In the first two cases (the central banks of the CFA franc[1] zones and the Eastern Caribbean), sovereign states outsource the monetary policy and banking supervision advisory role to the regional organization, but retain their power to license new banks and enforce sanctions. In the third case (the Eastern Caribbean Supreme Court), sovereign governments outsource justice to a regional organization.

In all cases, the relationship between the national governments and the regional bodies required crafting a set of governance rules to facilitate the operation of the regional bodies and to align their incentives with those of the government client shareholders.

Key to the operation of multicountry central banks are rules for the distribution of seigniorage among their members. Profits made by the Eastern Caribbean Central Bank (ECCB) are distributed in proportion to each country's share in the total demand for money; enforcement of the rule is facilitated by the bank's quasi-currency board policy (a policy that inhibits countries from free-riding on others through borrowing in excess of their quotas or discounting low-quality commercial bank bills).

The Central Bank of West Africa (BCEAO) and the Bank of Central African States (BEAC) in contrast, failed to maintain a similar discipline in their operations during part of the 1970s and most of the 1980s, instead using indirect mechanisms to extend credit to some of their members beyond the statutory limits, thus undermining monetary and fiscal discipline (Stasavage 1997).

The comparison among the performances of the multicountry central banks opens important questions: Are the differences in performance between the ECCB and the African central banks the consequence of differences in the design of governance rules or of differences in prevailing ideas as to what monetary policy can or cannot do? Do differences in size (GDP, population) among member countries matter for the governance of the regional institutions?

For the Eastern Caribbean Supreme Court, whose status in relation to the executive and legislative power is clearly linked to the strong tradition of independence of the judiciary in the region, the key questions today are: Will the creation of the Caribbean Court of Justice strengthen this independence? How will the difference in size among countries influence events?

Note

1. Historically CFA stands for *Colonies françaises d'Afrique* (French colonies of Africa). See chapter 3 for further information.

Reference

Stasavage, David. 1997. "The CFA Franc Zone and Fiscal Discipline," *Journal of African Economies* 6 (1): 132–67.

CHAPTER 2

Banking Supervision in OECS Member Countries

Edgardo Favaro and Frits van Beek

In 1983, the seven small island states in the Eastern Caribbean that had joined in creating the Organization of Eastern Caribbean States two years earlier agreed to form a multicountry central bank, the Eastern Caribbean Central Bank (ECCB), and to vest it with the responsibility for banking supervision in their territories. The decision was intertwined with political independence and the need to replace colonial institutions with new, national institutions. It was also a response to structural changes in the banking industry.

To be sure, the countries that signed the ECCB Agreement Act of 1983 had had more than three decades of experience with regional currency board arrangements, but much of that experience was based on a governance structure supported by colonial rule and a banking industry dominated by branches of foreign banks that were self-regulated and self-supervised by their head offices.

It was a bold step for these countries to take: at the time, there were only two examples in the world of multistate central banking arrangements to look at and learn from (both in Africa, under the tutelage of

Edgardo Favaro is a lead economist at the World Bank. Frits van Beek is a consultant to the World Bank.

France), and none of multicountry supervision. Financial stability required close oversight of bank operations, but why make it the responsibility of a central bank, operating under quasi-currency board rules?[1]

Background

Political

Independence came to the Eastern Caribbean subregion in the 1970s and early 1980s. Grenada became independent in 1974, Dominica in 1978, St. Lucia and St. Vincent and the Grenadines in 1979, Antigua and Barbuda in 1981, and St. Kitts and Nevis in 1983.

In 1981, these six countries, together with Montserrat (which has remained a British Overseas Territory), signed the Treaty of Basseterre and created the Organization of Eastern Caribbean States (OECS) to promote political and economic cooperation. To further this aim, these countries supported creation of multicountry institutions in justice, money, defense, and aviation, where there had already been a long history of cooperation.

The Eastern Caribbean Supreme Court (ECSC) dates back to 1967. The ECSC is a superior court of record for the nine current member states of OECS (the six independent states and the three British Overseas Territories of Anguilla, the British Virgin Islands, and Montserrat). (See chapter 5.)

The common currency arrangement dates back to the British Caribbean Currency Board (BCCB), established in 1950, and the subsequent Eastern Caribbean Currency Authority (ECCA), established in 1965.

The Regional Security System (RSS), including the six independent OECS members and Barbados, was established following the Grenada crisis of 1983; its historical roots go back to the years of the West Indies Associate States Council of Ministers, established in 1967.

The Eastern Caribbean Civil Aviation Authority dates back to a 1957 decision of the U.K. government to appoint a Director of Civil Aviation to advise the governments of the Windward and Leeward Islands on all matters relating to civil aviation.

The Eastern Caribbean Common Market dates back to 1968.

Monetary System, Banking, and Banking Supervision

In the transition from colonial rule to independence, the monetary system evolved from a currency board to a quasi-currency board, and the banking system saw a gradual increase in the importance of domestic banks.

The BCCB was set up in Trinidad in 1950 to serve Trinidad, British Guiana (now Guyana), Barbados, and the current OECS member states. The BCCB was a pure currency board: by statute, every West Indian dollar it issued had to be backed fully by a deposit in sterling of the equivalent (EC$4.80 per pound sterling at that time) into its account in London.

In 1965, the BCCB was replaced by the ECCA, following the withdrawal of British Guiana and Trinidad and Tobago to establish their own central banks upon independence. "Unlike its predecessor, the ECCA was under no obligation to provide 100 percent sterling backing for the currency which it issued. Under the 1965 ECCA Agreement the foreign exchange cover for the EC dollar was set at 70 percent, but this requirement was reduced to 60 percent 10 years later. Grenada, not an original ECCA signatory, joined the Authority in 1968" (www.eccb-central bank.org). Thus the ECCA was a quasi-currency board with certain, limited monetary powers.

The first banks in the islands were branches of foreign banks: Barclay's (United Kingdom), Royal Bank of Canada, and Bank of Nova Scotia (both from Canada), but starting around 1950, domestic financial institutions gradually increased in importance. The first domestic banks were the cooperative banks (1950s) and the government and postal savings banks. In the 1970s, most of the countries established national banks with full or part government ownership.

The United Kingdom Colonial Office relied on the British banks' head offices for supervision; Barclay's Inspectorate, for example, went around the world to ensure that all its branches were sound. "Barclay's inspection process was very thorough," says ECCB Governor Sir K. Dwight Venner.

By contrast, there was little or no regulation or supervision of domestic financial institutions. The ECCA did not have any responsibilities in the area of banking supervision, although its research department did off-site analysis. Most of the islands had enacted acts to regulate banking activity (for instance, St. Kitts had a 1967 Banking Act), there was a tax on banks, and there were also minimum capital requirements, but overall there was a regulatory vacuum (ECCB staff).

ECCA requested support from the central banks of Barbados or Trinidad and Tobago when there was need for supervisory action or intervention. But on at least one occasion, the outside supervisors were refused access to the premises by the bank in question: "In 1980 ECCA had worries about the Bank of Commerce of St. Kitts and Nevis, which was part of the clearing system, but it did not have the authority to do anything about it. We asked the authorities of Bank of Commerce for authorization to inspect its operation and were given permission, but when supervisors from the Central Bank of Trinidad and Tobago arrived to do the inspection, the bank's authorities changed their mind and did not let them in. In 1981 the bank failed" (Errol Allen, former Deputy Governor of the ECCB and of the ECCA). This experience underscored the importance of introducing modern legislation to regulate banking activities, a process that became intertwined with the process of converting ECCA into a central bank.

Monetary Institutions and Banking Regulation after Independence

Establishment of the ECCB

Deliberations on establishing a central bank for the Eastern Caribbean Currency Union (ECCU)[2] began in 1969–1970 when Barbados announced its intention to leave the existing currency union (ECCA) and create its own central bank. The OECS governments had decided already in 1970 that ECCA should be transformed into a central bank, but it was not until 1976 that ECCA secured the assistance of the International Monetary Fund (IMF) in drafting a central bank agreement "suitable to the needs of the area," which was circulated to governments in 1977. In 1978, a joint ECCA/IMF mission visited the islands to discuss the project with the participating governments (Holdip 1992).

"The process of bringing the central bank into fruition took a long time; it had to proceed in phases, and the devil proved to be in the details, as each of the member countries wanted different things," says Errol Allen. Among the more contentious issues were the foreign exchange backing and the profit-sharing formula. Some countries, led by Grenada, wanted to reduce the reserve cover to 40 percent, arguing that "the funds should be used to develop these countries." In the end, the reserve cover was kept at 60 percent (annex I to the ECCB Act).

Other countries, led by Dominica, wanted changes in the formula used by ECCA to allocate profits to the member countries—for example, by linking it to GDP or population. "Profit sharing was another issue of contention. Currency in circulation was one base to divide profits; the other base was an imputed equity component. The principle that prevailed was that profits accrue in proportion to the market share each country had in total currency in circulation. But the final formula also respected the formula used to divide profits accruing to ECCA" (Errol Allen; annex II to the ECCB Act).

The process gained momentum after the signing of the Treaty of Basseterre on June 18, 1981, creating the OECS. The treaty includes "Currency and Central Banking" as one of the areas in which "the Member States will endeavor to co-ordinate, harmonize and pursue joint policies" (Article 3.2[i]).

The governments requested technical assistance from the IMF, which was provided jointly by its Central Banking Department (now the Monetary and Finance Department) and its Legal Department. The latter played a major role in drafting both the ECCB Agreement Act and later (see below) the Uniform Banking Act (UBA).[3] IMF experts joined ECCA management and board members on missions that visited each of the participating governments to review the draft legislation and iron out any differences. In addition, in 1982–1983, the Central Banking Department of the IMF provided a nine-month attachment for the deputy managing director of ECCA to learn about international best practices in central banking. Basic agreement among the countries was reached at the IMF/World Bank Annual Meeting in Toronto in the fall of 1982.

The agreement to establish the ECCB was signed on July 5, 1983, by the governments of Antigua and Barbuda, Dominica, Grenada, Montserrat, St. Kitts and Nevis, St. Lucia, and St. Vincent and the Grenadines; the central bank started operations on October 1, 1983. Anguilla (like Montserrat, a British overseas territory) joined the ECCB in 1987, when it became an associate member of the OECS.

The ECCB was set up as a central bank, but retained some currency board characteristics and has in fact generally followed quasi-currency-board practices (see below). Setting the foreign exchange reserve coverage of the Eastern Caribbean dollar at no less than 60 percent of its demand liabilities implied an aggregate limit of 40 percent of demand liabilities on the extension of credit to member governments and the commercial banks. To insulate the ECCB from pressures to expand credit, the Act placed strict limits on the amounts of credit that the Bank could extend to individual member governments through a number of prescribed instruments (van Beek et al. 2000).

Today, the ECCB is one of only four multistate central banks in the world (box 2.1). The other three are the Bank of Central African States (BEAC) and the Central Bank of West African States (BCEAO), for the two African-franc currency unions linked formerly to the French franc and

Box 2.1

Banking Supervision in Central and West Africa and in the EMU

There are only two other regional banking supervision bodies in the world (neither was in existence in 1983): the Banking Commission of Central Africa (COBAC), for the six member countries of the Economic and Monetary Community of Central Africa, and the West African Regional Banking Commission, for the eight member countries of the West African Economic and Monetary Union. These commissions were established in 1990, in association with the Central and West African currency unions, respectively.

Like the ECCU members, the member countries of the two African currency unions have maintained for themselves certain basic powers, including the authority to issue or revoke banking licenses. The independent status of the regional bodies means that bank supervision in each member country involves coordination among three parties (the national government, the regional commission, and the common central bank), rather than two (as in the ECCU). (See chapter 4 on Banking Supervision in the CFA Franc Countries.)

Banking supervision in the European Monetary Union (EMU) has remained the responsibility of the individual member countries, but in the European Union (EU) context, arrangements for cross-border inspection based on ownership criteria are being put into place, and harmonization of the national regulatory frameworks based on Basel I and II has advanced rapidly.

Source: Authors.

now to the euro (see chapter 4), and the newcomer European Central Bank (ECB), for the euro area (European Monetary Union [EMU]). Before the inception of the ECB, the ECCB was the only multistate central bank where the convertibility of the common currency is fully self-supported and the parity has not been changed.

Building Supervision Capacity: The Initial Steps

To address the general lack of capacity for regulation and supervision in their territories, the member countries undertook to enact banking legislation and agreed to vest bank supervisory authority, including the power to issue prudential guidelines, in the ECCB, while maintaining final national authority over such basic matters as issuing or revoking bank licenses.

There were several reasons for vesting the supervisory power in the ECCB. Pooling the countries' scarce resources was one of them: centralized supervision could reduce the cost and increase the quality of supervision services. A belief that monetary stability depended on financial stability also played a role. According to Mignon Wade, Counselor of the ECCB and former Senior Director of its Bank Supervision Department, the founding members recognized from the beginning that it was important "to establish relations with commercial banks (which were minimal under the predecessor ECCA), in order to avoid a surprise bank failure early on the watch of the new central bank." But practical considerations were also important in the decision: financing the development of high-quality bank supervision requires resources that are predictable. Vesting the responsibility for bank supervision in an institution that had its own resources (from seigniorage) reduced the scope for political interference in daily activities.

Apparently, none of the ECCB members pushed for alternative arrangements. Apart from the zero solution of having each country set up its own supervision authority, two such alternatives come to mind: One would have been the creation of a separate subregional authority outside the central bank to conduct supervision in cooperation with the governments and the new ECCB, a model that was later adopted by the two African currency unions (see chapter 4). (There are no indications that the creation of a separate regional body was ever on the table.) The other would have been to outsource bank supervision to the Bank of England, the Bank of Canada, or the Federal Reserve of the United States—not likely to be attractive to newly independent countries.

The framework for regulation of the commercial banks has two main legislative components: the ECCB Agreement Act of 1983 (and its amendments) and the banking acts of the member states. Article 3 paragraph 2(e) of the ECCB Act gives the bank the power to "regulate banking business on behalf of and in collaboration with Participating Governments." Article 35(1) specifically gives the ECCB the right to require financial institutions to open their books for inspection to enable verification of compliance with the directives issued. The ECCB exercises these powers through its Bank Supervision Department, which began operating when the ECCB came into being on October 1, 1983.

Multistate arrangements for banking regulation and supervision are rare. For such arrangements to be effective, it is critical that the underlying regulatory and commercial legislation be uniform in the participating states. "If the initial conditions differ too much across the countries, the multistate approach may well fail in the absence of carefully worked out transition arrangements" (Governor Venner). As discussed below, lack of uniformity in national banking legislation became an issue early on in the experience of ECCB supervision. More generally, because of legal restrictions, countries have traditionally been loath to share the highly confidential results from bank examinations with other countries. Under the ECCU system, such information is freely discussed by the Monetary Council and the Board of Directors of the ECCB. The ECCB itself, however, until recently was severely constrained in what information it could make available to outside parties and the public.

Evolution of the Monetary and Financial System in the Past Two Decades

The Financial System

The financial system in the ECCU is quite deep (the ratio of M2 to gross domestic product (GDP) is relatively high at more than 90 percent in 2003–05), and ownership is diversified.[4] The system is dominated by commercial banks, with each territory having at least four banks, two or more of them part of a foreign-owned international banking group (the exception is Montserrat, which has one locally owned and one foreign-owned bank). In all, there are 39 commercial banks, of which 26 are units of one of three international banks and one regional banking group. Four of the locally owned banks are fully or majority government owned. The foreign-owned banks have more than 55 percent of the combined market (measured by loans); the government-owned have 15 percent, and the domestic private banks 30 percent (IMF 2004).

In addition to the commercial banks, the financial system comprises near-banks (credit unions and building societies, mortgage banks, and finance companies), insurance companies, national development banks, the part-funded national (social) insurance systems, and a wide array of offshore financial services companies.

Historically, the system has been inefficient because of a proliferation of small-size institutions (that in the case of commercial banks contribute to high interest rate spreads), and interterritory fragmentation, reflecting the tendency of financial institutions to limit their investments to their country of domicile, in part because of various licensing, disclosure, and tax constraints. Recent legislative reforms leading up to the establishment in 2001 of the Eastern Caribbean Stock Exchange

(ECSE), the Regional Government Securities Market in 2002, and the Eastern Caribbean Home Mortgage Bank in 1996—as part of the ECCB's initiative to establish a single financial space—have eliminated many of these restrictions.

The Monetary System

The ECCB has been effective at maintaining exchange rate stability and low inflation over two and a half decades. The key has been strict adherence to quasi-currency-board rules. While required by statute to maintain reserve coverage "not below 60 percent of demand liabilities," in practice the ECCB has kept credit extension to a minimum and has typically maintained the foreign-exchange-backing ratio in a range of 90–95 percent (the ratio averaged more than 94 percent during 2000–05).

"Independence is our strength," says Wendell Lawrence, former Finance Secretary, St. Kitts and Nevis. But what does "independence" mean when the highest decision-making authority of the bank, the Monetary Council, consists of eight ministers, one from each of the participating governments? "There is safety in the fact that eight members have to agree for the ECCB to move. Political influence has to go through the Monetary Council, and what is the probability of all ministers going crazy at the same time?" says Janet Harris, Finance Secretary, St. Kitts and Nevis. Lawrence adds, "The fact that there has to be unanimity in the Monetary Council has been critical to maintain discipline."

To date, the ECCB has had only two governors and two deputy governors. The current Governor, Sir K. Dwight Venner, was appointed in 1989, upon the retirement of Sir Cecil Jacobs, who had also served as Managing Director of the ECCA (since its inception). Mr. Errol Allen, who was Deputy Managing Director of ECCA, served as Deputy Governor of the ECCB from 1983 until his retirement in 2005.

That most ECCU member countries governments showed, in the 1980s, sizable surpluses on their current fiscal operations and only small overall deficits helped restrain pressures to expand credit. The constant exception was Antigua and Barbuda, which has a long history of running fiscal deficits, and (sometimes) Dominica and Grenada, which also encountered fiscal difficulties (both countries had several programs with the IMF in the first half of the 1980s).

Starting in the mid-1990s, however, countries began to borrow heavily from regional and local banks to finance growing fiscal deficits. Today, both Dominica and Grenada have programs with the IMF, and the ratios of debt to GDP of the six independent ECCU countries, at an average of more than 100 percent since end-2002, are among the highest in the developing world (IMF 2005).

Banking Supervision

"Uniformity of laws has been critical to effective ECCB supervision across member countries," says Governor Venner. During 1988–92, new banking legislation common to all of the states was enacted in each of the member countries. These acts, collectively referred to as the Uniform Banking Act (UBA), are uniform across the currency area, and their adoption strengthened the regulatory environment and served to standardize the ECCB's supervisory and regulatory procedures while setting the stage for the harmonization of banking business within the ECCU.

The initiative for adopting a Uniform Banking Act in each country was predicated on the need to facilitate the operations of a centralized regulatory authority. Differences in legislation across countries were large enough to make life difficult for the new supervisor and for the foreign banks (which, unlike the domestic banks, operate in multiple territories, some of them in all) and to be an obstacle to the ECCB's goal of creating a single financial space in the subregion. This prompted immediate action by the Monetary Council to push for uniformity. The domestic banks fought the UBA, especially on capital requirements, where the foreign banks were given a dispensation that they considered unfair (Governor Venner).

The UBA gave substantial authority to the ECCB for supervising the banking system. The ultimate authority in the application of the act, however, was vested in the minister of finance in each state, who was required to act in consultation with, and on the recommendation of, the ECCB.

All commercial banks and other institutions deemed to be carrying on banking business must be licensed under the UBA (in addition to the commercial banks, 13 finance companies are currently licensed under the act). As part of the ongoing supervision, licensed financial institutions are required to submit weekly, monthly, quarterly, and annual returns to the ECCB.

It was clear almost from the time that the UBA took effect in 1988–1992 that changes would be needed to strengthen the governments' capacity to enforce the law. For example, when a bank was found not to be complying with the legal requirements or the prudential guidelines, the ECCB would enter into a memorandum of understanding (MOU) or letter of commitment (LOC) with that bank, setting out a timetable with a series of actions designed to bring it back into compliance. But because the ECCB essentially had no powers to enforce these commitments, in practice certain banks simply failed to comply and remained under such undertakings for years on end (five years or more in some cases). Also, the ECCB could not impose provisioning on bank loans to the public sector that were not being serviced, a shortcoming that became critical when government borrowing from the banks began to rise in the mid-1990s.

Accordingly, and again with assistance from the IMF's Legal Department, various proposals for amending the UBA were drafted and approved by the Monetary Council from the mid-1990s on. But the countries were slow to enact these amendments. It was not until after the IMF/World Bank Financial Sector Assessment for the ECCU had been concluded in mid-2004 that countries began to pass Revised Banking Acts. St. Vincent and the Grenadines and St. Lucia (which had difficulties with the legal drafting style) were the last countries to do so, in 2006.

"The new Banking Act gives us a lot of teeth," says Mignon Wade. Important new powers for the ECCB in the Revised Act pertain to cease-and-desist orders and to provisioning for government loans in the capital calculation (as specified in a circular issued to the banks amending the prudential guidelines under the authority of section 36 of the new Act).

Judging from the interviews, the banks in both the private and public sectors are supportive of the way the ECCB has carried out its supervision mandate—or, as Wendell Lawrence put it, "Banks in the OECS are afraid of the supervisor." The Bank is respected for having brought regulation and supervision in the subregion up to international best practices (sometimes exceeding the standards of the Basel Core Principles [BCP]), for the quality and thoroughness of its examinations, for the technical skills and professionalism of the examiners, and for its outreach to the banks through the annual Commercial Banks Conference, where it puts all the new issues in banking business and supervision on the table.

The ECCB relies on a variety of modalities for training its bank supervision staff. ECCB bank examiners regularly attend courses offered by the U.S. Federal Reserve, while the Bank also regularly invites other institutions to offer on-site training; participating institutions include the Bank for International Settlements (BIS), the Bank of England, the Caribbean Regional Technical Assistance Center (CARTAC), and the Center for Latin American Monetary Studies (CEMLA). It also sends staff to participate in programs offered by the Caribbean Group of Banking Supervisors and the Association of Banking Supervisors of the Americas and for attachment with supervisory authorities in such countries as Trinidad and Tobago, The Bahamas, the Cayman Islands, Guernsey, and Jersey (Mignon Wade).[5]

Testing the Capacity of the ECCB for Preventing Crises

Several banks experienced crises in the period before the ECCB was established, including the St. Vincent Corporate Bank and the First Bank of Barbuda; even so, only one bank failure occurred: the Bank of Commerce in St. Kitts and Nevis in 1980–1981.

The first and (so far) only crisis or near-crisis since the establishment of the Bank occurred in 1993 with the failure of the Bank of Montserrat (owing mainly to bad management practices). All eight countries quickly passed emergency legislation to enable the ECCB to intervene (this legislation is still on the books and can be used again). The intervention was done by an ECCB subsidiary established for the purpose (Caribbean Assets and Liabilities Management Services Limited (Ltd.), known by the appropriate acronym of "CALMS"), which acquired the bank's bad assets ($14.7 million) in exchange for a promissory note. The ECCB took the charge to prevent a systemic crisis. The government of Montserrat did its share by injecting capital and by becoming the bank's major shareholder. According to Governor Venner, the (very large and immediate) presence of the ECCB on the scene was critical to preventing a run on the bank. An important consideration in the operation was the principle of equitable treatment of the member countries, Montserrat being the smallest one, and of domestic versus foreign banks.

Recovery of the bad loans by CALMS was proceeding relatively well until the volcanic eruptions in 1996–1997 brought the island's economy to a halt. Recovery picked up again later, and following a recent payment of $2.9 million, the outstanding balance is now down to $7.6 million.[6]

In 1999, the regulators arranged for the Nevis Cooperative Bank, which was insolvent, to be acquired by the Royal Bank of Trinidad and Tobago Ltd. The acquired bank was subsequently renamed "RBTT Bank SKN Ltd." The failure of the Bank of Antigua was averted in 1990 when the government of Antigua and Barbuda agreed to its purchase by Allan Stanford, an American businessman and financier. (At that time, the Uniform Banking Act, which provided the ECCB with a regulatory role, had not yet been enacted.)

The National Commercial Bank (SVG) Ltd. (a wholly owned government company) has gone through an intensive and extended workout over the past several years. The government of St. Vincent and the Grenadines has made capital injections and also formed a recoveries company (a special-purpose vehicle). This company purchased the bad debts of public sector companies and corporations, including those of the bank, and has been very successful in its recoveries efforts. The government has signaled its intention to privatize the bank.

Several of the locally owned banks have lost one of their major correspondent banking relationships. The loss was associated, among other things, with their relatively small size. Accordingly, some 12 of these banks have formed a holding company to promote a strategic partnership among themselves, some of the objectives being to relate to third parties in one accord, to pursue syndicated loans, and to promote the banks as a virtual group (Mignon Wade).

Several of the national development banks (which are not under ECCB supervision) have also experienced difficulties; the one in Grenada was recently restructured, with assistance from the Caribbean Development Bank (CDB), and the one in St. Vincent and the Grenadines is being incorporated into the restructured NCB (Senior ECCB Staff).

In all these episodes, the banks in trouble were very small. All in all, it is fair to say that the system has not to date been tested by a full-blown financial crisis. "The bailout of the Bank of Montserrat was facilitated by the bank's small size. It would not have worked for a large domestic bank" (Wendell Lawrence). This limitation derives from the quasi-currency-board nature of the central bank, which severely limits its ability to act as a lender of last resort. Expanding credit to support a large domestic bank in trouble could significantly reduce the reserve backing of the Eastern Caribbean dollar.

The apparent stability of the demand for money in the Eastern Caribbean may be the result of, at least in part, the tradition of fiscal discipline and the long-standing relative isolation of these countries from world financial markets, and even from the regional Caribbean market (as Wendell Lawrence put it, "Jamaica's major banking crisis barely caused a ripple in the subregion."). This stability may be threatened, however, because both of these fundamentals have been changing since the mid- to late-1990s, as foreign banks, plus nonbanks from the region, especially from Trinidad and Tobago, have aggressively entered the subregion and as the fiscal and debt positions of the ECCU countries have deteriorated sharply (see above).

Relationship between the Governments and the ECCB

As noted earlier, each member country is responsible for licensing banks and for enforcing banking regulations; the ECCB has an advisory role in both areas (see Box 2.2). This arrangement has worked in practice so that, as some interviewees put it, "the Minister of Finance would never license a bank without the ECCB's agreement." (The case of Capital Bank International in Grenada is the single exception to this observation.) At the same time, the fact that each member government has kept authority to issue the licenses makes it difficult for them to disengage when they are called to take action. This reality has de facto defused tensions as to who should be responsible for licensing banks. Formal authority resides in the national governments, but the voice of ECCB is heard and respected.

Any multistate arrangement inevitably involves coordination costs. In the evolution of ECCB banking supervision, these have been especially evident in sometimes slow decision making and implementation. Although the 1993 emergency legislation was passed quickly by all the member countries (see above), the process of getting more-or-less uniform, ECCU-wide legislation passed by the eight national legislatures has more often been slow and difficult (Janet Harris). This was the case for the UBA and the Revised UBA, as described above, even though

---

Box 2.2

Governance of the ECCB

The Monetary Council, the highest decision-making authority of the Bank, comprises the eight Ministers of Finance of the participating governments. Each minister designates an alternate to serve on the Council in his or her absence. Chairmanship of the Council is rotated among the members on an annual basis. The Council meets three times a year.

   The Board of Directors comprises the Governor, Deputy Governor, and one Director appointed by each of the participating governments. The Governor functions as Chairman of the Board. The Board is responsible for policy and general administration of the Bank and meets five times a year.

   The Governor and Deputy Governor are appointed by the Monetary Council, normally for five-year terms, and can be reappointed.

Source: ECCB Web site.

Ministers of Finance (who are often also Prime Ministers) or their deputies sign off on these initiatives in their capacity as members of the Monetary Council. At the same time, as was noted in many of the interviews, the need for unanimous decisions by the Monetary Council on key issues has proved to be a great source of strength and confidence in the system.

The participating governments play a dual or perhaps ambivalent role in the working of banking supervision in the ECCU: they are partners with the ECCB in the arrangements for regulation and supervision, holding the ultimate authority over their implementation and effectiveness, and at the same time, they exercise the final decision-making authority over the ECCB as a multistate agency. Also, some of the governments have full or part ownership of local banks from which they borrow to finance fiscal deficits, which can give rise to "conflicts of interest" when such banks fall out of compliance; on the other hand, the authorities may welcome the ECCB's role as an "outside party" that helps fight the political interests, as in the case of the National Commercial Bank (SVG) Ltd. (Senior Government Staff).

Because the ultimate regulatory powers reside with the national governments, the system is political by its nature. But again, as stressed by many of the respondents, the inclusion of all eight Ministers of Finance on the Monetary Council provides a built-in protection against outright, overt political interference in the regulatory and supervisory role of the ECCB.

This balance of forces has been aided by the widespread respect the ECCB has earned over the years for its technical capacities, the quality of its work in banking supervision and monetary operations, and the way in which it has taken the lead in the economic and financial arena of the subregion. Present and past government officials, as well as private and public bankers and other parties, were unanimous in identifying this respect as the second pillar of the system.

Supervision of Nonbank Financial Intermediaries

The nonbank institutions are all licensed by the national governments, usually (but not always) by the ministries of finance. Regulation is not uniform across countries, and supervision is spotty at best.

"Outside the commercial banks, supervision is weak. There are great deficiencies in supervision of insurance companies, credit unions, and building societies" (Errol Allen). The ECCB provides support and monitors developments in the credit union, insurance, and development finance sectors, but exercises no control over their activities: these institutions are licensed and supervised by relevant government authorities in the respective territories. Development finance institutions are required to submit prudential returns to the ECCB.

There is consensus that regulation and supervision of nonbank financial institutions need to be strengthened if the integrity of the ECCU financial system is to be maintained.

The ECCB has become especially concerned about the insurance companies, which in recent years have been competing with the banks by accepting deposits at very high interest rates and are thought to have overextended themselves on risks. Little is being done to analyze their reports, although St. Lucia has started to do on-site inspections. A Harmonized Insurance Act has been prepared for adoption by the member countries; it has been passed already by Grenada and St. Vincent and the Grenadines.

The offshore sector is regulated by the Offshore Banking Acts in the respective countries, and supervision is primarily the responsibility of the national regulators. The number of offshore banks expanded rapidly in the mid-1980s, and governments often did not do due diligence before granting licenses.

These dynamics changed in mid-2000 when all the OECS countries appeared on at least one of the lists ("name-and-shame lists" or blacklists) that were issued by three international bodies in response to concerns that had arisen regarding supervision standards in the world's offshore financial centers (Financial Stability Forum [FSF]), money laundering (Financial Action Task Force [FATF]), and so-called harmful tax competition (Organisation for Economic Co-operation and Development [OECD]).

The Caribbean countries responded with a major effort, supported by technical assistance from the IMF under its worldwide Offshore Financial Center Assessment Program (created by the IMF for the purpose) and from the United Kingdom in the case of Anguilla and Montserrat (as well as for Bermuda and the British Virgin Islands), to strengthen their offshore banking legislation and supervision capacities and bring them in line with the BCP standards. As a result, by 2005 the OECS countries had all been removed from the FSF and FATF lists.

The ECCB has been influential in building the capacity of countries in the region to supervise their offshore banking sectors. Already in late 2000, the Nevis Island Administration had enacted legislation that entrusted the ECCB with supervision of all offshore banking businesses under its jurisdiction, in accordance with the provisions of Article 41 of the ECCB Act. Dominica, Grenada, and St. Vincent and the Grenadines have also amended their Acts to allow for varying degrees of participation by the ECCB in the regulation and supervision of their offshore sectors, and St. Kitts and Nevis and St. Lucia have indicated agreement to some form of ECCB involvement in the supervision of their offshore financial sectors.

Salient Issues of the Banking and Financial System Today

Regulation of Nonbank Financial Intermediaries: Centralized or Decentralized?

Initially, the thinking in the ECCB and at least some governments was to bring nonbank financial institutions under the aegis of the ECCB, although countries with offshore banks within their borders tended to be particularly protective of their powers over those operations. But, as the complexities of expanded supervision tasks became clear, concern grew that the ECCB might become overextended, so an alternative approach was sought. This led to the concept of a so-called Single Regulatory Unit (SRU) to be established in each country, as laid out in a report prepared by Bernard La Corbiniére under the auspices of CARTAC.

On the basis of feasibility studies done by CARTAC for Dominica and Grenada, the report recommended that each country set up a new statutory body to regulate the nonbank institutions, including in some cases the offshore sector. To that end, Antigua and Barbuda in 2002 amended the International Business Companies Act of 1994 to establish a Financial Services Regulatory Commission, and Grenada approved an Act on the Regulation of Financial Institutions (GARFIN). Anguilla, Montserrat, and St. Kitts and Nevis will also establish statutory bodies. For political reasons, Dominica, St. Lucia, and St. Vincent and the Grenadines have opted to bring their SRUs under their Ministries of Finance.

The reach of the SRUs varies across countries. In St. Lucia and St. Vincent and the Grenadines, the SRUs will regulate both the domestic nonbank and the offshore sectors, partly as a means of building skill sets in the countries, and in the process helping the ECCB in its supervisory tasks. In St. Kitts and Nevis, the onshore and offshore functions are likely to remain separated, given the dominance of Nevis in the offshore sector and its status in the federation.

The strategy of developing supervision capacity in each country separately, rather than in a multicountry institution that services the region as a whole, may be seen as a departure from the strategy that gave rise to banking supervision in ECCB. Mignon Wade disagrees: "There are several reasons why the ECCB cannot at this point take the responsibility to supervise nonbank financial intermediaries: First, there is the risk that the ECCB would lose focus on what is its main responsibility. Second, there are financial reasons: the cost of on-site supervision is high because of the geography. Third, there are practical reasons: centralized supervision is difficult if countries do not have a homogeneous legal framework. And it will take many years to get to that point."

Allen agrees with Wade: "Centralized supervision did not seem to be the best-suited solution, given the circumstances." "At this point, there is no political support for a centralized body. There is lack of uniform legislation, which would be a precondition for centralized supervision" (Senior Staff of a SRU).

Consistent with these views, the SRU initiative has concentrated on preparing harmonized acts to regulate the different nonbank financial institutions in each territory, such as the just-mentioned Harmonized Insurance Act and the Act to Regulate Money Transfer Services. For St. Kitts and Nevis alone, 33 pieces of proposed legislation came out of the project (a government lawyer).

The authorities in St. Kitts and Nevis are concerned lest the SRU approach prove to be a "step backward." Representing the smallest independent state, they do not have the capacity to implement or pay for it or to provide the needed training. At best, it could be implemented in stages. The difficulty of ensuring the independence of supervisors in a small island community would be another good reason for having a centralized regionwide supervisory body instead (Janet Harris).

The decision to take a decentralized approach to the regulation of nonbank and offshore financial institutions was driven by pragmatic and political considerations, including the imperative need to tackle the offshore sector under the threat of the blacklists issued in mid-2000 (Allen), the budget difficulties that the ECCB would have faced had it assumed the responsibility, the reluctance of some governments to relinquish perceived power (a Senior Financial Consultant), a perception of human and financial resource limitations, and a tendency of overextension in the ECCB (Wade and a Senior Financial Consultant). Unifying the national supervision activities in one regulatory body in each country would bring efficiency gains, the ECCB would support them with technical assistance, and they could support the ECCB in its on-site examinations in the respective territories (Errol Allen). In the end, the arrangement could prove to be a stepping-stone to a single regional body, either separate from or incorporated in the ECCB, once the single financial space of the ECCU becomes a reality (Governor Venner).

The Stability of the Financial Sector: External and Domestic Sources of Risk

The Financial Sector Assessment Program of 1999 identified the possibility of contagion from outside developments as the principal risk for the ECCU financial system. The risk of contagion had been lower in the past because of the lack of integrated capital markets and because of what one respondent called a "trusting public" that takes the integrity of the system and the capability of the central bank for granted. As well as the supervision system has worked to date, it will need to be strengthened as capital markets in the subregion develop further and become integrated in the broader Caribbean and North American financial markets (Wendell Lawrence). The view of the ECCB is that the system has a proven capacity to act quickly when a systemic emergency arises, allowing it to quell any contagion that might ensue.

The entry of Trinidadian banks and insurance companies into the financial space of the subregion is a potential source of risk to the system. Both banks and insurance companies are aggressive: the banks operate in the merchant bank tradition of seeking upfront transaction fees and are less well regulated than the ECCU banks (including offshore), and Trinidad and Tobago is only just now starting to regulate the insurance business (Wendell Lawrence). The recycling by Trinidadian banks of deposits in OECS social insurance funds to OECS governments could have played a role in the debt situation in the OECS (Janet Harris).

There are also domestic risks. As mentioned above, monetary and price stability had also been the result of fiscal discipline. To the extent that most countries in the region began to run systematic and large deficits from the mid-1990s on, the fiscal pillar of monetary stability has greatly eroded.

Most of the OECS governments' domestic debt is in the portfolio of the commercial banks or in the hands of the public; except for the social insurance funds, the nonbank financial intermediaries hold very little government debt. If governments encounter difficulties servicing their debts, the real value of bank assets will deteriorate, which may put pressure on the current monetary arrangement: a quasi-currency board backs high-powered money, not M2 or any broader monetary aggregate.

The new Banking Act (UBA) introduces the possibility of distinguishing the quality of government assets and establishes the obligation to provision government debt if and when the debt is not serviced. This provision may be important in the case of loans to public enterprises that stay on the books of national commercial banks. The St. Kitts-Nevis-Anguilla National Bank, for example, holds a large portfolio of nonperforming loans to the government of St. Kitts and Nevis and to the now-defunct state sugar company. While the loans to the latter are secured, the realization of the collateral would be protracted (Mignon Wade).

The new powers of the ECCB in the Revised UBA may strengthen its hands in relation to the governments, but as noted by Wendell Lawrence, these have not been tested yet, and in any case "the real issue is the sanctions to be taken, not who exercises them; in the end, though, it is the Ministers of Finance who should be taking the lead in ensuring that banks actually take the actions specified in the MOUs and LOCs."[7]

Reflections on the Orgins and Evolution of Banking Supervision in OECS

What does this examination of the OECS experience with banking supervision tell us about (a) what influences the creation and subsequent performance of an institution and (b) whether a similar regulatory model might be adopted in the context of nonbank financial intermediaries?

Origins

During the transition to independence, there was a vacuum regarding supervision of domestic banks; political independence made this vacuum visible, posing a challenge to the governments of the Eastern Caribbean countries. The ECCB was founded in response.

The decision to vest the central bank with the responsibility for regulation and supervision of banks implied that each member country delegated part of its sovereign power, something that politicians are usually reluctant to do. Factors that weighed in favor of a multicountry solution were the following:

- *History*. The Eastern Caribbean states had a tradition of supporting multicountry institutions for core state responsibilities: justice, money, and defense. (In areas where there was already a significant degree of autonomy in each island-state—education, health, taxation, and tariffs on international trade—idiosyncratic solutions prevailed.)
- *Structure of the industry*. Most banks were (and are) branches of international banks operating in several countries in the subregion. A uniform

regulatory framework reduced their operation costs, generating a *demand* for uniform regulation in the subregion.

Creating ECCB and a banking supervision department for the subregion did not imply that each country government entirely relinquished its jurisdiction in banking to the multicountry central bank. In fact, the member governments retained fundamental regulatory authority in the following:

- *Licensing of new banks.* This is the responsibility of the finance ministry of each member country; the ECCB has an advisory role. In principle, this division of responsibilities raises eyebrows, but in practice it has worked satisfactorily. Time and reputation have won a de facto veto power for the ECCB in this area.
- *Enforcement of the law and sanctions.* Following a bank inspection, the ECCB may issue an MOU or LOC; it cannot, however, enforce its recommendations. ECCB's role here is again advisory to the finance ministries.

The coexistence of national and multicountry institutions in banking regulation and supervision implies a built-in tension similar to that existing between state and federal governments in federal states or between independent central banks and ministries of finance in some countries. An important chapter of the story of banking supervision in the OECS subregion is the story of how this tension may be managed.

Evolution

The decision to pool resources and supervise banks through the ECCB had a clear appeal in exploiting economies of scale. But for this to work in practice, the governments of the member countries and the management of the ECCB had to develop pragmatic processes and procedures that minimized friction:

- *Establishing a legal framework.* A uniform legislative framework governing bank operation has been critical to the efficiency of the multicountry regulatory solution. Had that framework remained heterogeneous, the effectiveness of the regional institution would have been considerably impaired.
- *Budget.* The capacity to perform the supervision function depended on a stable source of funds to build the necessary cadre of human capital

and physical resources. The fact that the ECCB had its own resources through seigniorage and that the Monetary Council authorized sufficient spending budgets over the past 25 years strengthened independence.

- *Time.* Time has been necessary to familiarize banks, finance ministers, and banking supervision staff with the rules and to build reputation.
- *Rules.* Rules—in particular, the unanimity rule in the Monetary Council governing the relationship between national and subregional authorities—have been important in ensuring the independence of the central bank.
- *Judicious management of power.* Wise rules have been accompanied by wise management of tensions inherent in the coexistence of national governments and multistate institutions. Parties have favored cooperation over collision.

Regulation of Nonbank Financial Intermediaries

The creation of SRUs in each country, rather than pooling resources and establishing a multicountry regulator, might look like a step backward.

But it would be wrong to rush to that conclusion. At that time, many of the conditions propitious to founding the ECCB were lacking for nonbank entities. Here are two examples:

- *There was an absence of unified legislation covering insurance and other financial activities across countries.* This would have been a serious obstacle to exploiting the benefits of pooling national resources in a single multistate body.
- *Member countries were reluctant to commit the resources required to build up and maintain a multistate regulatory agency.* The new agency might not have been able to secure a budget adequate to build the necessary technical cadre and push for a unified legislation in the nonbank financial sectors.

Annex 2A. List of Interviewees

Name	Affiliation
Dwight Venner	Governor, ECCB
Errol Allen	Former Deputy Governor, ECCB
Mignon Wade	Counselor, ECCB
Wendell Lawrence	Former Finance Secretary, St. Kitts and Nevis
Janet Harris	Finance Secretary, St. Kitts and Nevis
Hugo Pinard	Former Country Manager, Royal Bank of Canada
Isaac Anthony	Director of Finance, St. Lucia

Edmund Lawrence	Manager, National Bank of St. Kitts and Nevis
James Simpson	Senior Staff ECCB
Trevor Brathwaite	Deputy Governor of the ECCB
Douglas James	Manager, Offshore Regulatory Office, St. Vincent and the Grenadines
Fidela Clarke	Director General/Regulator, Financial Services Department, St. Kitts and Nevis
Bernard LeCarbonniere	Former Finance Secretary, St. Lucia
Robert Effros	Former Counsel, Legal Department, IMF

Notes

1. A pure currency board issues (or contracts) money against a change in international net reserves; a quasi-currency board also allows (within strict limits) the issuance of money against a change in domestic credit.

2. The Eastern Caribbean Currency Union (ECCU) is made up of eight countries sharing a common currency under the aegis of the Eastern Caribbean Central Bank. The currency is the Eastern Caribbean dollar.

3. The IMF has supported the ECCB in all areas of its operations, both through its Article IV surveillance of the six member countries that are independent and regional ECCU surveillance (in place since 1998) and through its technical assistance (TA) services, including those provided by the Caribbean Regional Technical Assistance Center (CARTAC). In the area of banking supervision, TA was provided for the drafting of the UBA and of subsequent amendments incorporated in the revised banking act, for the assessment of ECCB standards against the Basel Core Principles (BCP), for the strengthening of the offshore sector, and for the development of the Single Regulatory Units (SRU) framework (see below).

4. M2 is the sum of currency plus demand and time deposits in the consolidated financial system.

5. The Caribbean Group of Banking Supervisors, established in 1984, seeks to foster cooperative efforts to implement international best practices among its members.

6. Data as of March 2007.

7. An MOU is a memorandum of understanding; an LOC is a letter of commitment.

References

Holdip, M. P. 1992. "The Eastern Caribbean Central Bank: An Historical Analysis of a Sub-Regional Monetary Institution." Master's thesis, University of the West Indies.

IMF (International Monetary Fund). 2004. "Eastern Caribbean Currency Union: Financial System Stability Assessment, including Report on the Observance of Standards and Codes on Banking Supervision." Country Report 04/293, International Monetary Fund, Washington, DC.

————. 2005. "Eastern Caribbean Currency Union: 2005 Article IV Consultation: Staff Report and Public Information Notice on the Executive Board Discussion on the Eastern Caribbean Currency Union." Country Report 05/304, International Monetary Fund, Washington, DC.

van Beek, Frits, José Roberto Rosales, Mayra Zermeño, Ruby Randall, and Jorge Shepherd. 2000. "The Eastern Caribbean Currency Union: Performance, Progress, and Policy Issues." Occasional Paper 195, International Monetary Fund, Washington, DC.

CHAPTER 3

Banking Supervision in the CFA Franc Countries

Christian Brachet

This case study describes the emergence and development of banking supervision in the countries in the *Colonies Françaises d'Afrique* (CFA) franc zones. The story has special relevance for small states. They face high fixed costs in the provision of public services and can benefit from the added credibility that supranational regulatory authorities sometimes bring. This study addresses the policy response by members of the two zones to the challenges of financial sector supervision (in the context of the crises that beset banking systems from the late 1980s). It helps to think about the benefits and costs of multicountry bank supervision and regulation; the conditions that influence the choice between national and multicountry institutions over time, especially for countries with limited financial and human resources; the possibility that a group of developing countries may import de facto monetary and price stability from an industrialized country through a multicountry central banking agreement; and the conditions that make such an agreement viable.

Christian Brachet is an employee of the International Institute for Africa. The assistance of Christian François, also an employee of the International Institute for Africa, whose familiarity with the franc zones and its history has been of considerable help, is gratefully acknowledged. See annex 3B for a list of people who have contributed through interviews or comment in the course of research.

The CFA franc is the currency of six countries in Central Africa and eight in West Africa (table 3.1).[1] Three of these countries, Equatorial Guinea, Gabon, and Guinea-Bissau, are small states. The two CFA franc zones have been in existence since late 1945, following a series of adaptations to the arrangements that had governed the Franc Zone until 1939. (See annex 4A for a brief review of the historical background and the evolution of monetary arrangements.)

The historical origins of the CFA franc zones and of BEAC (*Banque des Etats de l'Afrique Centrale*) and BCEAO (*Banque Centrale des Etats de l'Afrique de l'Ouest*), the two regional central banks, are similar to those of the monetary arrangements in the Eastern Caribbean that gave origin to the Eastern Caribbean Central Bank. In both cases, the creation of multicountry central banks made it possible to circumvent weak capacity at the country level. And in both cases, the creation of a multicountry central bank did not imply the withdrawal of national governments from the financial sector; in fact, they remain responsible for the

Table 3.1. CFA Franc Zones: Basic Data, 2005

Trading Countries	Area (sq km)	Population (thousands)	GDP CFA francs (billions)	GDP U.S. dollars[1] (billions)	GDP U.S. dollars[1] (per capita)
CEMAC					
Cameroon	475,442	16,322	8,771	16.6	1,019
Central African Republic	622,984	4,038	751	1.4	353
Congo, Republic of	342,000	3,999	3,129	5.9	1,484
Gabon	267,667	1,534	4,508	8.6	6,177
Equatorial Guinea	28,051	650	3,759	7.1	10,968
Chad	1,284,000	9,749	3,088	5.9	601
Total	3,020,144	36,292	24,006	45.5	
UEMOA					
Benin	115,762	8,439	2,334	4.4	525
Burkina Faso	274,122	13,228	2,985	5.7	428
Côte d'Ivoire	322,463	18,154	8,451	16.0	883
Guinea-Bissau	36,125	1,586	161	0.3	192
Mali	1,240,192	13,518	2,896	5.5	406
Niger	1,267,000	13,957	1,712	3.2	233
Senegal	197,161	11,658	4,537	8.6	738
Togo	56,785	6,145	1,049	2.0	324
Total	3,509,610	86,685	24,125	45.7	

Source: Banque de France, Annual Report on the Franc Zone.
[1]US$1 = CFAF 527.25.

licensing of banks and the enforcement of sanctions to this day. There are also differences: ECCB has always operated as if it were a currency board, BEAC and BCEAO have not; the Treasury of France is lender of last resort to the financial system, ECCB is on its own.

The history of banking regulation in Central and West Africa also resembles that of the Eastern Caribbean. Before independence, most banks were branches of international banks, and prudential supervision was largely done by the inspection departments of those banks. After political independence, prudential regulation in Central and West Africa was not uniform across countries, and the few existing norms were not always enforced. Weak oversight was in accordance with the characteristics of the local banking sectors and with the international norm that obtained in the 1950s and 1960s. The importance given to banking supervision in the Eastern Caribbean (see the case study on Banking Supervision in OECS Member Countries, chapter 3) was informed by two decades of experience and deep changes in local and international banking systems between the 1960s and 1980s.

The creation of regional mechanisms for bank supervision in Central and West Africa was principally the product of the crises that beset the banking systems of the zones from the late 1980s. These both contributed to, and fed on, the broader economic and financial imbalances that led to the devaluation of the CFA franc (CFAF) on January 12, 1994, and the subsequent tightening of fiscal policies and extensive restructurings of the banking sector. Regionally based banking supervision also followed from the belated realization that national supervision mechanisms were inconsistent with lender-of-last-resort responsibilities vested in regional central banks (and ultimately the French Treasury).

Looked at after the fact, these regional arrangements have certainly led to important savings of financial and human resources, compared with the largely nation-based systems that prevailed until 1990. But their main claims to success have been the improvements in corporate governance in an industry in which it had been severely lacking, the professionalization of supervision and, substantially, the depoliticization of a process that had originated in the banking crises of the 1980s.

Monetary Arrangements and Institutions since Independence

Background—It is with independence in the late 1950s/early 1960s that the zones became fully collaborative arrangements, freely entered into, between the newly sovereign states and France. The arrangements were, and still are, characterized by (a) an open-ended guarantee by France of the convertibility of CFA francs into French francs—now the euro—as a counterpart to the pooling of at least 50 percent of the foreign exchange reserves of each zone into operation accounts maintained with the French Treasury;[2] (b) the free transferability of funds, within existing exchange regulations, between the zones and France; (c) a fixed exchange rate of the CFAF to the French franc, then to the euro once it replaced the franc on January 1, 1999; and (d) a series of mechanisms intended to ensure that member countries conduct policies in a manner consistent with the peg and with the guarantee of convertibility provided by France. Most important, at the operational level, are the required maintenance of a minimum 20 percent foreign exchange cover ratio for the central banks' sight liabilities and a limit on outstanding central bank advances to member countries' treasuries equivalent to no more than 20 percent of fiscal receipts in the previous fiscal year. This limit has been set to go down to zero during 2003–2013 in the Monetary Union of West Africa (UMOA), but remains unchanged in the Monetary Union of Central Africa (UMAC) (see annex 4A). Providing, as they did, a guarantee of relative financial stability through anchoring the exchange rate and maintaining, with safeguards, the role of the French Treasury as the de facto lender of last resort, these mechanisms explain to an important extent the virtually seamless transition from the pre- to the postindependence arrangements.

Although it did not lead to substantive changes in the principles governing the zone, independence led to the first formal revamping of the zone's institutions since the war. The official *Instituts d'Emission* established at that time were converted in 1959 into full-fledged central banks, with substantial African participation in their executive organs, although they remained headquartered in Paris and retained significant French board representation for both BCEAO and the then BCEAC (later renamed BEAC), including a French chairman for BCEAC.

For West Africa, the BCEAO regrouped Upper Volta (which subsequently became Burkina Faso), Dahomey (now Benin), Côte d'Ivoire, Mauritania, Niger, Senegal, and Togo (this last, in 1963). Mali (formerly French Sudan) initially refused to join the BCEAO, left the Franc Zone, and established its own central bank and currency—but it subsequently rejoined. Mauritania pulled out of the arrangement in 1973, while Guinea-Bissau, a former Portuguese colony, joined the UEMOA, UMOA, and BCEAO in 1997.

In equatorial Africa, meanwhile, the BCEAC regrouped the Central African Republic (formerly Oubangui-Chari), Chad, the Republic of Congo, Gabon, and Cameroon. Equatorial Guinea, a former Spanish colony, joined the central bank and the regional arrangements in 1985.[3]

The 1972–73 Reforms—A second wave of postindependence adaptations occurred in 1972–73, when the two zones acquired features that are close to current arrangements and their institutions became more formally "Africanized." In late 1972, the BCEAC changed its name to BEAC; France relinquished the position of chairman of the board, which passed to a representative of one of the member countries (on an annual rotating basis); the size of the board itself was reduced from 16 to 12 directors (13 since Equatorial Guinea joined the zone), with the number of French representatives falling to 4, then to 3 in November 1974. The new bank gained a measure of independence for the management of up to 35 percent (now rising gradually to 50 percent) of its foreign assets; and from April 1975, the French Treasury granted an exchange guarantee (in terms of special drawing rights [SDRs]) to the BEAC's foreign holdings in the operation account (now limited to the required statutory holdings). Effective in 1977, BEAC headquarters was moved from Paris to Yaoundé, Cameroon.

The statutes of the BCEAO, for their part, were modified in November 1973, effective in October 1974. Bank management, headed by the governor and its board, was placed under the control of the Council of the Ministers of Finance of the UMOA, with rotating chairmanship, and the board itself was set at 14 members (16 since the entrance of Guinea-Bissau), including 2 for France. The same rules applied to the arrangements with France as for the BEAC. In 1978, BCEAO headquarters was moved from Paris to Dakar, Senegal.

The economic and financial crises that engulfed the two zones in the late 1980s through the early 1990s (see below) brought recognition that their long-term survival depended on their becoming truly integrated economic areas and led to important institutional reforms in the 1990s. In addition to a major devaluation of the CFA franc and to the adoption of stern adjustment policies, these reforms entailed full removal of impediments to intraregional trade, adoption of a common external tariff, coordination of fiscal stances, and establishment of regional surveillance mechanisms to enforce economic policy discipline consistent with the peg. Thus were born in the west the Economic and Monetary Union of West Africa (UEMOA) on January 10, 1994; and in equatorial Africa,

Box 3.1

Legal Frameworks

Inter-African texts
BEAC

(a) Convention of Monetary Cooperation between the five states, November 1972 (extended to Equatorial Guinea in January 1985), providing for the establishment of the Monetary Committee of the BEAC area and of the central bank (BEAC). This text was amended and replaced by the UMAC convention of July 1996.

(b) Statutes of the BEAC (annexed to UMAC convention; last amended in July 2003).

BCEAO

(a) Treaty between the six original member states, November 1973 (extended to Mali in June 1984 and to Guinea-Bissau in May 1997), redefining the UMOA and establishing the BCEAO.

(b) Statutes of the BCEAO (annexed to UMOA Treaty; last amended in September 1990).

Texts governing the relations between the zones and France
BEAC

(a) Convention of Monetary Cooperation between the member states of the BEAC and the French Republic, November 1972 (amended January 1985 to accommodate the entrance of Equatorial Guinea).

(b) Operation Account Convention between the Minister of Economy and Finance of France and the President of the Board of the BEAC, March 1973.

BCEAO

(a) Cooperation Agreement between the French Republic and the Republics of the UMOA, December 1973, extended to Mali in June 1984 and to Guinea-Bissau in May 1997.

(b) Operation Account Convention, December 1973, between the Minister of Economy and Finance of France and the President of the Council of Ministers of the UMOA.

Sources: BEAC, BCEAO, and Banque de France.

Box 3.2

UMOA/BCEAO: Institutional Arrangements and Governance Structures

The executive organs of the UMOA/BCEAO comprise the following:[a]

(a) The Conference of the Heads of State, established by the Treaty of November 14, 1973, reforming the UMOA. The supreme authority of the union, it meets once a year in each state in turn and under the chairmanship of the host country. It decides unanimously on any issue not resolved by the Council of Ministers (see (b) below) and on the adhesion/withdrawal to/from the Union of any new or existing members.

(b) The Council of Ministers, established by the same treaty. It consists of two ministers by member country and is chaired by ministers of finance on a rotating basis for a period of two years. The governor attends, with a consultative voice. The council meets at least twice a year and decides on monetary and credit policy for the UMOA.

(c) The BCEAO itself, which is the monetary authority of the UMOA. Its main executive organs are the following:

– The governor. He or she is appointed for six years by the Council of Ministers and in principle is to come from each member country in turn (in practice, all governors have been Ivorian citizens). In addition to his or her responsibilities for the management of the bank, the governor oversees the implementation of the treaties, agreements, and conventions relative to the BCEAO; determines the agenda of the board; and implements board and Council of Ministers decisions. He or she represents the bank in relations with third parties and, importantly, has joint signing authority with the Chairman of the Council of Ministers.

– The two deputy governors. Appointed for five years by the board, they assist the governor in the discharge of his or her duties. The functions in principle are also to be rotated between member countries.

– The Executive Board. Originally consisting of 16 members—two each per country, plus two for France—it has grown to 18 with the entrance of Guinea-Bissau into the UMOA. The board, chaired by the governor, meets at least four times a year (or as often as needed) and is responsible for defining the main orientations of monetary policy within the union.

(continued)

Decisions normally are taken by simple majority; a few require a majority of 6 out of 7 members; changes in the statutes of the BCEAO, which must also be ratified by the Council of Ministers, require unanimity.

- The National Credit Councils. Chaired by the minister of finance of each member country, they consist of two state representatives, four independent personalities appointed by each government, and, since 1988, a representative from France. The councils support the director of the local BCEAO agency and implement the guidelines set by the UMOA Council of Ministers and the BCEAO board on the financing of economic activity in each member country.
- The directors of the national BCEAO agencies, who are the equivalent of the BEAC national directors.
- The central directors, who are the department heads.
- The national controllers and the commissioners. The national controllers, appointed by the minister of finance in each member country, oversee the accounts of the national agencies. Their observations are centralized by a commissioner-controller (appointed by the Council of Ministers of the union), who also verifies the accounts of BCEAO headquarters.

Source: BCEAO.
a. As of December 31, 2006.

the Economic and Monetary Community of Central Africa (CEMAC) in 1996.[4] These institutional adjustments were accompanied by reforms of the operational monetary policy frameworks.

Arrangements—The legal arrangements governing the zones (box 3.1) and the institutional frameworks, including the governance structure of the two central banks (boxes 3.2 and 3.3), thus consist of two series of texts: the first, inter-African, on the modalities of cooperation between the member states of each of the two zones and on the statutes of their respective central banks; the second on the rules governing the relations between each monetary union and France (box 3.4) and on the modalities of operation of the operation accounts. In recognition of the sovereign participation of member states, all countries have equal representation in the supreme organs of the unions (that is, in the Conferences of the Heads of State and in the Councils of Ministers). This equality also extends to the composition of the board of the BCEAO and to the number of French executive directors (however, the board of the BEAC differentiates between the larger and the smaller countries).

Box 3.3

UMAC/BEAC—Institutional Arrangements and Governance Structures

The executive organs of the UMAC/BEAC comprise the following:[a]

(a) The Conference of the Heads of State.

(b) The Ministerial Committee (two ministers per country). The executive Secretary of the CEMAC and the Secretary General of the COBAC attend as observers; the BEAC Governor acts as reporter.

(c) The Executive Board of the BEAC, consisting of 13 directors (and an equivalent number of alternates), four for Cameroon, three for France, two for Gabon, and one each for the Central African Republic, Chad, the Republic of Congo, and Equatorial Guinea. The board meets at least four times a year or as often as needed, under the chairmanship of the governor and in the presence of the vice governor and censors, who have a consultative voice. Decisions normally require a simple majority; a few require a qualified majority of 3/4; changes in the BEAC statutes require unanimity.

(d) These executive organs oversee BEAC management, which comprises the following:

- The governor, appointed for five years (renewable) by unanimous decision of the Heads of State, on a proposal from the Gabonese government. The governor carries out the decisions of the board and is responsible for the implementation of the statutes and the management of the institution, including personnel appointments and revocations not in the purview of the Board.
- The deputy governor and the secretary general, appointed in the same conditions, on proposal from the Congolese and Chadian governments, respectively.
- The national directors of the BEAC, appointed by the board on a proposal of the governor.
- The central directors, who are the department heads.

(e) The national monetary and financial committees, which support the national directors and consist of the minister of finance, chairman, the ministers representing the country on the Ministerial Committee, the executive director(s) of the BEAC for the country, one personality appointed *intuitu personae* (in his or her personal capacity) by the local government, and the BEAC governor. They meet in the presence of at least two of the censors, including the French censor.

(continued)

(f) The College of Censors, which consists of one official each from Cameroon, Gabon, and France and oversees the accounts of the bank, the regularity of its operations, and the implementation of the budget.

(g) The Audit Committee, consisting of the three censors, one Executive Director, and one independent personality appointed *intuitu personae*.

Source: http://www.beac.int/cobac/cbcobac.html
a. As of December 31, 2006.

Box 3.4

The Mechanisms of Coordination with France

The institutions described above remain proper to each CFAF zone. In addition, twice a year, usually ahead of the BWI's Spring and Annual Meetings, all ministers of finance of the Franc Zone, including from the Comoros, meet with their French counterpart to review international developments and prospects, examine developments within the zones, and decide on possible modifications in the structures and method of procedure of the zones.

Source: Author.

The Banking Systems: From Independence to the Crisis

The banking systems—During most of the colonial period, and much of the French Union period until 1959, the banking systems of the zones consisted mostly of branches or subsidiaries of French banks. Banks in the CFA franc zones operated largely under self-imposed principles of prudent lending in the context of the general rules established by the Bank of France and enforced by banks' internal inspection departments and the French Bank Control Commission (precursor of the current Banking Commission). The quality of loan portfolios was also continuously monitored, bank by bank, and in effect loan by loan, by the criteria established by the Bank of France to determine eligibility to its rediscount window. There were few, if any, local banks.

With independence, three developments—all eventually with adverse consequences—took wing. One was a sharp, and often compulsory, increase in state participation in banks, including subsidiaries of foreign banks, or even their outright nationalization (for instance, all banks in Cameroon had to have a minimum 33 percent government participation until the late 1980s; and all banks in Benin and Equatorial Guinea were state-owned until 1989). A second was the emergence of commercial banks of purely local, and generally mixed (public-private), ownership, often minimally capitalized. A third was the establishment of a number of state-controlled development banks designed to finance long-term investment projects (nine in the UMOA and five in the BEAC area in 1989.) This reflected the prevailing interventionist slant of economic policy making, an approach also manifest in the mushrooming of state-owned enterprises (SOEs).

Supervisory arrangements—Supervision and the development of the requisite regulatory and prudential apparatus, however, lagged behind. The few existing regulations and applicable accounting principles were broadly informed by the system then prevailing in France; however, they were not uniform and often remained unenforced. Oversight was lodged in part in an inspectorate general (BCEAO) or control department (BEAC) of the central banks, but mostly in a control commission/directorate in each country's ministry of finance, supported by the local agency of the central bank. Banking supervision in general was weak; state-owned banks (and state participations) weighed heavily on the banking industry; and political interference in lending decisions at the national level was widespread. But the role of the regional authorities remained purely technical and advisory, and responsibility for supervision ultimately resided with the ministry of finance.[4] In this environment, regional supervision was lax, or light and spotty, while, in the words of a commercial banker, "... national involvement leaned far more toward management of state participations than toward enforcement of prudential rules."

System vulnerabilities—To the extent that, during that period, credit was largely "directed" and tightly supervised by the two central banks, with rediscounting ceilings decided per country and per bank, the monetary authorities in effect decided on a case-by-case basis on the type of credit that would be eligible for refinancing, establishing in the process a de facto rating of individual borrowers. Discretionary and distortionary as it was, the system might have offered a measure of protection against deteriorating loan portfolios had it not been for important loopholes:

- The increased reliance on commercial bank borrowing by governments as they were reaching their statutory ceilings on central bank advances—borrowing not subject to provisioning against losses even if not serviced (a feature that continues to this day, despite recent attempts in the UMAC to modify the rules).

- The automatic eligibility to the rediscount window, outside of the national/individual bank ceilings, of specific types of paper, prominently paper representative of export crop prefinancing (the so-called *crédits de campagne*—an important feature of the UMOA countries, where cocoa, coffee, and cotton are dominant cash crops); and the attendant lack of professional verification of the quality of signatures and the viability of the underlying operation.
- The sizable equity participation of the state in commercial banks and representation in their executive organs. This typically made for heavy-handed interference in bank decisions and financing of nonviable ventures. It also opened the door to large-scale connected lending and at times a true perversion of banking practices. Last but not least, it much weakened the ability of the national supervisory authorities and of the small and understaffed inspection directorates of the two central banks to act against credit abuse. To quote a commercial banker: "No Minister of Finance, or his representative, will ever be prepared or able to warn or push for sanctions against a fellow minister who also happens to be a bank CEO, even if his bank is in serious breach of prudential rules."
- The growing abuse of state-owned development banks to complement, or make up for, shrinking investment budgets—either directly or through enforced lending to state-owned enterprises or agencies, more often than not for nonviable projects.

Unfolding of the crisis—The seeds thus sown found a fertile soil in the extraordinarily severe economic and financial crisis that engulfed the two CFAF zones during 1985–93—and fueled it further. Over this eight-year period, real per capita declines in the CFA franc zone ranged from 20 to 50 percent; imbalances in fiscal and external payments mounted dramatically; arrears in domestic and external payments—in effect debt defaults, but also defaults on current payments—piled up; banking systems turned insolvent virtually everywhere, or survived by means of blatant breaching of prudential rules, supervisory forbearance, and support from the monetary authority that was well beyond appropriate limits; and policy response to domestic and external shocks was at best uneven, most often weak—falling well short of what the situation demanded.

There were many causes for this collapse, and the ensuing literature has been abundant.[6] First was the abrupt downturn in the terms of trade of most of these countries; second, the increasingly expansionary fiscal policies of most members; third, the resulting real appreciation of the CFAF;[7] fourth, the timidity or absence of microeconomic reforms that might have supported early enough the redirection of resources to tradables; and fifth, the widespread default on foreign and domestic payments obligations, including obligations to banks, as the margins under the ceilings on central bank advances were being used up.

This last set of developments was the tipping point for the fiscal and banking crises. Governments and agencies withdrew their deposits from banks; and accumulated arrears further impaired bank liquidity as government/SOE suppliers reduced cash balances while ceasing to service bank loans. The public took fright and stepped up deposit withdrawals, velocity of circulation of money accelerated, and capital fled. The resulting liquidity crisis compounded the banks' already damaged solvency and profitability, and the banking systems of the zone began to implode. As Senegal's Minister of Finance observed to an IMF mission in 1988, "banks are being eaten up by worms."[8]

Devaluation—A sharp correction in the external value of the CFAF, accompanied by stringent supporting domestic policies, became inescapable. Late in the night of January 11, 1994, after a series of marathon sessions, the heads of state of the zone, gathered in Dakar, announced a devaluation of the two currencies from CFAF 50 to CFAF 100 per French franc (75 in the case of the Comorian franc), effective on January 12.[9] This was the first, and so far only, modification in the parity of the CFA franc since 1948. In the weeks that followed, all countries except Togo, which was in the midst of a domestic political crisis and acted only later in the year, adopted adjustment programs—including a large component devoted to restructuring their banking systems.

The international community acted speedily to support the operation. The IMF approved some 11 standby or ESAF (Enhanced Structural Adjustment Facility) arrangements before the end of 1994 for a total of about SDR 1 billion; the World Bank and the AfDB/AfDF (African Development Bank/African Development Fund) approved a variety of adjustment support operations, for totals of US$1.8 billion and US$0.4 billion, respectively, and the European Union for US$0.5 billion; France extended exceptional assistance of more than US$1.2 billion; other donors, mostly bilateral, of US$0.3 billion; and debt relief reached

US$9.8 billion. New project loans reached US$1.8 billion (*Source:* IMF, January 1995, unpublished).

After the Devaluation: The Resolution of the Banking Crisis and the Birth of Regional Supervision

The devaluation was, politically, traumatic within the zone. Most populations had never known another regime and treated the CFAF and the French franc as virtual substitutes. But, because of generally prudent fiscal and wage policies in most CFAF countries, the exchange rate correction set them on a course of resumed growth and much improved fiscal and external performance, in sharp contrast with the previous eight-year period. Output growth has averaged more than 5 percent since 1995; after the initial wave of price corrections in 1994, inflation has remained, on average, close to that of the anchor currency country (now the euro area); with the help of the Heavily Indebted Poor Countries (HIPC) Initiative, the debt overhang has been about worked off, or nearly so; balance of payments positions have improved considerably; and the combined net foreign asset positions of the two central banks have grown to more than US$15 billion at the end of November 2006 (with the foreign exchange cover ratio approaching 93 in the BEAC), levels unheard of in the past (table 3.2).[10]

Most important, the financial sector landscape has been transformed and strengthened in both subzones. Admittedly, in the UMOA, the bulk of the effort started well before the devaluation, and BCEAO initiatives had laid down a large part of the bank restructuring process, or at least of its conditions for success, in the late 1980s. The key actor in this effort was Mr. Alassane Ouattara, then BCEAO Governor—later (from April

Table 3.2. CFA Franc Zones: Net Foreign Position of Monetary Authorities
(*billions of CFA francs*)

	2000	2001	2002	2003	2004	2005	2006
BCEAO	1,348.2	2,000.8	2,594.7	2,894.5	3,029.8	3,195.4	3,611.7[a]
Assets	2,522.3	3,103.8	3,655.4	3,735.3	3,729.4	3,768.9	. . .
Liabilities	1,174.1	−1,102.9	−1,060.7	−840.8	−699.6	−573.5	. . .
BEAC	547.7	484.4	696.7	675.4	1,232.9	2,625.8	4,651.5[b]
Assets	929.8	849.8	1,049.7	991.1	1,535.6	2,911.1	. . .
Liabilities	−342.0	−365.2	−353.0	−315.7	−302.4	−285.3	. . .

Sources: BCEAO, BEAC, and Banque de France.
a. August 2006.
b. October 2006.

1990) Chairman of the Coordination Committee on the Stabilization and Recovery Program in the Presidency of Côte d'Ivoire, and then Prime Minister from 1990 to 1994.

Strategy in the UMOA—With active support from President Houphouët-Boigny, who enjoyed unchallenged moral and political authority in French-speaking Africa, and from the Bank of France and the French Treasury, Mr. Ouattara embarked on a campaign to persuade other UMOA heads of state of the urgency of tackling the distress in their banking systems. He called for the following:

- A clean break with past practices in bank management and supervision—including the imposition of rigorous limits on lending to associates, shareholders, and bank executives; strengthened powers for the monetary authorities to force shareholders to increase capital contributions to institutions facing difficulties; greatly improved internal controls; and enforcement of strict criteria of competence and honesty in selecting bank executives and managers
- The adoption of a new, harmonized banking law (October 1990; revised in 2000) and the standardization of accounting plans (effective in early 1996); the adoption of uniform prudential regulations and strengthening of prudential norms; and the establishment of a regional banking commission immune to national political interference
- The closing of money-losing state-owned development banks
- A large-scale restructuring of commercial banking systems, including scaling down government participation (to 25 percent or less) and reducing government involvement in management decisions; streamlining operational costs; reorienting deposits toward institutions facing liquidity constraints, and accelerating repayments of government debts; the assumption by governments of banks' (consolidated) debts to the BCEAO; abandonment of some official deposits and claims; direct state reimbursements of depositors and some capital contributions; and calls on existing or new investors to recapitalize banks that could be rescued
- The adoption of indirect instruments of monetary policy in lieu of the directed credit of earlier periods
- Changes in the legal and judiciary environment through adopting new procedures of arbitrage, better mechanisms to foreclose on collateral, and alignment of banking legislation with the regional business law (enshrined in the regional OHADA Treaty of 1993)

Sizable external financing was lined up: in particular, large Financial Sector Adjustment Loans (FSALs), or FSAL-like loans from the International Development Association (IDA), and similar support from other multilateral or bilateral donors, usually in the context of IMF-supported programs. The restructuring was radical and determined. By 1996, the number of banks in operation in the UMOA had fallen to 52, from 105 in 1986; and the total estimated fiscal cost of the operation amounted to around CFAF 1.3 trillion, or almost 16 percent of regional 1993 GDP. Foreign banks, for their part, had contributed some CFAF 120 billion in new equity. By then, the crisis was also well on its way to a resolution—at least in its systemic dimension, for there remain several individual problem banks (see below)—and the number of banks in operation indeed started to rise again.

At the same time as the restructuring program was launched, and after much debate,[11] the decision was made to overhaul past supervision arrangements and establish at the regional level the Banking Commission of the UMOA (April 24, 1990). The commission began operating on October 1, 1990, when the new banking law—*Loi portant Réglementation Bancaire*—which had to be ratified by all seven countries, became effective (table 3.3).

Table 3.3. CFA Franc Zone Banking Commissions: Regulatory Apparatus, Modus Operandi, and Powers

BC-UMOA	Central African Banking Commission (COBAC)
1. Legal and regulatory framework	
Convention of April 24, 1990, establishing the banking commission	Convention of October 16, 1990, establishing the COBAC
Banking law of February 24, 1990, and subsequent amendments (common framework; ratified individually by each member country)	Convention on the harmonization of banking regulations in the states of Central Africa (January 17, 1992); ratified individually by each member country
Prudential framework (June 27, 1991; update of June 17, 1999; became effective January 1, 2000)	Prudential framework (12 regulations issued from 1993 to 2004)
Accounting plan for banking profession in the UMOA (January 1996; revised July 2004)	Accounting plan for credit institutions (February 15, 1998) (effective July 1, 1999, in Cameroon and January 1, 2000, in the other five member states)
Common regulations on external financial relations	Exchange regulations (April 29, 2000)
Uniform law on payment instruments	Regulations on payment systems, instruments, and incidents (April 4, 2003)
Common regulations on payment systems	

(continued)

Table 3.3. CFA Franc Zone Banking Commissions: Regulatory Apparatus, Modus Operandi, and Powers *(continued)*

BC-UMOA	*Central African Banking Commission (COBAC)*
Common directive on AML/CFT	Regulations on AML/CFT (April 4, 2003, and April 1, 2005)
Periodic instructions and circulars from BCEAO and BC-UMOA	Periodic instructions and regulations from COBAC
2. Industry coverage	
Banks	Banks
Other financial institutions: leasing, consumer credit, and venture capital corporations; savings and loan associations and other mutual savings banks	Other financial institutions: leasing, consumer credit, and venture capital corporations; savings and loan associations and other mutual savings banks
	Microcredit institutions
Excluded: insurance companies, pension funds, brokerages, notaries, postal services, and microcredit institutions (overseen for time being by BCEAO and national authorities)	Excluded: insurance companies, pension funds, brokerages, notaries, and postal services
3. Method of procedure	
Ongoing supervision (*contrôle sur pièces*) (based on regular—usually monthly—information from banks)	Ongoing supervision (*contrôle sur pièces*) (based on regular—usually monthly—information from banks)
Control in situ (*contrôle sur place*)—every two to three years	Control in situ (*contrôle sur place*)—every two to four years
4. Powers	
	Regulatory
Administrative	Administrative
• Formal consultation on granting of license, approval of external auditors, and modifications in composition of share capital	• Formal consultation on granting of license, approval of external auditors, and modifications in composition of share capital
• Inspection and controls	• Inspection and controls
• Cautioning	• Cautioning
• Injunction to take specific action	• Injunction to take specific action
Disciplinary	Disciplinary
• Warning	• Warning
• Reprimand	• Reprimand
• Prohibition of certain operations	• Prohibition of certain operations
• Revocation of external auditors	• Revocation of external auditors
• Suspension or dismissal of managers/executives	• Suspension or dismissal of managers/executives
• Withdrawal of license, relayed to national minister of finance, who makes a formal decision and may appeal to Council of Ministers of UMOA	• Withdrawal of license, notified to National Minister of Finance; bank affected may appeal to Board of the BEAC

Sources: Banking Commission, UMOA; COBAC.

A more checkered experience in the UMAC—The resolution of the banking crisis was more difficult and protracted in the UMAC. This was partly because the banking systems of the subzone were, if anything, in even poorer shape than in the West, but also because national authorities were initially far less ready to take corrective action.

In the words of Mr. Adam Madji, the first Secretary General of the Central African Banking Commission (COBAC), "by the early 1990s, the situation of the banking systems of the zone had become critical. Out of the 40 banks in existence in 1990, 9 had ceased operations, only 1 complied with prevailing norms, 20 were in precarious positions, and 10 were de facto insolvent" (Madji 1997). The causes of the situation were broadly the same as in the UMOA, but they were compounded by widespread problems of governance, mismanagement, and poor internal controls in a majority of banks. Indeed, Mr. Madji added that, based on subsequent assessments by COBAC inspection teams, " ... more than 90 percent of bank failures were traceable to internal deficiencies—the 'adventurism of managers'—and to weaknesses in internal control systems." To this, as in the UMOA, one had to add the inadequacy of supervision mechanisms— the somewhat powerless Control Directorate of the BEAC and the politically manipulated and largely dysfunctional National Bank Control Commissions. Mr. Oye Mba, then Governor of the BEAC, and Mr. Mamalépot, his successor from 1990, however, were convinced of the need to proceed speedily, finding further encouragement in the initiatives launched in the UMOA. The COBAC thus was established in October 1990, or only shortly after the Banking Commission of the UMOA; and the Convention on the Harmonization of Banking Regulations (Banking Law) was adopted in January 1992.

Alongside these two measures, policies focused on a major overhaul of the banking systems. The attendant financing needs were initially estimated at about CFAF 530 billion (9.3 percent of regional 1993 GDP)— of which 209 billion to finance liquidations—with the Cameroonian banks alone accounting for more than 90 percent of the total. Plans centered on (a) reimbursing the totality of private creditors of those institutions destined for liquidation—with priority given to small savers—via separate recovery structures similar in inspiration to those set up in the UMOA (such as the "*Société de Recouvrement des Créances*" [SRC] in Cameroon) or via straight government assumption of debts; (b) engineering the needed liquidations, where these were inescapable, or demergers when part of the bank operation could be salvaged; and (c) restoring the solvency, profitability, and liquidity of the institutions that could carry on by calling on existing or new shareholders. The cost of the operation was to be supported by governments, either through direct budget contributions or consolidation of BEAC claims on the states or through abandonment of public sector deposits and fiscal claims.

In practice, the results, despite the improvement in liquidity positions facilitated by the devaluation, fell far short of expectations. In 1996, six years after the restructuring program had been launched and despite heavy support from external lenders, most prominently the World Bank, the overhaul of the banking systems was far from complete. Only 11 banks were judged sound and in broad compliance with prudential norms, 11 others remained "fragile," and 9 more still "critical." Total financing needs were estimated at more than CFAF 100 billion, and 24 banks were still in the process of liquidation—11 in Cameroon, 4 in Central African Republic (CAR), 3 in Gabon, and 2 each in the other three countries.

It is only with the prospect of eligibility for the HIPC Initiative and the more determined implementation of corrective policies in the late 1990s and early 2000s that progress in resolving the crisis became measurable.[12] Twenty banks have now been liquidated or are in the process of liquidation; four foreign banks have withdrawn; all development banks except the Gabonese Development Bank (BGD)—never seriously imperiled because of a history of prudent management—have closed; and a number of new banks have emerged. Estimates of the total cost of the operation vary, partly because a few liquidations remain incomplete, but it is estimated to have been on the order of CFA francs 800 billion to 1,000 billion, or 13–15 percent of 1993 GDP.

Yet, the banking system in UMAC still has some way to go before it can be deemed healthy again. As discussed further below, noncompliance with a number of prudential norms means that several institutions still need sizable additions to equity capital; and while the last commercial bank deemed in delicate position in the Republic of Congo has just been sold to a large foreign group, there remain concerns with three or four institutions in Cameroon, as well as a large bank in the Central African Republic, where the current civil unrest and tensions with a neighboring country complicate the search for a potential foreign investor.

Current Supervision Systems—Operation

The establishment of two regional commissions has contributed to depoliticizing banking supervision. This view is unanimously held by both the official and the private sectors, and the latter is prompt to recognize the professionalism of inspectors and of the supervision process in general, even if disagreements may surface at times, especially regarding the need for provisions against losses. In the words of a commercial banker, "it has returned deontology to the profession and integrity to the process." But the financial systems of the zones remain little developed and technically rather rudimentary, especially in the UMAC. Observers accordingly believe that further training will be required to deal with future developments, such as the upgrading of payments systems and (eventually) the move to the Basel II "New Accord" of 2006.

Cost savings—The move to regional arrangements has also brought about gains in efficiency and professional capacity, as well as savings on the costs of supervision—at least at the aggregate level. What was originally dispersed between inspection/control directorates in the two central banks and among 13—and eventually 14—national directorates in member countries has been regrouped into two institutions: the Banking Commission for the UMOA, employing some 100 staff, and the COBAC, employing 50.[13] Professionals have replaced political appointees or civil servants from national ministries; locally based foreign technical assistance has now given way to in-house training; and the corps of inspectors obeys a higher code of professional ethics than when supervision was nation based.

Administrative and financial arrangements—The French model largely inspires the system. In both zones, the chairmen of the commissions are the central bank governors (table 3.4). The secretariats general and their staff remain central bank staff, while the commissions and the secretariats depend on central bank budgets.[14] If anything, the Secretariat of the BC-UMOA feels even more closely integrated into the central bank, partly because regulatory powers have remained largely in the hands of the Council of Ministers of the UMOA and of the BCEAO—although two-way consultations are intense—and partly because the governor appoints the secretary general (SG). In the COBAC, in contrast, the SG is appointed by the Conference of the Heads of State, to which he also reports and whose meetings he may attend as observer, including in the absence of the ministers of finance. This apparent greater independence notwithstanding, the COBAC Secretariat General continues to face resource and staffing constraints that are judged to have hampered its effectiveness (World Bank and IMF 2006).

Table 3.4. CFA Franc Zones Regional Banking Commissions—Governance Structures

	BC-UMOA	COBAC
Founding convention	April 24, 1990	October 16, 1990
Start of operations	October 1, 1990	January 1, 1993
President	Governor, BCEAO	Governor, BEAC
Members	• 8 (1 each) representatives of UMOA member countries • 1 representative of French Treasury • 8 members appointed *intuitu personae* by the Council of Ministers of the UMOA on a proposal from the Governor • Decisions by simple majority, with Governor casting decisive vote in case of split	• 3 BEAC censors • 7 members appointed *intuitu personae* by the Council of Ministers of the UMAC • 1 representative of the French Banking Commission • External personalities as needed (consultative voice only) • Decisions by qualified majority (2/3 of votes cast)
Secretariat General	• Secretary General (appointed by the Governor) • Deputy Secretary General • General Counsel • Department of Inspection • Department of Surveillance and Banking Studies • Department of Administration • Internal Comptroller • Total staff 102 (as of end-2006), of which about 60 are inspectors	• Secretary General (appointed by the Conference of the CEMAC Heads of State, to whom he or she also reports) • Deputy Secretary General • Department of Inspection • Department of Surveillance • Department of Regulation and Research • Department of Microfinance • Legal and Administration Department • Total staff 48, of which 17 are inspectors

Sources: Banking Commission of the UMOA, and COBAC.

Powers—Although the authority to extend bank licenses resides with each minister of finance, the decision in both zones is subject to formal agreement for assent (*avis conforme*) of the banking commissions. Regulatory powers of the banking industry are otherwise lodged in the Council of Ministers and the board of the BCEAO in the UMOA, and in the COBAC in the UMAC. Administrative and disciplinary powers are both with the commissions, with decisions taken by a simple majority in the BC-UMOA and a qualified majority of two-thirds in the COBAC. (The commissions do not have the power to impose financial penalties on institutions in defiance of the norms, although the possibility has been discussed in the UMOA). Disciplinary sanctions, of immediate application, are the exclusive power of the commissions, except that license withdrawals in the UMOA must be formally notified to the interested party by the national minister of finance within one month of the decision by the banking commission; the minister, however, may appeal the decision to the Council of Ministers of the union. In the UMAC, all disciplinary decisions are of the COBAC, also with immediate effect, except for a one-month delay after notification to the minister of finance of a license withdrawal. But all administrative and disciplinary decisions can be appealed by the bank involved to the Executive Board of the BEAC, which has the final say and decides by qualified majority.

Method of procedure—Decisions follow from the normal off-site (that is, ongoing) and on-site inspection process, which is decided by the commissions as part of their regular work program and conducted by the secretariats general. (The BCEAO may also proceed with in situ inspections at its own initiative, after notification to the BC or, inversely, at the request of the BC itself, to whom it then reports.) The conclusions (and initiation, in the case of the COBAC) of in situ inspection missions are notified to the central bank, to the minister of finance of the country where the bank is incorporated, and to the board of that bank. Criminal cases are referred to the judicial authorities. The findings of the commissions on bank compliance with prudential and other norms are published at the aggregate level in the commissions' annual reports (table 3.5).

Although this method of procedure remains at the core of the Commissions' activities, there are a few signs that analysis of bank financial soundness is beginning to include a greater variety of methods, reflecting the evolution of the industry and influences from other quarters (other supervisors, Basel/FSI environment, and so on.) The COBAC, in particular, has made increasing use of internal ratings of bank performance under the prudential norms (SYSCO system).[15]

The commissions thus operate in a much more professional and transparent environment. As described in tables 4.3 and 4.5, the legal framework has been progressively fleshed out; the structures are well established and fully functioning; the regulatory (in the case of the COBAC), administrative, and disciplinary authority of the commissions is generally (though not entirely) unchallenged; and the conditions have been laid out for preventing recurrence of systemic crises of the type the two zones faced in the 1980s. Initial frictions between the industry and what was seen as an unduly rigid approach to compliance with norms

Table 3.5. UMOA and UMAC: Operational Norms and Prudential Framework

	UMOA	UMAC
A. General dispositions		
Minimum capital		
Commercial banks	CFAF 1 billion[a]	Determined by national monetary authority
Other financial institutions	CFAF 300 million[a]	
Special reserve addition	15% of net annual profits (compulsory)	n.a.
Provisioning rules		
Claims on government and government agencies	0%	0%, but proposal by the COBAC to establish differential rates, according to degree of compliance with CEMAC fiscal convergence criteria
Government-guaranteed private risks	No obligation, but provisioning recommended up to 100% over five years (capital and interest)	Optional
Nonguaranteed doubtful or contentious claims		
Without tangible guarantees	100%[b]	25% first year 75% first two years 100% in three years
With tangible guarantees	0% first two years 50% in three years 100% in four years	15% first year 45% first two years 75% first three years 100% in four years
Unpaid interest		
On leasing operations	100%[b]	. . .
On other risks	100%,[b] if for three months or longer	. . .
Unrecoverable claims	Loss to be fully recognized[b]	Loss to be fully recognized[b]
Internal controls requirements	Yes	Yes
Agreement to appointments of managers and external auditors	Yes	Yes
Publication requirements	By June 30, communication to BCEAO and Banking Commission of annual statements, and publication in official gazette	In accordance with OHADA dispositions for public companies
Reporting requirements to banking commissions	Monthly, quarterly, semiannually, annually	Monthly, quarterly, semiannually, annually

(continued)

Table 3.5. UMOA and UMAC: Operational Norms and Prudential Framework *(continued)*

	UMOA	UMAC
B. Prudential norms		
Norms related to net capital base (fonds propres nets)		
Definition of *fonds propres nets*	Yes[c] (with more rigorous definition of *fonds propres effectifs* to account for additional risks, such as risk concentration)	Yes[c]
Solvency ratio (net worth over weighted credit risk)	8%	8%
Risk concentration		
Individual norm (lending on single signature)	75% of bank net worth	45% of bank net worth
Global norm (combined lending on signatures equal or greater than 15% each of bank net worth)	Eight times bank net worth	Eight times bank net worth
Fixed assets coverage (net worth plus permanent resources to fixed assets)	No less than 100%	No less than 100%
Lending to shareholders, associates, executive directors, management, and staff	No more than 20% of net worth	No more than 15% of net worth
Equity participation in nonbank enterprises	Not to exceed 15% of bank net worth and 25% of enterprise equity capital	Not to exceed individually 15% of net worth, and 45% overall
C. Other prudential ratios		
Liquidity coefficient (ratios of liquid assets to liquid liabilities, as defined by central bank/ banking commissions)	75%	100%
Long-term transformation ratio (ratio of MLT resources to MLT assets)	75% (MLT = at least two years' residual maturity)	50% (MLT = at least five years' residual maturity)
Portfolio structure ratio (ratio of assets qualifying for "classification agreements"[d] by central banks to total assets)	60%	45%

Sources: BCEAO, BC-UMOA, BEAC, and COBAC.

n.a. = not available.

a. Net worth must be at least equal to regulatory capital.

b. In same financial year.

c. Specified by BCEAO/BC-UMOA; and by COBAC instructions.

d. Assets judged by central banks to be backed by adequate signatures and collateral.

have been largely overcome. And there is a sense among banks—albeit perhaps more in the UMAC than in the UMOA regions—that the secretariats general have become more open to dialogue and to taking on board bankers' views when legitimate.[16]

Supervision Systems: Outstanding Issues

All is not as well as could be, though. Multicountry arrangements face risks of free-riding or of settling for the lowest acceptable standard,[17] and in both zones, the prudential framework is still not fully compliant with Basel I, especially regarding credit risk concentration. The applicable limit to large exposure remains at 75 percent of regulatory capital in the UMOA and 45 percent in the UMAC (50 percent for a "strategic company"), well above the 25 percent called for by the BCA. The commissions explain this flexibility by the overwhelming weight of certain sectors or activities (and of the companies operating in these sectors) in countries that remain primary commodity producers (for example, forestry in the UMAC or cash crop exporters in the UMOA), as well as by the riskless nature of certain types of export prefinancing; but it is recognized that it nonetheless increases systemic vulnerabilities.[18] Moreover, some banks remain in breach even of these high ratios, which weakens the credibility of the regulators. In other areas, rules remain excessively lax (for instance, the three- to four-year delay allowed for full provisioning against nonperforming loans in the UMAC—three maximum in the UMOA).

Compliance with existing norms, although improving, continues to fall well short of requirements, and many banks still need to build up their capital base (table 3.6A and table 3.6B). At end-2005 (end-2004 in the UMAC), more than one-fifth of banks did not comply with the minimum capital adequacy ratio in both zones (with one country's banking system displaying a combined negative net worth); almost two-thirds did not meet the limit on single large exposure (and one-fourth in both cases failed to meet the aggregate limit on such exposures, with a particularly large deviation in Côte d'Ivoire). One-fourth of banks failed to comply with the minimum liquidity coefficient in the UMOA, and 15 percent in the CEMAC; the "transformation" norm was not met in 40 percent of the cases in the UMOA and 30 percent in the UMAC. The requirement to cover fixed assets—in principle, no less than minimum required capital— was not met in one-fifth and one-third of the cases, respectively; and the limit on lending to shareholders, associates, and executives/managers/staff

Table 3.6A. Number of Banks in Compliance with Prudential Norms and Solvency Ratios (2004)

UMAC	Cameroon	Central African Republic	Chad	Equatorial Guinea	Gabon	Congo, Republic of	Total
Total number of banks	10	3	7	3	6	4	33 .
Average solvency ratio, in percent	11.2	12.4	15.3	13.0	23.3	15.9	14.8
Risk coverage	7	2	5	3	5	2	24
Minimum capital	8	2	5	3	5	3	26
Fixed assets coverage	6	2	4	3	5	2	22
Risk distribution							
Global norm	7	2	5	3	5	3	25
Individual norm	2	1	2	1	5	1	12
Liquidity coefficient	8	2	7	2	6	4	29
Transformation norms	5	2	5	3	6	2	23

Source: COBAC.
Note: Banks in operation only; noncompliance indicates need for increase in regulatory capital.

was exceeded in one-fourth of the cases in the UMOA. Considerable regulatory forbearance remains therefore characteristic of the systems, partly because national authorities resist facing possible bank closures with their attendant fiscal costs.[19] The evidence hence is that certain norms may need to be stiffened, others perhaps revised, but also that the commissions still have some way to go to enforce their disciplinary powers and act decisively whenever norms are breached.

The dispositions governing the Single Agreement (*Agrément Unique*),[20] whereby a bank having secured a license in a given country should be free to set up branches in another, have remained a dead letter. In the UMOA, Banking Commission (BC) officials claim that the cases that have so far come to the attention of the BCEAO have typically failed to meet the attendant requirements, especially regarding the level of regulatory capital for the head office. Many industry representatives, though, believe that other factors may have been at play. In the UMAC, the main reason clearly has been deep-seated resistance by the national authorities, or their preference for allowing subsidiaries on their territories rather than branches.

Another indication in the UMAC that national authorities remain somewhat reluctant to let go of their prerogatives is that three commissioners—in principle to be appointed *intuitu personae* (in their personal

Table 3.6B. Number of Banks in Compliance with Prudential Norms and Solvency Ratios (2004)

UMOA	Benin	Burkina Faso	Côte d'Ivoire	Guinea-Bissau	Mali	Niger	Senegal	Togo	Total
Total number of banks	9	8	16	1	10	8	12	6	70
Average solvency ratio, in percent	9.0	11.0	12.0	38.0	17.0	13.0	11.5	-3.9	11.4
Risk coverage	n.a.	n.a.	n.a.	n.a.	n.a.	n.a.	n.a.	n.a.	51
Minimum capital	6	8	12	1	9	5	11	3	55
Fixed assets coverage	8	8	12	1	9	5	12	3	58
Risk distribution									
Global norm	6	7	8	1	10	6	12	3	53
Individual norm	4	1	4	1	6	4	6	3	29
Liquidity coefficient and transformation norms									
Liquidity coefficient	7	4	12	1	7	7	10	5	53
Transformation norms	6	4	8	1	9	4	8	1	41
Limitations on lending to shareholders, managers, and staff	8	7	12	1	6	5	9	4	52

Source: Banking Commission, UMOA.

n.a. = not available.

Note: Banks in operation only; noncompliance indicates need for increase in regulatory capital.

capacity)—continue to be directors in their own national ministries and thus presumably beholden to national political considerations. This may account in part for the delay in actions in relation to banks that are in breach of prudential norms. Doubts thus remain that the commission is really independent. Yet those delays are also frequent in the UMOA even though the college of independent commissioners is much larger, which would a priori make for more independence of the supervision authorities.

Given the universe of institutions it has to cover (114 financial institutions, excluding microfinance, at end-2006—of which 91 are banks), the BC-UMOA is generally seen as adequately staffed; but in the COBAC (which has to cover more than 50 institutions, of which 33 are banks, plus almost a thousand microcredit institutions [MCIs]), staffing levels so far have fallen short of requirements. On-site inspections are generally carried out at two- to three-year intervals by the BC-UMOA, and more frequently if circumstances require, but because of staffing constraints tend to stretch to two to four years in the case of the COBAC. These constraints also affect the timely issuance of implementing regulations for prudential norms. The Secretariat General of the COBAC hopes, however, for a significant increase in the number of inspectors in line with the recommendations of the World Bank-International Monetary Fund (WB-IMF) 2006 Financial Sector Assessment Program (FSAP) mission.

Licenses have been granted generously in the UMOA in the past few years, and a number of new banks[21] have emerged, especially in Senegal. (Only 93 financial institutions, of which 72 are banks, were in existence in the UMOA at the end of 2004.) There has been concern of late over the liquidity problems some of these banks have encountered in Côte d'Ivoire; several have proved unable to meet their compensation obligations on a daily basis and have followed imprudent lending and provisioning practices; one recently faced insolvency and was placed under receivership by the BCEAO, after fewer than four years of operation. The number of banks operating in the CEMAC, in contrast, has remained stable at around 32 or 33 in recent years.

Legal environment—The uncertainty of the legal environment and the weaknesses of the judiciary remain a pervasive concern, partly because proper land and commercial registries are inadequate or lacking. More important, recurrent difficulties in foreclosing on collateral; long and onerous appeal procedures; inadequate economic, business, and other specialized training of magistrates; and a perceived systematic bias in favor of debtors ("to be solvent is one of the most serious faults in the region," claims a banker) are repeatedly cited as impediments to the normal conduct of banking activities—let alone the diversification of bank products and the deepening of financial intermediation. And the opportunities for corruption, given low remuneration levels and the insufficient funding of the judiciary, are also a concern.

The Banking System at the End of 2006

Stronger though they may be than 15 years ago, the financial systems of the two zones remain little developed, especially in the UMAC. Total financial assets stand at about 30 percent of GDP in the UMOA—about the average in sub-Saharan Africa—but barely 19 percent in the UMAC, one of the lowest ratios in the world.[22] Banks account for the bulk of the total, with nonbank institutions—cooperatives, mutual credit institutions, leasing companies, and venture capital firms—playing a marginal role in the UMAC and only a slightly larger one in the UMOA (1 and 2 percent of the market, respectively).

The weight of foreign capital in the private banks of the UMOA is high (more than 55 percent), especially in the larger banks, where there is a strong presence of French and Belgian groups—*Société Générale, BNP Paribas, Crédit Agricole/Calyon* (formerly *Crédit Lyonnais)*, and *Belgolaise (FORTIS)*. Other foreign groups include Citibank and, more recently, Atlantic Financial Group (AFG) and Financial BC SA. But two regional banking groups, the Africa Financial Holding/Bank of Africa (AFH/BOA) and Ecobank, have also developed a large presence and have operations in six and seven of the member states, respectively.

Public sector participation in commercial banks in the UMOA is on the rise again, after declining significantly in the years that followed the banking crisis. It now averages around 20–21 percent, reaching or exceeding 25 percent in Burkina Faso, Côte d'Ivoire, Mali, and Togo. There are some new or revived state-owned (often specialized) development banks, such as the BNDA in Mali, the BTCI in Togo, and the CNCAS in Senegal, as well as housing banks—and, since 2005, eight new *Banques Régionales de Solidarité* designed to cater to activities that have difficulties accessing normal bank credit. All state banks are governed by the same rules as private banks, but not all are in a healthy situation: two, in Côte d'Ivoire and Mali, have turned into serious sources of concern, despite much prodding for corrective action by the BC-UMOA and the World Bank. This creeping reemergence of a significant government presence in the industry, and the poor or deteriorating shape of some development banks, make some observers wonder whether the seeds of the difficulties experienced in the 1980s are not being sown again.

The situation in the UMAC stands in partial contrast. State development banks have disappeared in all countries but Gabon, but state participation in commercial banks remained high through the 1990s, only to decline sharply, to around 17 percent, in the past few years. Foreign-controlled banks—23 out of 33—account for almost 60 percent of both capital and financial assets, again with a large French presence (including the *Natexis/Banques Populaires* Group in Cameroon and Congo.) New banks with African capital, however, are developing rapidly and spreading their network at the regional level (CBC and Afriland First Bank, from Cameroon, and BGFI Bank, based in Gabon.)

Conclusion

Regional bank supervision in the CFAF zones has certainly been a direct by-product of the banking crises of the 1980s and early 1990s. But it is also a logical consequence of the monetary unions; it therefore must be seen in the broader context of the efforts now under way to impart a regional dimension to economic policy making and management in the two subzones.

Even if policy implementation has frequently lagged behind the adoption of texts or treaties, the progress made since the early 1990s, together with the wake-up call of the 1994 devaluation, depict an altogether different economic and financial landscape from the one the regions had known in the three decades that followed independence. Intraregional trade barriers have been nearly dismantled (or are in the process of becoming so); common external tariffs have been adopted; indirect taxation has been revamped, with value-added taxes in place in most countries; regional infrastructure projects, especially on transportation networks, have been launched; the mechanisms of multilateral surveillance on domestic policies are now well known and oiled, if with limited results so far; and, but for the countries facing domestic or foreign security issues, a degree of fiscal policy convergence has been achieved. Although many challenges need to be faced in the period ahead, none of these achievements can be dismissed, nor the central role that the two monetary authorities have played in bringing them about. Indeed, they have largely been the engines of reform. The monetary unions and regional banking supervision have been but two, and closely related, pieces of the construction. But they have shown the way forward.

Annex 3A. Historical Background and Evolution of Monetary Arrangements

The monetary history of the French colonial empire and of its institutional arrangements from the 17th to the 18th centuries was checkered, reflecting the vagaries of political and economic events, both at home and abroad. But by the early 1920s, and certainly on the eve of the Second World War, the empire was nearly unified into a single currency zone, even if there were several different authorities of issue, and the monetary signs varied in denomination.[23] (Issuing privileges had been granted mostly to private financial institutions such as the Banque de Madagascar, the Banque de l'Indochine, the Banque de l'Afrique Occidentale, and so on.) To quote Mérigot and Coulbois (1960, 298 ff.), "In general terms, transfers were made easily, but for the cost of a modest commission equivalent to the postal communication fee."

This monetary union did not withstand the beginning of hostilities in 1939 and the events of the Second World War. The imposition of generalized exchange controls in September 1939 reintroduced a clear distinction between the metropolitan franc and the currencies of the overseas territories. And the armistice of 1940 (bringing metropolitan France and part of the colonies into the monetary orbit of Germany while others— mostly in the Western Hemisphere and in the AEF [*Afrique Equatoriale Francaise*]—soon joined the Free French of the London Committee) led to the so-called "rupture of 1940," which also sealed a rupture at the level of the monetary institutions.

Developments during the Second World War, plus the de facto alignment of different parts of the old Franc Zone with the Vichy authorities or with the London Committee, and then the Algiers provisional government, and their authorities of issue, were enormously complex. Describing them would exceed the scope of this note. Suffice to say that they led to an important redirection of external trade, with the "free" territories moving increasingly into the orbit of the British sterling and U.S. dollar zones (with an authority of issue which had become in December 1941 the "*Caisse Centrale de la France Libre*"—and then the "*Caisse Centrale de la France d'Outre-Mer-CCFOM*" from February 1944—dependent on the London Committee), and the inflation differentials betweens various parts of the old empire and between these parts and both the metropolitan power and the rest of the world diverging considerably.

In the aftermath of the war, two issues were of primary concern to the French authorities: one was to reestablish a meaningful relationship of the French franc with British sterling and the U.S. dollar (the then dominating reserve currencies), which would take account of relative price differentials during the war years; the second, to bring some order to the multiplicity of francs that circulated in various parts of the old colonies and territories. The devaluation of the French franc (FF) of December 26, 1945—to FF 119.10 per U.S. dollar and FF 480 per pound sterling, from 43.80 and 176.625, respectively, in September 1939—was meant to address the first issue. It was accompanied by a decision to differentiate between the relative economic situations of overseas possessions, especially in the light of their inflation experience during the war years.

The "Franc Zone" was thus split into three "subzones": (a) metropolitan France (French franc); (b) the zone of the *Colonies Françaises du Pacifique* (CFP franc); and (c) the zone of the *Colonies Françaises d'Afrique* (CFA franc), which encompassed the territories of the AOF (*Afrique Occidentale Française*) and Togo, and AEF (*Afrique Equatoriale Française,* including Cameroon), Madagascar and the Comoros, Réunion, the French Coast of the Somalis, but also, and strangely enough, St. Pierre and Miquelon. Other, ad hoc, arrangements were put in place for the members of the Franc Zone elsewhere in the world. The three texts of December 26, 1945, were quite complex, but the essence for the CFA zone was that the adoption of a rate of 1.7 FF per CFA franc meant a devaluation of the CFAF in terms of the U.S. dollar of only 28.6 percent compared with its prewar value, considerably less than that undergone by the French franc (63.2 percent). It is unclear (price data were scarce and hardly reliable) whether this lesser devaluation implied a significant loss of competitiveness. But it seems to have been sufficiently corrected in real effective terms by the successive devaluations of the French franc in the postwar years—and despite an increase in the value of the CFAF to CFAF 1 = FF2 in October 1948 (or CFAF 50 per new French franc after the monetary conversion of 1958)—for the fixed rate to have remained unchanged between 1948 and the mid-1980s, when serious signs of overvaluation emerged.

For practical reasons, the metropolitan currency continued to circulate legally in the zones until such time as the authorities of issue—which remained until 1955 the BAO in AOF and the CCFOM in AEF—were able to issue the new CFAF notes and coins. The liberty of transfers within the zones and between the latter and France was reestablished in early 1946. But exchange regulations and controls in relation to the rest of the world remained in general application throughout the Franc Zone, and the CFAF followed the French franc throughout all the monetary adjustment operations that followed the unfortunate episode of October 1948. To that extent, the monetary unity of the Franc Zone within the French Union—the new name for the French colonial empire—after the war was largely reestablished.

Formal mechanisms of cooperation within the zone were introduced in 1951 with the establishment of a Technical Coordination Committee (which became the Monetary Committee of the Franc Zone in 1957) to coordinate credit policy, and with the opening of a compensation account for the currencies of the Franc Zone, the precursor of the current operation account, in the books of the French Treasury. In 1955, the BAO and the CCFOM lost responsibility for issuing the CFA franc, to the benefit of newly established official authorities of issue (*Instituts d'Emission*) for the AOF/Togo and the AEF/Cameroon, respectively.[24] But, in the main, the distinguishing and enduring characteristics of the current Franc Zone, which continue to this day, were firmly set out—a fixed parity CFAF/FF, unified exchange regulations (at least at the time), free convertibility and transferability within the zone, pooling of reserves, and, as a counterpart, an open-ended guarantee of access to foreign exchange by the French Treasury.[25]

There was thus no a priori limit to the two *Instituts d'Emission* running a net debtor position with the French Treasury, the de facto lender of last resort. But important safeguards—most still in place—were instituted: monetary policy action, in the form of raised interest rates and/or curtailment of rediscounts and of advances to governments, was to be taken as soon as the foreign exchange cover of the monetary authorities' sight liabilities fell below 20 percent for three months in a row; the advances themselves had to be kept, for each country, at or below 20 percent of fiscal receipts in the previous fiscal year; the monetary authorities could decide a "raking" of all other foreign positions (that is, foreign exchange held by commercial banks, the post offices, and state agencies and enterprises); and, eventually, failing all other options to bring the operation account back into the black, the interest rate charged by the French Treasury on the overdraft in the operation account would start rising gradually to penalty levels.

These safeguards, to a good extent, enabled the macroeconomic policy disciplines required and continued to work reasonably well, even in the two decades that followed the independences. But they suffered from two important weaknesses: They failed to address explicitly the need for factor mobility and cost flexibility within the zones, and they opened some room for moral hazard (that is, for some members to stray from the required policies at the expense of others). These weaknesses played an important role in triggering the economic and financial crisis that beset the CFA franc zones in the late 1980s.

Already during the 1940s and 1950s, and as they attained independence, some countries had withdrawn from the various types of monetary arrangements—within or outside the CFAF zones—they had maintained with France after the war. Syria and Lebanon severed links in 1948–49, Djibouti in 1949, the three countries of Indochina in 1954, and the Maghreb countries during 1956–62. In 1959–60, and in subsequent years, the sub-Saharan African countries followed suit, at the same time that France adopted a new constitution abolishing the French Union, but offering to maintain with her former African territories in the union a form of association in the framework of the French Community. Most countries of the old AOF and AEF—except Guinea (1958) and Mali (which subsequently rejoined)—initially chose to adhere to this association. Thus were defined the broad contours of the CFA franc zones as they are now known, even if the following decades saw a few additional modifications in membership.

Annex 3B. List of People Interviewed

This paper has also benefited from comments by Anne-Marie Gulde-Wolf, Bruno Cabrillac, Bernard Laurens, and Jean-Pierre Patat, to whom I am in debt. The paper draws on published information as well as on interviews with the following officials:

Name	Affiliation
Rigobert Andély	Deputy Governor, BEAC
Mahamat Mustapha	Secretary General, COBAC
Barthélémy Kouezo	Head, COBAC
Jean-Marie Ogandaga Ndinga	Head, COBAC
Alamine Ousmane Maye	General Manager, Afriland First Bank
Georges Djadjo	General Manager and Executive Director, CBC-Cameroon
Jean-Pierre Coti	Director, CBC-Cameroon
Jean-Pierre Schiano	General Manager, BICEC
Jacky Ricard	Director, BICEC

François Hoffmann	General Manager and Executive Director, Union Gabonaise de Banque
Moukaram Chanou Alao	Vice-President, Citibank N.A. Gabon
Gilbert Mve Assoumou	Director, Citibank N.A. Gabon
Alassane Ouattara	Former Governor, BCEAO; former Prime Minister, Côte d'Ivoire
Jean-Claude Brou	Director, BCEAO
Mahamadou Gado	Advisor, BCEAO
Ellého Tete-Benissan	Director, Banking Commission-UMOA
Babacar Fall	Head, Banking Commission-UMOA
Patrick Mestrallet	General Manager and Executive Director, CBAO, Senegal
Mbassor Sarr	Financial Manager, SGBS, Senegal
Souleymane Soumare, Imencio Moreno, and Modou Seye	Directors, BST, Senegal
Mark Guigni	Ecobank Côte d'Ivoire
Bernard Labadens	General Manager and Executive Director, SGBCI, Côte d'Ivoire
Patrick Pitton	General Manager and Executive Director, BICICI, Côte d'Ivoire
Ambroise Fayolle	Assistant Secretary for International Affairs, France Treasury
Bruno Cabrillac	Financial Counselor for Africa, France Treasury
Rémy Rioux and Alice Terracol	Head and Deputy Head, respectively, France Treasury
Alain Duchateau	Director for International and European Relations, Bank of France
Anselme Imbert	Deputy Chief, Franc Zone Service, Directorate General of Economic Studies and International Relations, Bank of France
Nicolas Peligry	Deputy Chief, Banking Commission
Herve Leclerc	Inspector, Banking Commission
Roland Tenconi	Former Director, IMF

Notes

1. "CFA franc (CFAF)" stands (since November 1972) for the *Franc de la Coopération Financière en Afrique Centrale* in Equatorial Africa (organized since 1999 into the UMAC, or *Union Monétaire d'Afrique Centrale*), and (since November 1973) for the *Franc de la Communauté Financière d'Afrique* in the Monetary Union of West Africa (*Union Monétaire Ouest Africaine*, or UMOA). The two CFA francs—issued by the BEAC (*Banque des Etats de l'Afrique Centrale*) in the UMAC and by the BCEAO (*Banque Centrale des Etats de l'Afrique de l'Ouest*) in the UMOA, respectively—have been pegged to the French franc (FF) at the same exchange rate of CFAF 100 = FF 1 since January 12, 1994, and since the introduction of the euro (€) into the European

Monetary Union on January 1, 1999, to the euro at CFAF 655.957 = € 1. (See annex 4A for a history and review of the evolution of monetary arrangements.)

2. The ratio was 65 percent until September 2005 in the UMOA; in the UMAC, it will go down in steps from that level to 50 percent (on July 1, 2009). Another quid pro quo of maintaining this minimum ratio in the operation accounts is the remuneration of creditor positions by France at above-market rates.

3. Elsewhere in what remained of the Franc Zone, countries withdrew altogether (Madagascar, 1962); established their own separate bilateral arrangement with France (Comoros, 1974); or became full-fledged French Overseas Departments (DOMs, such as Réunion, French Antilles, Guyana, and St. Pierre and Miquelon) or French Overseas Territories (TOMs, such as Mayotte, Nouméa, the various Pacific and Indian Ocean islands, and the Austral and Arctic islands). The French franc, now the euro, is the currency of the DOMs and of some territories, whereas the CFP franc, pegged to the euro, continues to circulate in the remaining TOMs.

4. A convention on the Central African Monetary Union (UMAC), which complements the CEMAC Treaty, was signed on July 6, 1996, and became effective in 1999. Like the much older UMOA Treaty in West Africa, it updates and gives a coherent content to the monetary arrangements governing the relations among the CEMAC countries. Thus, in practice, as well as in the texts, each economic and monetary union now provides for a monetary union (UMOA and UMAC) and for an economic and customs union. For ease of discussion, unless otherwise required, the two zones are identified here as the UMOA and the UMAC.

5. As described in a note from the Secretariat General of the COBAC on "*La Commission Bancaire de l'Afrique Centrale (COBAC): Organisation, Pouvoirs, et Perspectives*," "... the states remained in command for the entire chain of control over their banking systems. All regulations applicable to the banking profession and the granting/withdrawal of agreements emanated from governments; the control in situ was at the initiative of the states; and the Ministers of Finance could appoint their own representatives on the inspection missions. Even though the Governor of the Central Bank could notionally address instructions or recommendations to banking institutions undergoing such inspections, initiating disciplinary procedures remained entirely at the discretion of the national authorities" (undated).

6. Among many others, see Parmentier and Tenconi (1996); Fielding (2002); BNP Paribas (2001); Devarajan and Hinkle (1994); Daumont, Le Gall, and Leroux (2004); and Clément et al. (1996). See also the extensive writings of Sylviane Guillaumont-Jeanneney and Patrick Guillaumont on the CFAF zone, both on the pre-and postdevaluation periods.

7. The IMF estimated at the time that the equilibrium real effective exchange rate (REER) had fallen by between 30 and 65 percent, with the highest

appreciation in the largest economies, from its average level in 1981–83 (when fiscal and balance-of-payments positions were seen as broadly sustainable in most countries).

8. Cited by the Director of Economic Studies, BCEAO (at the time, an IMF staff member).

9. Accounts of the meetings—ostensibly convened to solve the financial problems of Air Afrique, the regional airline—can be found in *Jeune Afrique* and other African publications of the time.

10. The position of the BCEAO remained significantly stronger than that of the BEAC until 2003, but the latter's has improved rapidly since then—and outstripped that of the BCEAO in the second half of 2006—because of the continuously high level of oil export receipts in five of its member states.

11. There was much resistance in some countries to letting go of the prerogatives of the so-called "national monetary authorities" (mostly ministries of finance) in supervising their own banking systems. Intense discussions took place on whether existing regulations and supervision practices could not merely be updated and strengthened. In the end, as recalled by a BCEAO official, the argument that national authorities could not continue to be "judge and party" carried the day.

12. With the exception of the countries that fell into civil strife (such as the Republic of Congo or the Central African Republic) or of important temporary slippages in policy implementation (such as in Gabon, a non-HIPC-eligible country, in 1998).

13. Too few indeed in the latter, in the view of the last World Bank-IMF FSAP mission, partly because of the heavy demands of supervision of the microcredit institutions.

14. The advantages and drawbacks of this setup have been the subject of some debate. Outside observers have noted that the commissions would enjoy greater independence if financed by a fee levied on financial institutions, which would then also have a stake in the quality of supervision. The BEAC/COBAC and BCEAO/BC-UMOA authorities, on the other hand, tend to see such arrangements as open to major conflicts of interest.

15. In a welcome departure from existing rules, the SYSCO system also proposes to require provisioning against fiscal risk, with graduated percentages of provisions, depending on the degree to which national treasuries comply with the convergence criteria established by the CEMAC in its multilateral surveillance over member states' fiscal performance. The initiative, however, is meeting with resistance from national authorities. These ratings, accordingly, remain internal to the COBAC for the time being, and unpublished.

16. A joint COBAC-Banks Regional Seminar on Corporate Governance in the Banking Industry (Libreville, October 2006) and the willingness of COBAC

staff to accommodate comments on an earlier contentious draft regulation were particularly well received.

17. Sources: interviews, November 2006; IMF (2006a) and the accompanying FSSA Report (IMF 2006b); and IMF (2003). (The 2004 and 2005 reports have not been published.)

18. The BC-UMOA also noted that precisely because of the risk concentration in the UMOA, it is making use of a definition of "effective own resources" (*fonds propres effectifs*) for regulatory capital that is more rigorous and restrictive than called for by the BCA.

19. There is no deposit guarantee scheme in the UMOA, although it is in discussion, and the arrangement adopted by the UMAC is not yet operational.

20. UMOA: July 3, 1997; UMAC: September 25, 1998.

21. The minimum statutory capital remains at CFAF 1 billion. Although in practice the BCEAO has required minimum paid-up capital of CFAF 1.7 billion to 3 billion (depending on the countries) before recommending agreement, these levels remain modest, given the banking risk in the zone.

22. One important reason why intermediation in the CEMAC is so shallow is that the monetary authorities maintain minimum deposit rates and maximum lending rates, both divorced from international market conditions. The former discourage efforts at capturing resources, while the latter prevent risk diversification.

23. What was then the de facto Franc Zone encompassed a very large area, extending from the Pacific colonies and territories to Indochina, the *Comptoirs* on the Indian Coast, the Indian Ocean possessions (Madagascar, Réunion, and so forth), the "French Coast of the Somalis" (now Djibouti), the Middle Eastern territories under mandate (modern Syria and Lebanon), the Maghreb, French Occidental (AOF) and Equatorial (AEF) Africa (including Togo and Cameroon, which were both under mandate), and the Western Hemisphere possessions (St. Pierre and Miquelon, French Guyana, and the French Antilles).

24. The maintenance of two subzones within the CFAF zone merely reflected the inheritance of the war and the existence in its wake of separate authorities of issue.

25. Although these arrangements are labeled "monetary," it has been argued with some reason that they are primarily of a budgetary nature; see Hadjimichael and Galy (1997).

References

BNP Paribas. 2001. "Challenges facing the CFA Franc." *Conjoncture* (October): 1–12. http://economic-research.bnpparibas.com/applis/www/RechEco.nsf /0/63552E1AC0D7091EC1256BA30056B490/$File/C0110_a1.pdf?Open Element.

Clément, Jean, Johannes Mueller, Stéphane Cossé, and Jean Le Dem. 1996. "Aftermath of the CFA Franc Devaluation." Occasional Paper 138, International Monetary Fund, Washington, DC.

Daumont, Roland, Françoise Le Gall, and François Leroux. 2004. "Banking in Sub-Saharan Africa: What Went Wrong?" Working Paper 04/55, International Monetary Fund, Washington, DC. http://www.imf.org/external/pubs/ft/wp/2004/wp0455.pdf.

Devarajan, Shantayanan, and Lawrence Hinkle. 1994. "The CFA Franc Parity Change: An Opportunity to Restore Growth and Reduce Poverty." *Africa Spectrum* 29 (2): 131–51.

Fielding, David. 2002. *Macroeconomics of Monetary Union: An Analysis of the CFA Franc Zone.* United Kingdom: Routledge.

Hadjimichael, Michael T., and Michel Galy. 1997. "The CFA Franc Zone and the EMU." Working Paper 97/156, International Monetary Fund, Washington, DC.

IMF (International Monetary Fund). 2003. "Staff Report on Recent Developments and Regional Issues in the WAEMU (UEMOA)." Country Report 03/70, International Monetary Fund, Washington, DC. (The 2004 and 2005 reports have not been published.)

———. 2006a. "Article IV Consultation with the CEMAC." Country Report 06/317, International Monetary Fund, Washington, DC.

———. 2006b. "FSSA Report." Country Report 06/321, International Monetary Fund, Washington, DC.

Madji, Adam. 1997. Communication to a seminar on the "Mobilization of Long-Term Resources and the Financing of Investment," Libreville, March 24–26. www.cenbank.org/OUT/PUBLICATIONS/REPORTS/BSD/1999/BSDAR98.

Mérigot, Jean-Guy, and Paul Coulbois. 1960. *Le Franc 1938–1959.* Paris: L.G.D.J.

Parmentier, Jean-Marie, and Roland Tenconi. 1996. "Zone franc en Afrique: Fin d'une ére ou renaissance?" In *Logiques Economiques*, ed. L'Harmattan. Paris.

World Bank and IMF. 2006. "FSSA Reports." Financial Sector Assessment Program (FSAP)/Financial System Stability Assessment (FSSA), Washington, DC. https://www.internationalmonetaryfund.org/external/pubs/cat/longres.cfm?sk=19854.0

CHAPTER 4

The Regional Court Systems in the Organization of Eastern Caribbean States and the Caribbean

Sir Dennis Byron and Maria Dakolias

The quest for regional unification in the British colonies of the West Indies has a 300-year history, beginning in 1627 with regional grouping for the Leeward and Windward Islands, and culminating in 1958 when the colonies formed the West Indies Federation under the British Caribbean Federation Act of 1956. The territories that made up the federation in 1958 were Antigua and Barbuda, Barbados, Dominica, Grenada, Jamaica, Montserrat, the then St. Kitts-Nevis-Anguilla, St. Lucia, St. Vincent and the Grenadines, and Trinidad and Tobago. The act's original aim was to establish a political union that would ultimately become independent from Great Britain as a single state. The federation was short-lived, collapsing in 1962 because of internal political conflicts among the islands. The smaller Eastern Caribbean islands regrouped, under the Associated Statehood Act of 1967, as the West Indian Associated States (WIAS)—the immediate predecessor of the Organization of Eastern Caribbean States

Sir Dennis Byron is a permanent judge and president of the United Nations War Crimes Tribunal for Rwanda, and former chief justice of the Eastern Caribbean Supreme Court. Maria Dakolias is lead counsel at the World Bank.

(OECS). The act changed their status from colonies to states in free association with the United Kingdom (UK): each state had control over its constitution and internal self-government; the United Kingdom retained responsibility for external affairs and defense. The British monarch remained head of state, but the governor now had only constitutional powers and was often a local citizen.

With the coming of independence for the former British colonies in the 1970s and early 1980s, the OECS was created as a successor to WIAS on June 18, 1981, with the Treaty of Basseterre. The organization's founding members were six former British colonies of the Eastern Caribbean subregion—Antigua and Barbuda (which became independent in 1981); Dominica (1978); Grenada (1974); St. Kitts and Nevis (1983); St. Lucia (1979); and St. Vincent and the Grenadines (1979)—and a seventh, Montserrat, which remains a British Overseas Territory. The membership, in other words, was that of the original West Indies Federation minus the larger islands of Barbados, Jamaica, and Trinidad and Tobago. Two other British Overseas Territories—the British Virgin Islands and Anguilla—joined the organization as associate members in 1984 and 1995, respectively.

The OECS states have in common their geographical proximity, their small size and limited resources, and the shared language and cultural heritage of their history as former British colonies. Establishing a regional court would therefore be a natural step in the transition from colonialism to independence: a feasible federal mechanism for resolving disputes within the group of small islands known as the Leeward Islands (Byron et al. 2007, 3). The British government proposed the Eastern Caribbean Supreme Court (ECSC) as the solution to the problem of scarce resources of smaller states and the need to build independent institutions to take over responsibility from the colonial court. Appeals from the ECSC would continue to be heard by the Judicial Committee of the Privy Council in Britain. The court was established for the WIAS states (later to become OECS) in 1967.

Already 40 years old, the ECSC is an innovative example of sovereign countries outsourcing provision of justice to a regional court, and of a group of countries outsourcing the final appellate function to the Judicial Committee of the Privy Council in London. Its functioning required the design of a governance structure ruling the relationship between the court and sovereign member countries, the appointment of judges, and so on. Its positive contribution to the region can be gauged by the rule-of-law indicators (figure 4.1) that show the region ahead of

Figure 4.1. Rule of Law: World Bank Governance Indicators, 2005

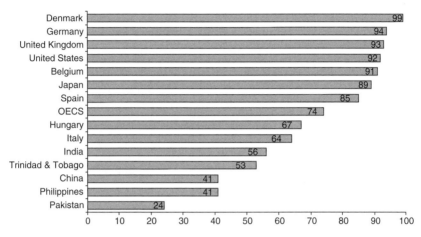

Source: Kaufmann, Kraay, and Mastruzzi 2006.

many countries, including Italy and Hungary. Its structure has fostered responsible governments, supported its objective of guaranteeing an independent judiciary, and secured individual human rights.

Despite the regrouping after the collapse of the West Indies Federation in 1962, economic integration and functional cooperation continued among the Commonwealth Caribbean States. The smaller states of WIAS retained their association with broader groupings, joining the Caribbean Free Trade Association (CARIFTA, 1965–72) and its successor, the Caribbean Community and Common Market (CARICOM, established in 1973), and becoming signatories in 2001 to the CARICOM Treaty (the Revised Treaty of Chaguaramas,[1] which established the Caribbean Community, including the CARICOM Single Market and Economy [CSME]).

With the formation of the CSME, the ECSC has entered a new stage. The "States Parties" to the CARICOM Treaty considered it important to have a specialized court for its interpretation and application of provisions of the treaty. Such a court would be more credible and effective than general jurisdiction courts in handling likely disputes and in ensuring uniform interpretation of the treaty in all the States Parties. Thus, the Caribbean Court of Justice (CCJ) was created with two fundamental jurisdictions: First, it interprets and applies the Revised Treaty of Chaguaramas. Second, it aims to replace the Judicial Committee of the

Privy Council of London as a final appellate court to hear appeals from the States Parties—including appeals from the Eastern Caribbean Supreme Court (ECSC). At the time of this report, only Barbados and Guyana have signed on to both its jurisdictions. It is thought that, in time, other Commonwealth Caribbean States will also sign on.

The creation of the CCJ implies a new stage of regional legal cooperation and of independence of small states. Its functioning will require the creation of a new governance structure ruling the management of the court and the relationship with member countries. Ultimately, the CCJ may replace the jurisdiction of the Judicial Committee of the Privy Council in London. As a regional court, the CCJ has the benefit of drawing on 40 years of experience from the ECSC, as well as the experiences of the short-lived—but very prestigious—Federal Supreme Court during the four years of existence of the West Indies Federation.

The Eastern Caribbean Supreme Court

The ECSC is the superior court of record for the nine current member states of the OECS—the six independent states of Antigua and Barbuda, Dominica, Grenada, St. Kitts and Nevis, St. Lucia, and St. Vincent and the Grenadines; and the three British Overseas Territories of Anguilla, the British Virgin Islands, and Montserrat. The functions of the court include the interpretation and application of laws of the member states of the OECS, deciding both civil and criminal cases and hearing appeals. The headquarters of the ECSC is in Castries, St. Lucia, with court offices in the nine member states. In February 2007, the ECSC celebrated 40 years of judicial activity.[2]

After the failed West Indies Federation in 1962, seven states formed a court structure under the West Indies Act of 1967 (West Indies Associated States Supreme Court Order).[3] The order established the ECSC, which includes the High Court and the Court of Appeal. Because the order preceded the independence of the six OECS states, references to the order are so embedded or entrenched in the constitutions of these states that it would be difficult for any of the states to amend its constitution without constitutional reform, referendums, or both (Saunders 2006). The provisions in the order establish the judicial appointment process, tenure, salaries, and the Judicial and Legal Services Commission, which is responsible for appointments, discipline, and removal of judges.[4]

Governance of the Judicial System

The ECSC's independence is enhanced by the very fact that it is a regional institution; no one state's executive or legislative arm can attempt with impunity to interfere in the court's operations. The stipulation that to make any changes, all member state governments must agree, is a safeguard of independence, as are the financial arrangements discussed below. For example, all members must agree on the budget and the retirement age for judges.

The selection of judges through the Judicial and Legal Services Commission of the ECSC further contributes to the court's judicial independence. The commission, established by the order of 1967, is made up of five members: chaired by the chief justice, it includes a justice of appeal or a High Court judge, a person who has been a judge of a court, and the chairpersons of the Public Service Commissions of two member states. The two Public Service Commission representatives are rotated every three years. Judicial appointments (except that of the chief justice) are made by the commission. To qualify for appointment as a justice of appeal, a person must be, or have been, a judge of a court in some part of the commonwealth for at least five years, or have practiced law for at least 15 years.[5] The requirements for a High Court judge are similar: a person must be, or have been, a judge in some part of the commonwealth or practiced law for at least 10 years. The chief justice is appointed by the British monarch, after the six prime ministers along with the three chief ministers for the colonies of the ECSC have unanimously agreed—a requirement that is a further safeguard of independence and avoidance of political interference.

Judges, as the requirements described above show, can be appointed to the ECSC from the pool of judges in the commonwealth, allowing for diversity on the courts. (This facility is not reciprocated by other commonwealth countries.) Expanding the pool of judges in this way is possible because, even though member states have their own laws that are interpreted by the ECSC, cases from other commonwealth jurisdictions are highly persuasive in matters before the OECS. Furthermore, lawyers trained in law in the Caribbean attend a regional law school, the University of the West Indies,[6] where they are exposed to the laws of various territories of the region. At present, 50 percent of the judges on the bench are from outside the OECS member states. The independence of the selecting commission is reflected in the diversity of judges: In the past 10 years, the ECSC has had nationals from Australia, Barbados,

Belize, Guyana, Jamaica, Trinidad and Tobago, and the United Kingdom. Currently there is a judge from Guyana. The commission does not respond to any particular legislature or executive for such decisions, with the result that the court has had the benefit of a variety of different experiences and perspectives on the bench.

The ECSC itself comprises the chief justice, who is the head of the judiciary, 4 justices of appeal, 18 High Court judges, and 2 masters. The number of judges on the court can be adjusted by order of the chief justice and approved by the member states.[7] The workload is demanding for the current number of judges, but the number compares well with that of other countries (figure 4.2). The number of judges per 100,000 inhabitants is an indication of how much access there is to justice. The poor and declining infrastructure will, however, be a challenge for keeping pace with demand for judicial services.

The "Code of Ethics for Eastern Caribbean Supreme Court Judges" has been in place since 2001 and provides five canons governing behavior in the following areas: integrity, impropriety, impartiality, extra-judicial activities, and political activity. Judges are expected to maintain professional competence, actively participating in continuing judicial education and training. To date, no judges have been removed for misbehavior. The standards of behavior, both on and off the bench, are higher for judges

Figure 4.2. Number of Judges per 100,000 Inhabitants, 2000

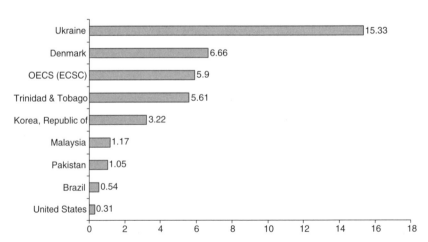

Ukraine 15.33
Denmark 6.66
OECS (ECSC) 5.9
Trinidad & Tobago 5.61
Korea, Republic of 3.22
Malaysia 1.17
Pakistan 1.05
Brazil 0.54
United States 0.31

Source: Legal and Judicial Sector at a Glance database: www4.worldbank.org/legal/database/Justice.
Note: Brazil and the United States have a federal court system and state or provincial court systems; the statistics here cover only the federal court system.

working in small states, who live and work in small communities. No judge in the OECS is anonymous (Byron 2002a). Judges have to be more accountable where everyone would know if they have misbehaved.

On the other hand, such intimate connections with a community obviously have their drawbacks, and the ECSC uses periodic rotation to protect against the familiarity inevitable in such small states (Byron 2002a). This practice is common for judges in smaller states, but it could be effectively used in larger communities as well.

Financial Arrangements

The member states have organized the financing of their regional courts to enhance their independence, from the point of view of the mechanisms both for financial contributions and for management of the budget. The ECSC is financed by contributions from the nine members of the OECS in varying proportions (table 4.1); its budget is managed by the judiciary. Each member state's percentage of the approved annual budget is set by the ECSC in concurrence with the authority (the Body of Heads of Government—the supreme body of policy direction of the OECS) and takes into consideration the number of resident judges and the number of court sittings in each member territory. The member states' contributions are as in table 4.1.

The budgetary exercise is a two-stage process. Draft annual budget estimates are prepared by the court and defended before the OECS budget committee, consisting of the directors of finance of the member states (Byron 2002b). The chief justice then presents the budget to the Conference of Heads of Government for its approval.[8] The decision to

Table 4.1. Contributions to ECSC from OECS Member Countries

Members	Share (percentage)
Anguilla	8
Antigua and Barbuda	13
British Virgin Islands	13
Dominica	11
Grenada	13
Montserrat	5
St. Kitts and Nevis	11
St. Lucia	13
St. Vincent and the Grenadines	13
Total	100

Source: ECSC Annual Report 2004–2005. www.eccourts.org.

approve the budget must be unanimous, and, once approved, the budget contribution becomes an international obligation on the part of the member states (Byron 2002a). To date, there has never been an instance where the budget has not been approved, and it has always been approved in a timely fashion (Byron 2002a). This does not, however, mean that member states always transfer their financial contributions promptly, and there is no sanction available to the ECSC: all that can be done to ensure transfer is for active court staff to follow up continually until the transfer is made. (Given the difficulty of collection, it is questionable whether the existing approximately EC $10 million in arrears can be forgiven.) Special arrangements have been made when a member state has suffered from a natural disaster, such as the hurricane in Grenada in 2004. In general, peer pressure by member states works to ensure that the funds are transferred, but it would help if there were some way for the ECSC to spend the committed funds without having continually to follow up for their transfer.[9]

The judiciary has been working to improve its control and management of the budget. Though internal audits were conducted earlier, they were not conducted on a regular annual basis until after 2000. Regular audits submitted to the governments of the member states, by supplying reliable statistics to forecast future workloads, have made preparation of the budget more efficient. Moreover, the resulting improved accountability and transparency have helped the chief justice to make a case for special allocations of additional funding for reforms. One example is a special allocation for purchasing a software system for the judiciary, granted in 2000. Once this was in place, the chief justice sought to have all judges communicate with him by e-mail, so that there was no excuse for them to fall behind in the reform process. The budget process for the ECSC is better than for many countries, but there is room for improvement: moving to a system similar to that of the Caribbean Court of Justice (see discussion of CCJ below) could be an added benefit and safeguard for independence.

Quality of Service

There has been a concerted effort since 1998–2000 to reform the efficiency, access to justice, and independence of the ECSC. These reforms have covered a proposed new court structure, new Civil Procedure Rules (CPR 2000 [Alleyne 2002]), improvements in the quality of judges through more transparent appointment processes, provision of judicial education, and introduction of a code of ethics, as well as capacity building for court administration and information technology. In 1990, there was no capacity for court management—support staff consisted of one multipurpose secretary. In 1991, the office of Chief Registrar was created and staffed with professionals. After the first court administrator was hired in 2002, the Department of Court Administration was established, and other court administrators were appointed for the various islands. Today there are 21 professional staff and 23 support staff working for the nine administration offices of the ECSC. All the reforms benefited from support at the highest level of the judiciary, with the result that today, in the words of one lawyer, "there is a judiciary that is more friendly" to litigants, where people can expect to be "treated with dignity."

As part of the reform, the High Court now intends to hold continuous hearings throughout the year in its criminal jurisdiction, and it is working to clear the backlog in criminal cases that built up as a result of there being only three sessions of the High Court per year in the criminal jurisdiction. The Civil Procedure Rules 2000 (CPR 2000) are modeled after the U.K. Civil Procedure Rules of 1998, which aimed to enhance efficiency and access by employing a case-management model that is judge driven. The process encourages the active involvement of litigants at every step of the proceedings, including their presence at all hearings, especially case-management conferences and pretrial review hearings. One significant change is that the course of litigation is now court-supervised: attorneys no longer have a right to extend deadlines without the court's permission (Alleyne 2002).[10] Information technology is being introduced so that judges can have access to case files from their desks and no longer need hard copies, and lawyers and the public have easy access to the status of cases. Stenographers have been employed to make the process more efficient, and a new system has been introduced for diverting appropriate categories of cases—minor offenses; offenses involving juveniles; offenses arising out of family disputes or involving neighbors, coworkers, or persons in relationship—into an alternative dispute resolution system away from the criminal justice system, along with practices such as reduced sentences for early guilty pleas, that allow cases to be disposed of quickly.

Before the recent reforms, some islands did not have a judge in residence—a single judge might be responsible for two or three islands. Now there is at least one judge per island to handle cases (except in Montserrat, which is served by the judge resident in Nevis). Such inefficiencies meant that some cases took as long as eight years from filing to disposition; now, many cases are resolved before the targeted 18 months to 2 years (Alleyne 2002). As a result of the reforms, the productivity of the ECSC has increased: a total of 1,112 cases were disposed of during 2003–2004, as against 874 cases during 2001–2003.[11] The clearance rate jumped from 44 percent in 2000 to 104 percent in 2004; once the number is above 100 percent, the courts are able to address their backlog (figure 4.3). For civil cases, the courts still have a way to go to meet the filing demand (see figure 4.4, which provides an international comparison). The reason may be that, as well as an overall increase in civil cases over the years—a more-than 400 percent increase in demand for many of the courts—there has been a change in the kind of cases filed: cases related to requests for damages and injunctions increased by more than 1,000 percent, and for land matters by more than 600 percent.[12] Infrastructure, however, needs to catch up with these developments, and this will be an issue in the future for most of the member states.

More reforms related to access to justice are contemplated. A comprehensive Strategic Plan for the ECSC has been prepared and is being considered.[13] The system of legal aid in many of the member states is limited, and a program is being developed to provide indigent parties free legal services. The new CPR 2000 has made accommodations, together with practical direction, for pro se litigants (that is, litigants who are not represented by a lawyer); this also assists in improving access to justice (Pemberton 2002), although there is the drawback that pro se litigants take more time of the court because they usually need extra guidance and assistance. In addition, a court-sponsored mediation program was

Figure 4.3. Clearance Rate for ECSC Court of Appeal: Civil and Criminal Cases
(percentage)

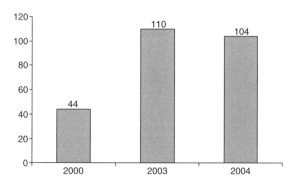

Source: Annual Reports of the ECSC, http://www.eccourts.org.

Figure 4.4. Clearance Rate for Civil Cases, 2002

(percentage)

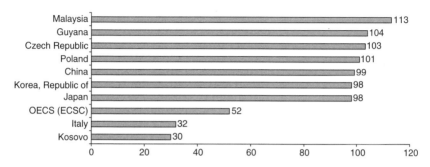

Source: Legal and Judicial Sector at a Glance database: http://www4.worldbank.org/legal/database/Justice; data for OECS from the Annual Reports of the ECSC: http://www.eccourts.org; data for Italy from CEPEJ (2002).
Note: Cases disposed of in First Instance Courts.

introduced to move cases more efficiently through the system and to help handle the backlog. This program was successful in some islands, but encountered some resistance from British Virgin Islands (BVI) lawyers, possibly because BVI lawyers' fees are hourly, rather than the flat fee charged by other lawyers in the region. Thus, lawyers in the BVI had more to lose if the speed of dispute resolution increased.

One further successful reform has been in judicial education. In 1998, the then Chief Justice Sir Dennis Byron established the Judicial Education Institute of the Eastern Caribbean Supreme Court. In 2002, the Institute, under the chairmanship of Justice Adrian Saunders, held its first formal judicial orientation program. The institute offers training and continuing education for High Court judges, masters, and registrars, as well as the magistracy. The curriculum follows international standards and is supported by the Commonwealth Judicial Education Institute, which provides connections among existing commonwealth judicial education bodies. The philosophy is that judges are the best trainers of other judges, to provide up-to-date education, canvass new ideas, and disseminate information. The opportunity for continuing education has been particularly useful for new judges, who are expected to start their judicial responsibilities right away, even though their background may have been in civil courts and their docket includes criminal cases. This became even more significant when, midway through the reform process, about 50 percent of the judges reached the mandatory retirement age. With so many new judges serving on the bench, it was critical that they be provided with adequate training to hit the ground running. Well-prepared judges are an important element to generate public confidence in the judiciary.

A new commercial division is to be established as part of the ECSC to take into account the growing volume of complex commercial cases, particularly from the British Virgin Islands. The BVI, with a population of 23,000, has about 750,000 offshore companies registered, which account for 48 percent of all offshore companies in the world. One-sixth of foreign investment in China is by companies registered in the BVI. One lawyer remarked that many foreign litigants "don't want to litigate in their home countries, but they do have confidence in the ECSC." There has been a more than 1,000 percent increase in civil cases in the BVI (figure 4.5). This demand for specialization has led to a proposal for the High Court to function differently, with the senior commercial judge to reside in the British Virgin Islands. Such a commercial division is seen in the BVI as integral to its success as a world-class financial center. An added benefit would be that judges would have the opportunity to specialize and then take that experience to other courts in the region; cross-fertilization of experience has been a positive outcome of the regional court.

Figure 4.5. Percentage Increase in the Number of Civil Cases Filed in ECSC High Court, 1967–2005

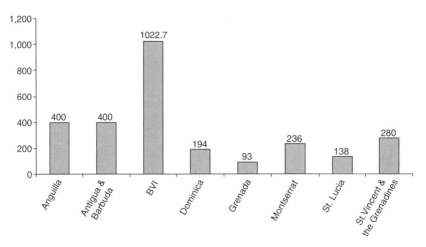

Source: Annual Reports of the ECSC: http://www.eccourts.org.

Currently, throughout the states of the OECS, the magistracy is still tied to the executive branches of the respective member states, very often under the attorney general's department, and is not completely under the judiciary's administrative authority. This creates a bifurcated judicial system that is inconsistent with established international standards. A new organizational structure for the magistracy is being proposed that would bring the magistrates into the trial courts of the High Court and would create four divisions: criminal (with traffic), civil (with small claims), family, and commercial. This change would contribute substantially to the independence and efficiency of the judiciary. At present, the magistrates and their staff are expected to behave as judicial officers, even though they are part of the executive branch. They are not considered fully independent or accountable and are not held in high esteem by the public. They have been on a separate pay scale and operate with poor administration. And yet "the magistrates preside over some 90 percent of all litigation in the region, and the average citizen is impacted by their work to a far greater degree than by the work of the 'higher' judiciary" (Alleyne 2007). By bringing the magistracy under the ECSC, the judiciary would be considered as one, allowing the chief justice to manage the system in a coherent fashion consistent with the reforms that have already been introduced at the ECSC level. This unification would expand the core staff operating under the existing court administration process, which should substantially reduce the delays and confusion that arise when, as now, each member state administers the magistracy differently. The creation of a unified judiciary would be accomplished by government process.

For further, much needed, reforms to take place, the order that established the ECSC may need to be revised. Several reforms could be considered. One prospective reform is a change in the mandatory retirement age for judges, currently fixed at 62 for High Court judges and 65 for appellate court judges. In independent nation states, it might be expected that disciplinary and removal procedures for judges would be handled by a regional process. A further reform might be to separate the judicial service from the public service to avoid the waste of resources that arises when civil servants are transferred after they have received extensive training in the judiciary.

It is not clear how the amendments required to revise the order could be effected—whether each member state would have to agree, and then what constitutional steps must be taken in each member state (Saunders 2006). For example, the St. Vincent and Grenadines Constitution requires a referendum of not less than two-thirds of the votes and two readings of the bill in the house to amend the order.[14] The very elaborate and onerous process required to amend the order is probably the result of British concern, at the time of granting independence, that the judiciary provisions of the constitution ought not to be easily tampered with by local politicians. In the United Kingdom, a change of this sort would require only a simple act of Parliament (although Australia, Denmark, France, Ireland, and Switzerland also require referendums and legislative approval for constitutional reforms; see table 4.2).

But the difficulty in revising the order may also have been a positive force for preserving judicial independence. Under the terms and conditions for salaries and appointments, for instance, salaries cannot be reduced, nor can the terms of appointment be made less favorable.[15] Salaries of the judges are respectable in comparison with those in other countries, and in comparison, for instance, with Germany's judicial salaries (figure 4.6). They have, however, remained the same for the past seven years, and there is a disparity in salaries between the different branches of government. For example, the salary of the Chief Justice of

Table 4.2. Legislative Process for Changing the Constitution

Country	Legislative Process	Referendum Option	Required
Australia	Absolute majority in both houses, majority approval by a majority of the states	Yes	Yes
Austria	2/3 majority in both houses	Yes	No
Canada	Majority approval in both houses, 2/3 majority of provincial legislatures	Yes	No
Denmark	Two successive parliaments must pass unamended	Yes	Yes
Finland	2/3 majority of parliament	No	No
France	Majority approval in both houses	Yes	Yes
Hungary	2/3 majority of parliament	Yes	No
Ireland	Majority approval in both houses	Yes	Yes
Italy	Majority approval in both houses (twice)	Yes	No
South Africa	Either 3/4 or 2/3 approval of assembly, possible approval of six provinces needed	No	No
Spain	3/5 majority in both chambers	Yes	No
Sweden	Majority approval by two successive terms	No	No
Switzerland	Majority approval of parliament, majority approval of the cantons	Yes	Yes
United States	2/3 majority in both houses, 3/4 approval of state legislatures	Yes	No

Source: Dakolias 2006.

Figure 4.6. Salaries of Judges
(purchasing power parity dollars, 2002)

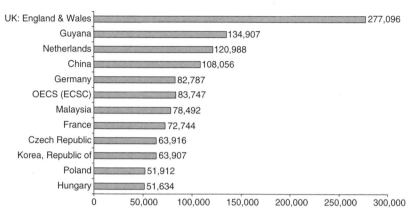

UK: England & Wales	277,096
Guyana	134,907
Netherlands	120,988
China	108,056
Germany	82,787
OECS (ECSC)	83,747
Malaysia	78,492
France	72,744
Czech Republic	63,916
Korea, Republic of	63,907
Poland	51,912
Hungary	51,634

Sources: Legal and Judicial Sector at a Glance database: http://www4.worldbank.org/legal/database/Justice; data for the United Kingdom, the Netherlands, Germany and France from CEPEJ (2002).
Note: Estimated annual salary of highest appellate court judges (purchasing power parity dollars of 2002).

the ECSC is less than that of the prime minister; this is significant if the two branches are considered to be equal. Other countries such as the United States compare the chief justice's salary to that of the vice president and the Speaker of the House.

The Caribbean Court of Justice (CCJ)

With the formation of the CARICOM Single Market and Economy (CSME),[16] there arose an urgent need for consistency throughout the region in the interpretation and application of the relevant rules governing commerce and trade. The CCJ, in its original jurisdiction, serves this role. "Almost from its genesis, the CCJ has been regarded as the critical factor for any future integration process" (Anthony 2003). The establishment of such a legal institution follows naturally from regional integration in the area of trade, the free movement of persons, goods, and capital that is included in the institutional and legal framework of the CSME. The theoretical context is that for the CSME to achieve its economic goals in the long term, it must be reinforced by a judicial framework that will ensure legal consistency, uniformity, and certainty.

Until the establishment of the CCJ, there were no provisions among the states for the transfer of sovereignty to any supranational regional institution, and no body of community law that would take precedence over domestic legislation or automatically apply in domestic jurisdictions.

In addition, there had been no entity that could adjudicate disputes arising out of the international agreements of the members of CARICOM (established in 1973) as to their rights and obligations. In 1994, the West Indian Commission,[17] in its report "Time for Action," advocated that a CARICOM supreme court should be one of the pillars of the CARICOM structures of unity.

Establishing new institutions is often difficult, and the CCJ has not been without controversy. The Agreement Establishing the Caribbean Court of Justice (AECCJ) was signed on February 14, 2001, and subsequently ratified by 12 countries: Antigua and Barbuda, Barbados, Belize, Grenada, Guyana,[18] Jamaica, St. Kitts and Nevis, St. Lucia, Suriname, Trinidad and Tobago, Dominica, and St. Vincent and the Grenadines. On April 16, 2005, the CCJ was inaugurated in Port of Spain, Trinidad and Tobago.

The CCJ is the Caribbean Supreme Court with two separate and distinct jurisdictions: It has an original jurisdiction to deal with disputes arising under the Revised Treaty of Chaguaramas of 2001, which established the CSME. It is also the court that replaces the Judicial Committee of the Privy Council as the final appellate court for the Commonwealth Caribbean. All CSME member states have signed on to the court's original jurisdiction; the appellate jurisdiction of the court is available only to the countries that have acceded to that aspect of the treaty. As of 2007, only Guyana and Barbados have signed on to both its jurisdictions.

The CCJ has exclusive jurisdiction in the uniform interpretation and application of the revised treaty.[19] This exclusive jurisdiction is needed to avoid conflicting opinions on important commercial issues to bring to an end uncertainty and unpredictability in the business climate of the region. The CCJ will also hear disputes between contracting states as to the rights conferred on them and their nationals and the obligations imposed upon the respective states by the treaty. The contracting states have undertaken to enact the necessary legislation to make CCJ judgments enforceable in the same manner as judgments from local courts, and the judgments from the CCJ are final and conclusive. This will provide affected parties with an effective redress mechanism. Provision has been made for individuals to institute proceedings before the CCJ if any right granted by the treaty to an individual of a member state is breached.

In the exercise of its original jurisdiction, the CCJ is today among four similar courts: the European Court of Justice (ECJ), the Court of Justice of the Common Market for Eastern and Southern Africa (COMESA

Court), the Court of Justice of the Andean Community (TJAC), and the Community Court of Justice in the Economic Community of West African States (ECOWAS).[20] The CCJ, it can be argued, strengthens the system of governance within the region and consolidates regional cooperation.

Financial Arrangements

The CCJ's capital and operating costs are financed through a trust fund capitalized at US$100 million provided by the Caribbean Development Bank. These funds were raised by that bank on the international capital market and turned over to a trust fund administered by an independent board of trustees. The Bank announced on June 19, 2004, that it had successfully floated a US$150 million note on the international capital market, from which US$96 million will be used to finance the operations of the CCJ. The board of trustees comprises financial and economic specialists, along with representatives from the regional bar and the bench. Their responsibility is to invest and manage the fund; they are accountable to the executive branches of the member states. The heads of government are obligated to the bank for the US$100 million according to their prorated share (table 4.3). Because their commitment is to the Caribbean Central Bank, a default by any one nation does not affect the funding of

Table 4.3. Trust Fund Contributions for CCJ

Members	Share (percentage)
Antigua and Barbuda	2.11
Barbados	12.77
Belize	3.44
Dominica	2.11
Grenada	2.11
Guyana	8.33
Haiti	1.68
Jamaica	27.09
Montserrat	0.42
St. Kitts and Nevis	2.11
St. Lucia	2.11
St. Vincent and the Grenadines	2.11
Suriname	3.92
Trinidad and Tobago	29.73
Total	100.00

Source: Revised Agreement Establishing the Caribbean Court of Justice Trust Fund, Annex. http://www.caribbeancourtof justice.org/legislation.html.

the CCJ. Therefore, the court is not vulnerable to the pressure of loss of funding that may result when a judiciary is dependent on another branch of government for financing. Moreover, the court is not required to interface with the executive branch on funding issues.

According to the Revised Agreement Establishing the Caribbean Court of Justice Trust Fund,[21] funds may also come from other sources. The resources of the fund consist of the contributions of members; income derived from operations of the fund or otherwise accruing to the fund; "and contributions of third parties being contributions which are not likely to prejudice the independence or integrity of the Court."[22] The fund shall not solicit nor accept any grant, gift, or other material benefit from any source except with the consent of all the members. Contributions of members shall be made for the purpose of the fund without restriction as to use. A fully operational CCJ is expected to need about US$4 million annually (Rawlins 2000). This arrangement— whereby the trust fund is expected to yield sufficient funds to handle the costs for the foreseeable future—is unique in the world. With such security of funding, the court has been able to attract some of the most experienced and knowledgeable court staff under procedures that are more flexible than civil service regulations.

The treaty provides that nonpayment of contributions to the budget of the court would result in the denial of access to its services by the defaulting member state. Agreement by CARICOM member states on such a sanction must be seen as a significant development in the history of the economic integration movement; historically, sanctions have tended to be nonexistent. While all the member states are currently paying for the CCJ, only two (Guyana and Barbados) are using it as the final appellate court replacing the Privy Council. "It would make financial sense for Contracting Parties to make the fullest possible use of the CCJ since they are already committed to paying for it" (De la Bastide 2006).

Governance

Like the ECSC, the CCJ does not confine selection of judges to the Caribbean region: candidates may come from outside the member states. The Regional Judicial and Legal Services Commission may appoint a judge with more than 15 years of experience. At present, two of the seven judges are from nonmember states: one from the United Kingdom and the other from the Netherlands. Although the majority are from the region, members of the public from one territory may still feel alienated from the regional system either because the territory is not represented adequately (or at all) on the bench and by court staff, or because court decisions are seemingly adverse to the interests of the territory. The same could be said for the ECSC, but it has a 40-year track record to prove its impartiality and independence to the public.

In contrast to other regional courts, the tenure of the judges in the ECSC and the CCJ is until retirement age. In the European Court of Justice, the judges are appointed by the ministers of government for a term of six years; in the Andean Court of Justice, they are elected by the states. The judges of the CCJ are appointed by the Regional Judicial and Legal Services Commission, an independent and impartial body. The president of the court is appointed by the heads of government of participating states on the recommendation of the commission acting on the advice of a tribunal established for that purpose.

Privy Council

Governance of the OECS or CARICOM judicial systems does not extend to the Privy Council, the final appellate court still widely used by most Commonwealth Caribbean states. Many former British colonies that in the past had channeled their final appeals to the Privy Council have, since the attainment of independence, abolished appeals to that body. Only a few remain today.[23] Canada created its own Supreme Court in 1875 to hear criminal cases, but it was not until 1949 that its relationship with the Privy Council ended.[24] Australia followed in the 1970s.[25] Ghana abolished the appellate jurisdiction of the Privy Council in 1960,[26] Malaysia in 1978 for criminal and constitutional matters and in 1985 for civil matters, Singapore in 1994,[27] Hong Kong (China) in 1997, and New Zealand in 2003.[28] For the Caribbean region, the Privy Council as the final appellate court of the Commonwealth Caribbean States can be said to have assisted in the transition phase between national independence of the states and their full institutional autonomy.

Since the 1950s, commonwealth appeals sent to the Privy Council have declined in number. In 2005, half of the appeals that the Privy Council heard annually came from the Caribbean region (table 4.4). At the outset, it should be noted that, certainly up to the mid-1990s, the interventions of the Privy Council in the region were rare, because the Privy Council historically dismissed many of the appeals that came from the ECSC. The statistics show that a large percentage of ECSC decisions are approved by the Privy Council and their reasoning adopted (table 4.4) (De la Bastide 1995). Between 1985 and 1994, the Privy Council upheld

Table 4.4. Number of Cases Appealed to the Privy Council

	1998	1999	2000	2001	2002	2003	2004	2005
Total number of cases appealed by ECSC members[a]	6	5	12	8	5	3	10	9
Total number of cases appealed by CCJ members[b]	39	23	33	29	32	30	40	28
Total number of overseas and domestic cases heard by Privy Council[c]	78	69	90	102	103	71	71	71

Source: Privy Council Web site.

a. ECSC members: Antigua and Barbuda, Dominica, Grenada, St. Kitts and Nevis, St. Lucia, St. Vincent and the Grenadines, Anguilla, the British Virgin Islands, and Montserrat.

b. CCJ members: Antigua and Barbuda, Dominica, Grenada, St. Kitts and Nevis, St. Lucia, St. Vincent and the Grenadines, Belize, Barbados, Jamaica, and Trinidad and Tobago.

c. The domestic cases are appeals under the Veterinary Surgeons Act of 1966 and under the Scotland Act of 1998. Other overseas cases that the Privy Council hears are cases from New Zealand, The Bahamas, Gibraltar, Mauritius, Isle of Man, and other British Overseas Territories.

102 decisions of the Courts of Appeal of Caribbean States, out of a total of 163.

The decisions that the Privy Council makes as to ECSC appeals notwithstanding, the composition of the Privy Council is not representative of the OECS. The Privy Council consists generally of British Law Lords. From the Caribbean, Sir Vincent Floissac, former chief justice of the Eastern Caribbean Supreme Court; Sir Edward Zacca, former chief justice of Jamaica; and Justice Telford Georges, former chief justice of The Bahamas, Tanzania, and Zimbabwe, have served on the Privy Council.[29] In July 2004, three additional Caribbean judges were appointed: Honorable Michael de la Bastide, Sir Dennis Byron, and Dame Joan Sawyer. To date, however, none of these three appointees has been asked to sit on any cases before the Privy Council, including those from the Caribbean. In 1974, Lord Denning had suggested that the Privy Council could become an itinerant court where British judges could sit in the Caribbean and Caribbean judges sit in England (Rawlins 2000, 13). This never happened, but the Privy Council did recently sit for the first time in The Bahamas.

Some lawyers argue that the Privy Council is a less expensive way for small states to provide for a final appellate jurisdiction. It is true that the United Kingdom funds the Privy Council, but because the judges sit in the United Kingdom, the lawyers and parties from the Caribbean have to pay their own expenses to appear before the Privy Council, in addition to paying legal fees for British solicitors. And, as anyone familiar with the city knows, working in London is an expensive proposition. In 1994, the government of Jamaica alone spent $12 million (Jamaican currency) in expenses to handle appearances at the Privy Council (Rawlins 2000, 42). Such a costly system limits access to justice for litigants, especially those without legal aid. In addition, if a Caribbean judge were asked to sit on the Privy Council, he or she may be required to pay her or his own way to London. The prohibitive costs that litigants must bear to access the Privy Council may be one of the main reasons that so few cases are appealed to that body.

Others argue that the distance of London insulates the judges on the Privy Council from regional and local pressures; however, this argument has not been substantiated by clear instances in which judges in the Caribbean have succumbed to such pressure. To the contrary, the independence of judges in the Caribbean is continually held up as a positive example of the rule of law in the region, and numerous examples can be cited to demonstrate the resolute manner in which the ECSC judiciary has upheld its judicial independence. Sometimes, even the Privy Council pays enormous deference to the judgments of the ECSC, a striking example of which occurred in the Credicom Asia case, in which the Privy Council as well as the New York Commercial Court both showed such deference (Archibald 2002).[30] Strong evidence of the public's trust in the independence of ECSC judges is that many parties choose to litigate in the BVI because they have confidence in the judges' ability to decide cases efficiently and impartially—an extra benefit that the ECSC contributes to the development of business in the BVI.

The question of insulation from pressure cuts both ways: the United Kingdom has substantial economic interests invested in the Caribbean. Having British judges as the ultimate arbiters of disputes that impinge on those interests could be a source of comfort to the United Kingdom. Moreover, currently British barristers enjoy lucrative fees from appearances before the Privy Council in appeals from the Caribbean. If the CCJ, instead of the Privy Council, were the final appellate court for all Caribbean states, this would surely result in a significant loss in earnings for these U.K. barristers because the rights of audience before the CCJ do not accommodate British barristers in the same way as the Privy Council does and Caribbean lawyers will invariably be more likely to appear before the CCJ than U.K. lawyers.

Furthermore, there is a basic issue of sovereignty in using the Privy Council. No member state of the OECS has any say in the institutional arrangements governing the Privy Council or how its judges are chosen.[31] It is internationally accepted that judges appointed to the bench should represent the diversity of a nation's population and views. In the ECSC, 43 percent of the judges are women, while in the United Kingdom, only 15 percent of the judges are women. The first woman appointed as a Law Lord occurred in 2004 (Dakolias 2006, 1184). By contrast, in that year, the head of the Guyana judiciary was a woman, Madame Justice Desiree Bernard, who now sits on the CCJ. The Law Lords or judges of the Privy Council do not come from the local population, are not familiar with the values and culture of the society on which they judge, do not even reside in that society, and cannot in any way be held accountable to the citizens of that society. The Privy Council is not even accountable to the European Court of Justice, as is the rest of the judiciary in the United Kingdom.

A final point is that the ECSC and therefore the Privy Council have the power and responsibility to strike down laws that are in conflict with OECS constitutions. What is curious is that the courts in the United Kingdom do not have this power or responsibility, because Parliament is supreme in the United Kingdom. So the Privy Council is given greater powers over the former colonies than the United Kingdom has bestowed on its own courts.

In constitutional and human rights cases where a balance has to be struck, as often must be the case, between the public interest and individual rights or between competing societal interests, the Privy Council judges are not in a good position to evaluate where the scales should tilt. They have little understanding of the mores and values of the local people nor any firsthand perception or appreciation of local conditions. And so they must necessarily fall back on their own training and their own experiences and the milieu in which they live. But it is precisely these things that some argue make them ill-equipped to render the most suitable judgment.

Highlights of the Courts' Jurisprudence

Deference by Privy Council

The Privy Council judges themselves understand the difficulties involved in their lack of awareness of local conditions and sometimes would refrain from rendering judgments on this basis. There is, however, no clearly articulated guidance on the circumstances and occasions in which they would take such a step, and so litigants may expend considerable sums of money in pursuing a final appeal, not knowing whether the Privy Council will ultimately determine the issues or decide that its ignorance of local conditions renders it unsuitable to rule on the points argued. At the same time, however, the Privy Council argues that it should remain the final appellate body for much of the Caribbean, perhaps as a matter of tradition. A few recent cases illustrate the problem.

In 2000, the Privy Council rendered its decision on the case of *Cable and Wireless (Dominica) Limited v. Marpin Telecoms and Broadcasting Company Limited* (see chapter 6).[32] Cable & Wireless had been granted exclusive licenses to provide national and international telecommunications services in Dominica, as well as in the majority of other states in the eastern Caribbean region. Marpin had been operating television stations and wanted to compete with Cable & Wireless in the provision of mobile telephone, e-mail, and Internet services. In 1997, Marpin entered into an agreement with Cable & Wireless under which Marpin acquired Internet access through lines and equipment supplied by Cable & Wireless. Marpin subsequently provided services without using the Cable & Wireless facilities; therefore, the latter withdrew the toll-free numbers allotted to Marpin for Internet access by customers.

The issue at trial was whether the granting of exclusive licenses to Cable & Wireless was constitutional. The High Court of Justice ruled that the exclusivity of the license was invalid, contravening sections 10 (1) and 7 (1) of the constitution, which provide for freedom of communication. Cable & Wireless appealed to the ECSC, which dismissed the appeal, agreeing with the decision of the High Court. The Privy Council allowed the appeal and remitted the case to the High Court for reconsideration and "appreciation of the local conditions." This was on the basis that the Privy Council could not decide whether Dominica's Telecommunications Act and the Cable & Wireless monopoly were reasonably justifiable to protect the rights and freedoms under the constitution in question. Allowing the ECSC to make decisions has created an environment where local economic conditions are taken into account.

The case of *Basdeo Panday v. Kenneth Gordon* was a libel case involving a former prime minister of Trinidad and Tobago, Basdeo Panday, and Kenneth Gordon, chairman of a large media house that operates several newspapers and a television station. The Privy Council in its judgment recognized the cultural distance between the Law Lords' appreciation of what is defamatory in libel cases and what would be considered a defamatory statement in the region. The judgment states: "How words of this character would be understood, and what effect such words would have on those who heard them, are matters on which local courts are far better placed than their Lordships."[33] Accordingly, on the issue of amount of damages, their lordships state: "The seriousness of a libel and the quantification of an award are matters where judges with knowledge of local conditions are much better placed than their Lordships' Board."[34] On the above grounds,[35] the Privy Council dismissed the appeal. The Right Honorable Mr. Justice Michael de la Bastide (2006) has stated that the net result of this decision is that the appellant might have felt that he was denied the full benefit of a second-tier appeal. This is one of a series of cases in which Privy Council judges have acknowledged their unfamiliarity with local conditions.

For these and many other reasons, several constitutional commissions in the region have recommended that a regional court should replace the Privy Council as a final court of appeal—hence the CCJ. But the Privy Council has made it difficult for Caribbean states to redirect their final appeals to the CCJ. When Jamaica's Parliament legislated that final appeals would be filed in the CCJ rather than the Privy Council, the Privy Council decided that the law was inconsistent with the constitution of Jamaica on the premise that it does not guarantee the independence of the CCJ judges.[36] Ironically, the Jamaica Constitution does not guarantee the independence of the Privy Council judges either, but this anomaly was glossed over on the basis that "the independence of the Privy Council and its imperviousness to local pressure had never been in doubt." This decision represented a distinct setback to the CCJ because it limited Jamaica's ability to access the appellate jurisdiction of the CCJ, and it encouraged a false notion that Caribbean judges, unlike their counterparts in Britain, can somehow be suborned.

Only a popular referendum or a special parliamentary majority could replace the Privy Council. Jamaica might hold a referendum, but the outcome is difficult to predict. The Privy Council judgment also raises concerns about other states in the region with similar constitutions. In February of 2005, at the CARICOM summit in Suriname, the heads of government amended the CCJ treaty to prevent further Privy Council intervention in such matters.

Human Rights Jurisprudence That Has Created Controversy for the CCJ

Jurisprudence has developed over time in many areas, but in the area of human rights, it has taken on greater significance, especially as it relates to the establishment of the CCJ. Over the past 15 years, beginning with the judgment in *Pratt v. A.G.*[37] from Jamaica, several Privy Council decisions on the death penalty have had a profound effect on capital punishment jurisprudence in the Commonwealth Caribbean. This case held that a delay in excess of five years or more on death row constituted cruel and inhuman punishment, contrary to the Constitution of Jamaica, and in essence also violated Commonwealth Caribbean constitutions. The Privy Council and the Caribbean court concerned had conflicting views on whether a delay in execution violated human rights and on whether the death penalty generally violated the Caribbean constitutions. Persons on death row must be executed within five years of their conviction of murder, or not executed at all. Mercy Committees consider whether to sanction an execution. If the government has ratified a treaty that gives citizens a right to petition international human rights bodies, then the Mercy Committee must allow them a reasonable time to exhaust those remedies.

The death penalty has been abolished in most industrialized countries, but it is still legal in the OECS and in the majority of other courts that are members of CARICOM. However, mandatory death penalties have been abolished as being inconsistent with the constitutional right to humane treatment. Executions have not been carried out in Barbados since 1984 and in Jamaica since 1986. One of the most recent executions took place in 1999 in Trinidad and Tobago, when nine members of a gang involved in the drugs trade were executed by hanging at the state prison in Port-of-Spain.

This evolution in the law over a relatively short period produced serious consequences in the Caribbean:

First, in the period between 1994 and 2002, the Privy Council repeatedly reversed itself on the same point, leaving Lord Hoffmann in one case to berate his colleagues severely on this score.[38]

Second, the regional governments openly condemned decisions of their own final court, conduct not typical before the 1990s. Regional governments not only publicly and forcefully criticized the Privy Council, but they also denounced human rights treaties they had ratified and subsequently enacted constitutional amendments that restricted human rights.[39] This led some sections of the public to link the dissatisfaction of the governments with the judgments of the Privy Council with their entirely unrelated plans to establish a Caribbean final court of appeal. None of these matters helped the advancement of Caribbean human rights.

Third, and naturally, confidence in the regional judiciary and justice system was undermined because of the apparent disconnect in opinions between the local judges and the Privy Council.

All of these events did not contribute positively to the establishment of the CCJ. Although many observers regard this evolution of the Caribbean's human rights jurisprudence in a positive light, the fact remains that this process was not determined *by* the Caribbean peoples themselves, but instead largely *for* them. The constitutions of the independent states included a caveat that the preindependence laws of the states were not to be "trumped by the fundamental rights and freedoms laid out in the new Constitutions" (Saunders 2006, 28). The Privy Council's interpretation of the laws and the constitutions of the independent states has evolved (as has that of courts in many countries, including the United Kingdom, for their own laws and constitutions). In a 1976 case in Jamaica, for instance, the Privy Council upheld a death sentence, holding that the convicted man had no legal rights to complain about the delay in the execution.[40] In the 1980s, the Privy Council adopted a more international approach to human rights and the death penalty, based on cases from several countries, including the United States and India. Later in the 1990s, the Privy Council, again relying on international precedents, reversed itself, holding that human rights would be violated with delays in execution. This development in jurisprudence reflects developments in the United Kingdom, where the death penalty (abolished for murder in 1965) was finally removed from the statutes in 1998 and the Human Rights Act of 1998 was adopted. But these were developments within the United Kingdom, not the OECS—and, though some may argue that the OECS benefited from this application of international standards by having the Privy Council interpret the laws, others could say that the process of developing jurisprudence must be home-grown for it to take hold.

This process created a climate of concern that the emergence of the CCJ would undermine the evolution of human rights. The newly formed CCJ has been called a "hanging court"—one that will uphold the validity of the death penalty and depart from Privy Council decisions. Proponents of the CCJ cite an element of emotionalism related to this issue because the decision to establish the CCJ predates the controversy. So far, as expected, the CCJ has adhered to the precedents from the Privy Council, and the judges have cited Privy Council cases in their judgments (see below).[41] Public support for the establishment of the CCJ has suffered as a result of the death penalty cases (Byron 2000). At the end of the day, public trust is critical for legitimacy of the institution.

Early Jurisprudence from the CCJ

Since inauguration in April 2005, the CCJ has heard eight applications for leave to appeal and seven substantive appeals as of the end of June 2007. No case in the original jurisdiction has as yet been filed, but this is expected to happen in due course. Most regional courts have a slow start before the number of cases filed increases. The ECJ[42] heard an average of 26 cases per year in its first 10 years, a number that increased to an average of 401 per year between 1987 and 1997 and 498 per year between 1997 and 2005. The ECSC too has had a dramatic increase in the number of cases over the years (figure 4.7).

It is too early to make any predictions about the future of the CCJ— the court needs time to demonstrate its effectiveness and to build public trust. However, its early cases show an appreciation of local conditions and values and an appropriate respect for precedents. An example of the former is the 15-year-long libel case of *Barbados Rediffusion Service*

Figure 4.7. Percentage Increase in the Number of Cases Filed: ECSC High Court and Court of Appeal Caseloads Compared with Those of the European Court of First Instance and European Court of Justice

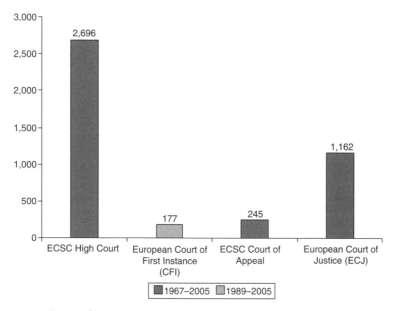

Sources: Annual Reports of the ECSC: http://www.eccourts.org; Annual Reports of the ECJ: http://curia.europa.eu/.
Note: The European Court of Justice began hearing cases in 1953. The percentage increase from 1953 to 2005 is 11,575%.

Limited v. Asha Mirchandani, Ram Mirchandani, and McDonald Farms Ltd.[43] The libel allegedly occurred when a radio station, as part of a live broadcast of the semifinals and finals of the 1989 Pic-o-de-Crop Calypso Competition, broadcast three calypso songs that criticized the quality of a poultry farm's produce. The farmers claimed that the songs alleged that their farm processed chickens in unsanitary conditions and allowed diseased chickens to be distributed. These songs allegedly destroyed their business, and they had to close the farm in 1990 as a result. The CCJ quashed the decisions of the lower courts. The case had cultural aspects and unique local issues: Calypsonians are traditionally political satirists and were often censored during colonial rule. Their music evolved in Trinidad as a means of spreading news and denouncing corruption.

The fears that had been originally expressed regarding the likely approach of the CCJ toward capital punishment cases and respect for the evolved jurisprudence over the past 15 years have proven thus far to be unfounded. In its two years of operation, the CCJ has demonstrated an equal appreciation of the usefulness of resorting to international jurisprudence as an aid to interpreting local constitutional provisions. In the decision of *Attorney General, Superintendent of Prisons, and Chief Marshal v. Jeffrey Joseph and Lennox Ricardo Boyce,*[44] the CCJ carefully reviewed many of the Privy Council precedents on the issues mentioned above, and the court gave considered reasons, sometimes not identical with those put forward by the Privy Council, as to why the new body of jurisprudence on capital punishment should in large measure continue to be observed.

In this case, the two respondents argued that the state was wrong to sentence them to death for the murder of a 22-year-old on the grounds that they had a pending appeal lodged before the Inter-American Commission on Human Rights (IACHR), where they had argued that the death penalty was inhumane. The Barbados authorities had read death warrants to the men on two occasions after the island's Prerogative of Mercy Committee refused to recommend commutation of their sentences. The respondents had argued that the Constitutional Amendment Act of 2000 provided convicted persons with a right to petition international bodies or courts regarding their death sentences.

The CCJ held that the exercise of the prerogative of mercy could be reviewed by the courts on the ground of procedural fairness. According to one Barbados lawyer, Dale Marshall, the judgment crystallized the status of the rights of convicted persons to petition international human rights bodies. The CCJ held that convicted persons may have a legitimate expectation that the state should wait for a reasonable time for reports from international bodies and that the Barbados Court of Appeal was bound to follow the decisions of the Privy Council in two previous cases, one involving the Jamaican government, which established that at least for a reasonable period, the state is under a duty to await the outcome of the process before human rights bodies. On the issue of the sentence imposed, the CCJ unanimously upheld the decision of the Court of Appeal of Barbados to commute both death sentences to life imprisonment. As this case demonstrates, precedents are being followed by the CCJ, and the court is providing legal reasoning that will be used by the lower courts.

In the case of *Tyrone da Costa Cadogan v. the Queen*,[45] the CCJ dismissed the application by Tyrone Da Costa Cadogan for special leave to appeal against the decision of the Court of Appeal of Barbados. The appellant had been sentenced to death by hanging for murder and argued that the conviction should be quashed. Specifically, he argued that (a) the court of appeal should have considered the issue of diminished responsibility, (b) his former counsel was incompetent, and (c) there was prejudice to him from lack of public funding. The court of appeal submitted that in its judgment there was no merit to the appeal. The CCJ dismissed the new grounds on the basis that (a) there was no medical evidence for abnormality of mind impairing the mental responsibility of Tyrone Da Costa Cadogan, (b) the manner with which the former counsel pursued the case did not raise issues of incompetence and therefore miscarriage of justice, and (c) the fact that there is lack of public funding for the services of a non-government-employed psychiatrist is not significant because free services are available from a government-employed psychiatrist, which on the evidence could render an impartial and competent opinion. The CCJ here is respecting the reasoning of the lower court even when the death penalty is at issue.

Conclusion

The executive yields enormous power in the small states of the OECS, given that there is only a slight separation between the legislative and executive branches of government. This power is generated by the parliamentary system, which allows for members of the legislative branch to be appointed as members of the executive branch, coupled with the demographics of the region, where a small group of politicians hold political power in both the legislative and executive branches for many years. This can lead to great pressure on the judiciary. But the ECSC was established, was functioning, and could not be tampered with by the executive, and its independence derived from being a regional entity. This allowed the judiciary to curb any tendency toward excess on the part of the executive. This environment stands in stark contrast to many developing countries where judiciaries are purely national and governments continually tamper with them, thereby using the judiciary as an instrument to advance the political necessities of the day.

An institution established to resolve regional disputes faces some difficult hurdles. In particular, the population of an individual state can feel alienated from the regional body because there are no judges or court staff from their own state, because they have little information about the work of the body, or because they perceive that cases are decided against their interests. Over the past 40 years, it seems clear that the ECSC has been able to surmount these obstacles by building public trust in the institution's capacity to deliver justice fairly, efficiently, and transparently. The court publishes an annual report, holds radio discussions, and keeps an open door to listen to issues raised by the bar and the public. Only one member state has ever withdrawn from the court: Grenada withdrew as a result of a coup from 1979 to 1983, but returned sometime later to continue its relationship with the court (Alleyne 2007). And the chairman of the OECS has indicated that although the governments may not always agree with the decisions of the ECSC, there is never a question as to whether they should comply with the court's decisions. It is this respect for the integrity of the court that ensures its sustainability.

A particular challenge for small states is the high per unit cost of providing justice services. As regional courts, the ECSC and the CCJ offer a solution to the problem by economizing scarce resources, both financial and human (the limited number of judges and other legal experts), and rationalizing what began as a limited demand for such legal services by spreading the cost. In addition, the exercise of the original jurisdiction of the CCJ as the sole tribunal for interpreting and applying the revised treaty will play an important role in unifying the applicable law and establishing certainty and predictability for investors in the region, as well as further improving the capacity for pooling regional resources. Two Caribbean states that will have the most difficulty accessing the court are Suriname (whose laws are based on the Dutch legal system) and Haiti (based on the French civil law system). As a first step in overcoming these difficulties, the rules of the CCJ, which govern proceedings in which the original jurisdiction of the court is invoked, are in the

process of being translated into Dutch. There is also a Dutch judge sitting on the court.

The CCJ is showing no signs so far of falling at any of the hurdles described earlier. It is building a reputation, and that takes time—it is too early to tell how often it will be used in its original jurisdiction (no action in this jurisdiction has as yet been filed) and when other states, apart from Guyana and Barbados, will send appeals to the court. It could be that the public may feel that the CCJ is too remote and out of touch with realities—like the Privy Council. Conversely, the public may believe that the region is not yet ready to replace the Privy Council because, as one judge explained, "it is difficult to convince the population to differ from the U.K." But there are grounds for optimism for this new regional institution in the effective precedent provided by the ECSC in its experiences of regional cooperation built upon mutual interests in fostering economic and social development.

Annex 4A. List of Interviewees

Name	Affiliation
Justice Denys Barrow	Justice of Appeal, ECSC
Justice Hugh Rawlins	Justice of Appeal, ECSC
Guy Ellis	Press Consultant, ECSC
Kimberly Cenac-Phulgence	Chief Registrar, ECSC
Geraldine St. Croix	Statistician, ECSC
Irvin Ferdinand	Accountant, ECSC
Aloysia Gabriel	HR Manager, ECSC
Mark Ernest	IT Manager, ECSC
Francis Compton	Regional Mediation Coordinator, ECSC
Gregory Girard	Court Executive Administrator, ECSC
Justice Albert Redhead	High Court Judge [Ag.] (Presiding Judge of the Criminal Division), ECSC
The Rt. Hon. Sir Vincent Floissac	Former Chief Justice
Claudet Valentine	Information Services Manager
Llewellyn Gill	External Auditor
Nicole Sylvester	President of the OECS Bar
Dancia Penn	Queen's Counsel, Former Deputy Governor, BVI
Sir Dwight Venner	Governor, ECCB
Dr. Joseph Archibald	QC—Senior Legal Practitioner based in the BVI
Hon. Baldwin Spencer	Prime Minister of Antigua and Barbuda and President of the Organization of the Eastern Caribbean States (OECS)
Justice Adrian Saunders	Judge of the CCJ
Justice Anthony Ross	Managing Judge, ECSC
Terence Byron	Legal Practitioner based in St. Kitts and Nevis

The authors would like to thank all the interviewees. In addition, we would like to thank those who offered their observations and comments for the preparation of this paper, in particular Chief Justice Brian Alleyne, Sir Vincent Flasse, Eldon Mathurin, Rolande Simone-Pryce, Frits van Beek, Christian Brachet, Kenneth Mwenda, Jaime Jaramillo, and Olivier Cattaneo. We would also like to thank Katerina Leris for her research assistance.

Notes

1. Revised Treaty of Chaguaramas Establishing the Caribbean Community, including the CARICOM Single Market and Economy, July 5, 2001. http://www.caricom.org/archives/revisedtreaty.pdf.

2. http://www.eccourts.org/.

3. West Indies Associated States Supreme Court Order no. 223 of 1967. Eastern Caribbean Supreme Court Order with Amendments, December 31, 2001.

4. http://www.eccourts.org/aboutecsc/history.html.

5. Order of 1967.

6. The first year can be pursued at any one of the four campuses; the second and third years are only offered on the Barbados campus. http://www.mona.uwi.edu/admissions/programmes/mona_law.htm.

7. Part II, section 5 of the order of 1967.

8. Annual Reports of the ECSC. http://www.eccourts.org.

9. In addition, while the judiciary will not be self-financing, it does generate revenue through court fees, traffic fines, and criminal fines that go to the local government of the member states. These fines and fees could be deposited into a trust fund for the courts.

10. This refers to matters filed after January 2001, when reforms were introduced.

11. Annual reports of the ECSC. http://www.eccourts.org/publications/annual reports/.

12. Figures from ECSC Statistics Office, referring to the High Courts in Anguilla, Antigua and Barbuda, and Montserrat during 1967–2005.

13. http://www.eccourts.org/publications/annualreports/AnnualReport2004-2005.pdf.

14. Section 38 of the Constitution of St. Vincent and the Grenadines, 1979.

15. Part III, section 11 (b) of the order of 1967.

16. The member states of the CSME are Antigua and Barbuda, Barbados, Belize, Dominica, Grenada, Guyana, Haiti, Jamaica, Montserrat, St. Kitts and Nevis, St. Lucia, St. Vincent and the Grenadines, Suriname, and Trinidad and Tobago. Revised Treaty of Chaguaramas Establishing the Caribbean Community,

including the CARICOM Single Market and Economy, July 5, 2001, art. 3. http://www.caricom.org/archives/revisedtreaty.pdf. This is a potential market of 14 million people.

17. The commission was established by the heads of government of CARICOM to formulate proposals for advancing the first Treaty of Chaguaramas, which established the Caribbean Community and Common Market (CARICOM) in 1973.

18. Guyana had abolished appeals to the Privy Council since 1970 in civil and criminal cases and in 1973 in constitutional matters. The court of appeal became the final court.

19. See CCJ 2001, Article XII.

20. http://www.ecowas.int/.

21. Revised Agreement Establishing the Caribbean Court of Justice Trust Fund, article IV. http://www.caribbeancourtofjustice.org/legislation.html.

22. Ibid.

23. Brunei, Zambia, Mauritius, Tuvalu, Kiribati, the British dependent territories in the Caribbean, the Channel Islands, and the Commonwealth Caribbean (Rawlins 2000, 10). For a full listing of the jurisdiction of the Privy Council, see http://www.privy-council.org.uk/output/Page32.asp.

24. The new act applied to actions commenced after the date of its commencement. In effect, the last Canadian appeal to the Privy Council was not decided until 1959.

25. Privy Council (Limitation of Appeals) Act of 1968, Privy Council (Appeals from the High Court) Act of 1975, and Australia Act of 1986.

26. The Courts Act, 1960, article 42 (1), declared the supreme court to be the final court of appeal, abolishing the appellate jurisdiction of the West African Court of Appeal and the Judicial Committee of the Privy Council.

27. Judicial Committee Repeal Act of 1994.

28. Supreme court set up by act of Parliament in 2003: Supreme Court of New Zealand Act. Appeals to Privy Council terminated as of January 1, 2004.

29. In the past 20 years, judges from the Caribbean have sat for appeals on the Privy Council in the following cases: In 2003, Senior Judge Edward Zacca sat among eight English lords in an appeal case from Jamaica related to the death penalty issue: *Lambert Watson v. the Queen* (Privy Council appeal no. 36 of 2003); also in 2000, in an appeal from the British Virgin Islands, *Geoffrey Cobham v. Joseph Frett* (appeal no. 41 of 1999).

30. Credicom N.V. and Colony Credicom L.P. and Colorado Credicom L.L.C. Civil appeal no. 4 of 1999.

31. Hon. Telford Georges, as cited in Rawlins (2000, 44).

32. Privy Council appeal no. 15 of 2000.

33. *Basdeo Panday v. Kenneth Gordon* (Privy Council appeal no. 35 of 2004), paragraph 10.

34. Ibid., paragraph 29.

35. The Privy Council also discussed section 4(e) of the Constitution of Trinidad and Tobago, which was one of the three grounds on which Mr. Gordon based his appeal against liability.

36. The constitutionality of these acts was challenged by the Independent Jamaica Council of Human Rights, the opposition Jamaica Labour Party, and certain other parties. The court of appeal unanimously ruled the amended legislation constitutional. The Privy Council reversed the decision and struck down the legislation in *Independent Jamaica Council for Human Rights (1998) Limited & Others v. Marshall-Burnett and the Attorney General of Jamaica.* [2005] U.K. P.C.3.

37. Pratt v. A-G. [1993] 43 W.I.R. 340 (P.C.).

38. *Neville Lewis v. the Attorney-General.* [2001] 2 A.C. 50.

39. Trinidad and Tobago announced its withdrawal from the American Convention on Human Rights on May 26, 1998.

40. *De Freitas v. Benny* [1976] A.C. 239.

41. *The Attorney General Superintendent of Prisons Chief Marshal v. Jeffrey Joseph and Lennox Ricardo Boyce.*

42. http://www.curia.europa.eu/en/instit/presentationfr/rapport/stat/st05cr.pdf.

43. CCJ appeal no. CV 1 of 2005.

44. CCJ appeal no. CV 2 of 2005.

45. CCJ appeal no. AL 6 of 2006.

References

Alleyne, Brian. 2002. "Overview of Civil Procedure Rules 2000." Eastern Caribbean Supreme Court Orientation Program for New Judges, February 25–29. On file with authors.

———. 2007. "The 40th Anniversary of the ECSC, February 2007." http://www.eccourts.org/ECSC40/sitting/Address-HisLordshiptheHonChiefJustice[Ag]BrianAlleyneSC.pdf.

Anthony, Kenny D. 2003. "The Caribbean Court of Justice: Will It Be a Hanging Court?" Address at the Norman Manley Law School, June 28. http://www.pm.gov.lc/former_prime_ministers/kenny_d_anthony/statements/2003/the_caribbean_court_of_justice_will_it_be_a_hanging_court_june_28_2003.htm.

Archibald, Joseph S. 2002. "The Changing Role of the Judge in Modern Society." Orientation Program for New Judges, February 25–29.

Byron, Dennis. 2000. "Judicial Reforms in the Eastern Caribbean and the Caribbean Court of Justice." St. Kitts Chamber of Industry and Commerce and the Foundation for National Development, June 17.

———. 2002a. "Hitting the Ground Running." Keynote Address, Eastern Caribbean Supreme Court Orientation Programme for New Judges, February 25. On file with authors.

———. 2002b. "Terms and Conditions of a High Court Judge." Eastern Caribbean Orientation Programme for New Judges, February 25–29. On file with authors.

Byron, Terence V., Probyn Inniss, Mark A. G. Brantley, and Toni Frederick. 2007. "Response to Address by the Honourable Acting Chief Justice." Supreme Court 40th Anniversary Celebration, St. Kitts and Nevis Local Committee, Historical Sub-Committee, February 27. http://www.eccourts .org/ECSC40/ sitting/Response-TerenceByron.pdf.

CCJ (Caribbean Court of Justice). 2001. "Agreement Establishing the Caribbean Court of Justice." Article XII. http://www.caribbeancourtofjustice.org/court administration/ccj_agreement.pdf.

CEPEJ (European Commission for the Efficiency of Justice). 2002. *European Judicial Systems 2002*. Strasbourg: Council of Europe. http://siteresources .worldbank.org/INTLAWJUSTINST/Resources/CEPEJreport.pdf.

Dakolias, Maria. 2006. "Are We There Yet? Measuring Success of Constitutional Reform." *Vanderbilt Journal of Transnational Law* (October).

De la Bastide, Michael. 1995. "The Case of a Caribbean Court of Appeal." 5 CARIB. L. REV. 401, 403.

———. 2006. "Putting Things Right and the Caribbean Court of Justice." The Seventh William G. Demas Memorial Lecture at Montego Bay, Jamaica, May 16. http://www.caribank.org.

ECSC (Eastern Caribbean Supreme Court). Annual Reports. http://www.eccourts .org/publications/annualreports/.

———. "Brief History of the Court." http://www.eccourts.org/aboutecsc/history .html.

———. Web site: http://www.eccourts.org/.

ECJ (European Court of Justice). "Tables and Statistics." http://www.curia.europa .eu/en/instit/presentationfr/rapport/stat/st05cr.pdf.

ECOWAS (Economic Community of West African States). Web site: http://www .ecowas.int/.

Kaufmann, Daniel, Aart Kraay, and Massimo Mastruzzi. 2006. "Governance Matters V: Aggregate and Individual Governance Indicators for 1996–2005." World Bank, Washington, DC. http://siteresources.worldbank.org/INTWBIGO VANTCOR/Resources/1740479-1150402582357/2661829-1158008871017/ gov_matters_5_no_annex.pdf.

Legal and Judicial Sector at a Glance database: www4.worldbank.org/legal/data base/Justice.

Pemberton, Charmaine A. J. 2002. "Civil Procedure Rules 2002: The Case Management Conference-Procedure." Eastern Caribbean Supreme Court Orientation Program for New Judges, February 25–29. On file with authors.

Rawlins, Hugh. 2000. "The Caribbean Court of Justice: The History and Analysis of the Debate." CARICOM Secretariat, Georgetown, Guyana. www.cari com.org/jsp/archives/ccj_rawlins.pdf.

"Revised Agreement Establishing the Caribbean Court of Justice Trust Fund." Annex. http://www.caribbeancourtofjustice.org/courtadministration/ccj_rev_ trustfund.pdf.

"Revised Treaty of Chaguaramas Establishing the Caribbean Community, including the CARICOM Single Market and Economy." July 5, 2001. http://www .caricom.org/archives/revisedtreaty.pdf.

Saunders, Adrian. 2006. "The Caribbean Court of Justice and the Evolving Human Rights Jurisprudence of the Caribbean." On file with authors. http://eccourts.org/publications/annualreports/ANNUALRE PORT2005-2006%5BFinal%5D.pdf (p. 28).

———. 2006. "The Entrenchment of the West Indies Associated Supreme Court Order 1967 in OECS Constitutions." On file with authors.

West Indies Associated States Supreme Court Order no. 223 of 1967. Eastern Caribbean Supreme Court Order with Amendments, December 31, 2001. On file with authors.

PART 2

Cases Studies on ICT Regulation and Outsourcing

Information and communications technology may be used to offset the negative implications of distance and small size. Unfortunately, many small states have telecommunication regulations that hinder competition, result in high telecommunication costs, and become an obstacle to accessing low-cost and high-quality international communications and worldwide knowledge.

Several of the chapters in this section illustrate the impact of a competitive framework in telecommunications (or the lack of) on usage. The cases of ECTEL and Samoa telecommunications describe the protracted transition from monopoly to competition and illustrate the benefits associated with this transition. In turn, the Cape Verde and USP case studies illustrate the costs a noncompetitive telecommunications market imposes on well-designed programs that use information and communications technology (ICT) services intensively.

Outsourcing is a way to overcome small size and capacity limitations, but is not always the least expensive solution. The chapter on e-government in Cape Verde describes the constraints the government faced when it designed and started to implement the e-government action plan.

The preferred government strategy was in-house provision rather than outsourcing. In this instance, the cost was arguably lower, and the quality of the design higher, for implementing an in-house rather than outsourced system.

Furthermore, outsourcing is not always feasible. ECTEL is an example of countries pooling resources to create a regional body and of outsourcing regulatory advice to the new organization. But what happens if, as in the case of Samoa's telecommunications sector, the regional option is not feasible today? Samoa's budget reform illustrates another aspect of the same problem. A supplier decides to stop servicing the budget software the government uses. Outsourcing the service (as had been done so far) was no longer feasible. An alternative, adaptable to Samoa's low transaction volumes, had to be sought. It was found in software used by local governments in larger states, customized to the realities of budget execution in Samoa.

Small size is also a driving force for simplifying regulation. To the extent possible, countries economize resources by relying on simple, easily monitored, rather than complex, regulations. The chapter on Samoa telecommunications sector reform illustrates how the law uses competition as a way to reduce the cost of monitoring market conditions.

CHAPTER 5

Telecommunications Regulation in the Eastern Caribbean

Edgardo Favaro and Brian Winter

Prologue

Mary Dean had a big problem with her telephone bill, just like many other residents of the tiny islands of the Eastern Caribbean. Half of her family lives abroad: her brother, her uncle, and her nephews among them. But until just a few years ago, she could afford to call them only every few months or so. "The phone was too expensive to use more often than that," said Mary, a waitress at a family-run Chinese restaurant behind a beach resort on the island nation of St. Lucia. "I never had enough money to call my brother. But things are better these days. Something changed."

What changed? This case study explores the larger, complex, global story of how Mary and other residents in the nations of the Eastern Caribbean region saw their telephone bills come down, their service improve, and more options emerge for telecommunications providers. It is the story of

---

Edgardo Favaro is a Lead Economist at the World Bank. Brian Winter is an employee of *USA Today.*

how a monopoly was broken and of newly independent countries developing in the wake of decades of colonial rule. The study illustrates how several small nations, united by history and culture—but diverse in many other ways—joined together to accomplish a single objective.

The central narrative concerns the creation and early life of the Eastern Caribbean Telecommunications Authority (ECTEL), which, in 2000, became the world's first multicountry regulatory telecommunications agency. The breakup of the Cable & Wireless (C&W) telephone monopoly and the creation of ECTEL facilitated the penetration of mobile-telephone technology into the Eastern Caribbean, with a remarkable positive impact on demand for services.

The questions raised by this story are of universal relevance beyond the shores of the Caribbean islands and outside the realm of the telecommunications industry. How are regional organizations formed? How much sovereignty must countries delegate when cooperating with others? And, finally, what is the future for regional organizations?

History

Until the late 1990s, a single company handled all telecommunications in the five countries that would one day form ECTEL: St. Lucia, Dominica, Grenada, St. Kitts and Nevis, and St. Vincent and the Grenadines. Cable & Wireless, a multinational company based in London, had been operating in the Caribbean region since the Victorian era, when these countries formed part of the sprawling British Empire. At the time, C&W's monopoly in telecommunications was guaranteed by local laws for several more years; in one case, its exclusivity license ran as far into the future as 2020.

C&W's charges for international telephone service were well above those in other countries of similar size and geography; these high costs were a burden to individual consumers and companies alike (see, for example, ITU [2006]).

Cable & Wireless Monopoly

The history of Cable & Wireless dates back to the 1860s, when its ancestral companies began erecting a massive telegraph network that connected London with the far-flung colonies of the British Empire, including those in the Caribbean. The company was for many years called "Imperial and International Communications," and its expansion largely mirrored that of the Empire, serving as the "nerve system"[1] of British colonial rule. Over the ensuing decades, C&W set up communications systems on virtually every continent as, by the end of World War I, the British Empire grew to include a quarter of the world's land mass and population. The company's presence became so ubiquitous in remote parts of the world that, according to C&W's Web site, the name "The Exiles" was adopted for themselves by C&W's British employees living abroad, who took the name from one of the company's first, most distant, and inaccessible telegraph stations within England.

The company began its operations in the Caribbean in 1868, when a telegraph cable was laid from Florida to Cuba. Over the next century, C&W would be almost entirely responsible for building and maintaining the Caribbean islands' communications links to the outside world. In a political and operational sense, C&W was often virtually inseparable from the colonial government—in fact, C&W was nationalized in 1947 and remained British government property until it was privatized by Prime Minister Margaret Thatcher's conservative administration in 1981.

The status quo began slowly to change in the late 1970s, when a movement for independence swept the former British colonies of the Eastern Caribbean subregion. But despite these countries' newfound independence from Great Britain, C&W remained their sole provider of telecommunications. The company's local units often continued to be managed by British expatriates who lived on the islands. By 1995, Cable & Wireless operated 15 separate telephone businesses in the Caribbean and mobile-telephone services in 10 Caribbean countries. In the five countries that would eventually form ECTEL, C&W held a monopoly guaranteed by law. "C&W was a British entity with a long tradition of being allowed unencumbered entry into the market," said Randolph Cato, now the director of economic affairs for the Organization of Eastern Caribbean States (OECS). "They were as much a part of the landscape in St. Lucia as a tree."

In the 1980s, C&W's arrangement in the Caribbean was hardly unique in the world. Building a fixed-line telephone system required an enormous initial investment, which then had to be recovered over time through service fees. Telecommunications was considered a "natural monopoly" because it was, in most cases, not economically feasible for a second company to come in and build a second fixed-line network. Around the globe, policy makers in most countries had decided that a sole provider of telephone services was the best option. This was just as true for the United States or the United Kingdom as it was for the countries of the Eastern Caribbean, where deregulation was only just beginning in the 1980s (see also chapter 9 on reform of telecommunications in Samoa).

Within the monopoly system, policy makers effectively had two options: a regulated monopoly or a publicly owned company to provide services. A third possibility, to auction the right to service a market, was not seen as desirable. The Eastern Caribbean states decided—some would say inherited—the first option, that of regulating a private company in a monopoly situation. But, here, the countries' relative size and short history since independence began to pose particular problems. Regulation is expensive. And it implied a level of technical knowledge that was difficult to find in the region. In sum, it was extremely difficult for each individual country in the Eastern Caribbean to find the staff, and then afford the salaries, for a team of technical experts who could have effectively regulated the telecommunications sector.

Faced with that reality, governments largely allowed C&W to regulate itself. "It was essentially an unregulated monopoly," said a source in the private sector. In theory, C&W would petition each country's ministry of communications for regulatory matters, and final authority rested with the finance ministry. "But in practice, legislation was often drafted directly by C&W and then approved with few or no changes by the government," said Eliud Williams, now the acting chief of ECTEL. Governments usually did not have the expertise or the political will to contest C&W's requests, and there was nobody to provide objective analysis or advice. So the perception was that the governments simply rubber-stamped whatever C&W requested. This arrangement, though not strictly formalized, had in truth gone on for years—particularly during the days when C&W operated within the framework of the British colonial system.

After independence, in the 1980s and 1990s, the cracks in the arrangement began to show. The young nations were struggling to develop their economies, and many officials did not believe that C&W had their best interests in mind. "Very little attention was paid to the development requirements of the island," said Eldon Mathurin, Chairman of the St. Lucia National Telecommunications Regulatory Commission. "Attributes like quality of service and penetration were not important in terms of the provider's perspective. Neither was affordability." C&W guarded its financial information rather closely; many officials believed that the company was reaping "excessive" profits from its operations in the Eastern Caribbean while keeping rates unduly high. Among the general public, some believed that removing or reforming C&W was a necessary part of the new nations' political maturity—two decades after independence, their telecommunications industry should not still be restrained by an anachronistic monopoly left over from the colonial regime.

In retrospect, the evidence that C&W was exploiting its monopoly position is not solid. A serious assessment of the extent to which C&W exploited its position would require much more comprehensive information about cost of production and prices in ECTEL countries and in comparable benchmark countries than is available here. The perception at the time that the company was exploiting that position has some support from indicators that the price of international phone calls was much higher in the region than in the United States and United Kingdom (table 5.1).

The monopoly conditions effectively restricted supply of services in ECTEL countries. The number of fixed-line and mobile-phone subscribers together (table 5.2) in ECTEL countries was, as of 2000, at about the average in small states worldwide; however, for mobile phones, the number of subscribers per 1,000 people was much lower than the average number of subscribers in small states (143) or than the average number in two benchmark countries in the region: Antigua and Barbuda and Jamaica. For instance, there were 142 mobile-phone subscribers per 1,000 people in Jamaica and 286 in Antigua and Barbuda, but only 17 in Dominica and 16 in St. Lucia.

The comparison of telecom density indicators in ECTEL countries with that of Jamaica and Antigua and Barbuda comes close to a natural experiment on the impact of market and regulatory conditions on the development of the sector. Jamaica and Antigua and Barbuda have geographical circumstances similar to those of ECTEL countries. By 2000, however, Jamaica had already for several years been deregulating the telecom sector. In Antigua and Barbuda, in turn, the provision of telephone services was the responsibility of a state-owned company.

Winds of Change

By the late 1990s, the relationship between C&W, its customers, and some of the subregion's governments had become "quite acrimonious" (a source in the private sector). The status quo would soon change forever,

Table 5.1. International Rates from OECS Countries

Rates per minute, EC$	2001	2003	2006
To: United States	3.25	1.65	0.90–1.65
To: United Kingdom	4.00	1.65	0.90–1.65
Comparison: United States to OECS	1.00	0.80	0.51

Source: TeleGeography (2006).
Note: 2.6875 EC$ = 1 US$ (ECTEL).

Table 5.2. Number of Telephone Subscribers and Internet Users in 2000

Country	Fixed & mobile subscribers per 1,000	Internet users per 1,000	Mobile-phone subscribers per 1,000
ECTEL			
Dominica	335	84	17
Grenada	352	41	42
St. Kitts & Nevis	522	61	27
St. Lucia	329	51	16
St. Vincent & the Grenadines	235	30	20
Other Caribbean			
Antigua & Barbuda	783	65	286
Jamaica	338	31	142
Small States	385	81	143
Larger States	349	76	165

Source: World Bank (2007).
Note: Small states are states with population below 2 million; larger states are states with population above 2 million.

though, because of a "perfect storm" of several events coming together at the same time: technological advances, public opinion, and global trends such as deregulation.

Since independence, public opinion had been slowly but gradually building against C&W, often by word of mouth. Interestingly, much of this perception was fueled by relatives living abroad, a common circumstance in the nations of the Eastern Caribbean. "Almost everybody here has a relative in the U.K., the U.S., or Canada," said Cato of the OECS. "People heard from their relatives that their telephone bills were extremely high in comparison." Pressure built as residents flooded local radio call-in shows—a popular form of political participation in this region, especially since the 1990s—with complaints. Simply put, customers wanted to be able to afford to talk more on the phone to their friends at home and their relatives abroad.

Meanwhile, the economic winds were changing worldwide. With the collapse of the Berlin Wall in 1989, combined with unprecedented improvement in global communications, there was a definite change in the world's economy—particularly, a migration toward the services industry. The young nations of the Eastern Caribbean knew they had to make a transition from agriculture (primarily bananas and sugar) to services (tourism and finance). "Diversification" became the watchword. And diversification would require a dramatic change in the economic infrastructure: in education, transportation, and especially telecommunications.

For example, banana plantations had not required a particularly sophisticated or economical telecommunications system—but an expanded banking system would. Even tourism required a more efficient telephone network because visitors from the United States or Europe expected a certain level of comfort, even if it was as simple as being able to call back home at reasonable cost.

The high cost of telecommunications on the islands was already making this transition difficult. To cite one particular example, a local businessman was attempting to create a call center in St. Lucia, but opted to conduct business via a satellite uplink at considerable cost "because C&W was uneconomical." This problem recurred elsewhere, and political pressure for change began to mount from the nations' influential businessmen. "C&W made many business models prohibitively expensive," Cato said, "so if you wanted to compete on a global level, then you had to address that." Policy makers soon realized that they could fall irrevocably behind in the new, globalized economy unless the status quo changed. "This was much more than an expensive phone bill," Cato said. "This was a macroeconomic problem."

Hand in hand with globalization came watershed improvements in technology. The proliferation of mobile telephones and the beginning of the Internet era completely changed how business was done in the telecommunications sector. It would transform what had been a classic monopoly industry worldwide into a competitive sector, broadening the range of products available and sharply reducing prices. It would now be economically feasible for more than one company to operate in telecommunications. In particular, because networks for mobile-telephone service were relatively easy for a new company to install, via transmission towers, the nations of the Eastern Caribbean became an attractive potential new market for both foreign and home-grown mobile-telephone companies.

By the late 1990s, many other governments around the world had overhauled their telecommunications sectors to reflect these changes. There was a decade of experience with deregulation in Australia, the United States, New Zealand, and the United Kingdom. The U.S. experience had begun with the forced breakup of AT&T by the government. That decision, combined with the spread of mobile-telephone technology, began changing the widely held view that telecommunications was a natural monopoly; the view that the sector could operate and thrive under competition started to dominate in policy circles. Under this new system, the role of the regulator drastically changed: it became a watchdog responsible for ensuring that business decisions by one company did not affect the capacity of other companies to enter the market or provide services. In the 1990s, deregulation also spread to South and Central America and to the Caribbean region. Many countries around the developing world saw their telephone sector opened to competition and, in many cases, state-owned enterprises were privatized. Many witnessed an improvement in service fees, quality, and breadth of services.

At this time, the Eastern Caribbean was still far from the cutting edge of progress in the sector, but, as Cato said, these developments "created a conducive environment to challenging C&W's authority."

The Spark for Change: The Formation of ECTEL

In the late 1990s, two watershed events changed the status quo. The first was the arrival of a second company, Marpin Telecommunications, to provide Internet service in Dominica. Marpin had operated as a broadcaster of four television channels on the island since 1983. In 1997, the Minister of Communications in Dominica ruled that Marpin's license as a broadcaster also authorized it to offer Internet services to the public. At first, Marpin operated its Internet service by leasing lines through Cable & Wireless in Dominica.[2] Then, in 1998, Marpin acquired its own gateway and sought to offer Internet services directly, bypassing C&W's network. C&W opposed this action, on the grounds that it violated its exclusivity deal as outlined by Dominican law, and retaliated by withdrawing the 800 dial-up service that enabled Marpin customers to dial up toll-free to the Internet.[3] The case ended up in court.

For the first time, a legitimate alternative to C&W had presented itself, and the future of the monopoly would be decided by the legal system. After several rulings in lower courts, the case arrived in 2000 at the Privy Council of the United Kingdom, which served as the highest court for Dominica and other nations of the Eastern Caribbean. The Council ruled against C&W, saying that the company's monopoly constituted an infringement of citizens' constitutional right to freedom of speech.

The decision, which became known simply as the "Marpin Case," led to a sea change in the thinking of the subregion's political leaders. The fear of a successful potential legal challenge by C&W to deregulation was severely diminished, and governments in the Eastern Caribbean were emboldened to take steps to end the C&W monopoly. The Marpin Case "radically changed the perception of exclusivity," convincing the region's leaders that C&W "would have no basis to seek compensation for loss of any perceived exclusive rights."[4]

Already in October 1998, immediately after Marpin's initial confrontation with C&W, the Organization of Eastern Caribbean States (OECS) had established an initiative called the Telecommunications Reform Project, which aimed to overhaul the existing system. "It was longhand for getting rid of the C&W monopoly," Cato said. A loan from the World Bank to Dominica, Grenada, St. Kitts and Nevis, St. Lucia, and St. Vincent and the Grenadines provided financing for the studies required to design a new competition-based telecommunications regulatory system.

Negotiations to end the monopoly began, with C&W arguing that any deregulation should be done gradually and governments looking for a much shorter timetable. In retrospect, both had solid arguments. C&W was trying to protect the substantial investments it had made in infrastructure in fixed-line telephony and other segments. These investments were *irreversible*: C&W could not, for instance, just rip its fixed-line network out of the ground in St. Lucia and then use it somewhere else—it was a sunk cost. The company was also asking for property rights—indeed, the existing law—to be respected. For their part, the governments were defending the rights of their citizens to access new technology—to catch up with changes that had occurred in other parts of the world and to allow a structural change that would be in the best interest of their countries' development.

The second watershed event arose from a confrontation between Cable & Wireless and the government of St. Lucia. It had always been clear that St. Lucia would be on the forefront of change—its exclusivity arrangement with C&W was set to expire in 2000, before that of the other states. The timing of the expiration was "good fortune," said Eldon Mathurin of the National Telecommunications Regulatory Commission (NTRC), in that new ground rules could be established without violating the old, expiring agreement, and St. Lucia would serve as a test case for other nations.

In the course of negotiations, C&W threatened to withdraw from St. Lucia and cut off telephone service if the St. Lucian government persisted with its negotiating stance. The threat was not credible, and C&W's heavy-handed tactics provoked a common reaction from all the countries in the subregion. The governments of the other four nations—Dominica, Grenada, St. Kitts and Nevis, and St. Vincent and the Grenadines— essentially made it known that if C&W left St. Lucia, the company would be forced to leave all the other states as well.[5]

This was an historic development for regional unity in the Eastern Caribbean, as well as for the telecommunications sector. The unity of these five countries of the OECS on this issue gave impetus to the idea of creating a unified regulatory entity to look after the telecom sector regulation for the five countries, as a whole, instead of each individual country trying to fight the C&W monopoly. From this, the seeds of ECTEL were sown.[6]

The Birth of the Eastern Caribbean Telecommunications Authority

After the experience in St. Lucia, the five governments realized that they had strength in numbers and that a new telecommunications regulator should reflect this fact. The intention was clear—this new regulatory body would be designed to help break up a monopoly, foster competition, and then regulate the sector—but figuring out exactly how to structure such an organization was a challenge.

There was ample precedent for regional cooperation in the Eastern Caribbean for the prime ministers to follow. The OECS had existed since 1981. It was followed by the creation of the Eastern Caribbean Central Bank (ECCB) and the Eastern Caribbean Supreme Court (ECSC) (see the case studies on these two regional bodies). There was also a long record of regional cooperation on other issues, including security, the civil aviation authority, health care reform, and banana sales abroad. "There has been a history of cooperation in the OECS that even precedes independence," Cato said. This was augmented by a long history of treating the region as one large pool of talent, given the relatively small scale of the islands. "You can't duplicate the level of the technical staff on each individual island," said Mathurin of the NTRC, citing an example: "If you have an extremely good pathologist in St. Lucia, there is no need for one in Dominica. There is no reason to duplicate (this expertise elsewhere) except for reasons of political vanity."

But even though models of regional cooperation were at hand, a tremendous amount of improvisation went into the decision to form ECTEL. The first document at the start of the telecommunications reform project made no mention of the possibility of an ECTEL or an organization like it. According to Cato, "The idea came about organically, over time. We said: 'You know what? If this is what works, then let's make it happen!'" The World Bank was cooperative on this point, and the charter reflected this spontaneity. "I don't know if any other loan or credit arrangement had so many amendments," Cato said.

The primary question became one of structure. Would ECTEL be an all-powerful regional body vested with executive power, an advisory body capable of only making recommendations to national governments, or some hybrid of the two?

The debate was essentially over how much sovereignty national governments would delegate. The other regional models were instructive, but only to a certain degree. In the case of the Eastern Caribbean Central Bank, the central bank had executive authority in matters of monetary and exchange rate policy, but it could be argued that it had no more than an advisory role regarding the regulation of the banking sector. And while local politicians had delegated considerable sovereign power to the ECCB, much of this was inherent in the nature of the exchange rate adopted by the central bank—by adopting a currency board system, the governments would in any case be sacrificing much of their control over monetary policy.

The advantages of sacrificing national sovereignty in telecommunications were much less obvious. In the broadest sense, a regulator administers the relationship between a government and service providers. An *effective* regulator identifies issues that may adversely affect competition in the sector, and it protects a stable environment for business, while encouraging investment. Meanwhile, an *ineffective* regulator is prone to adopt views favorable to incumbents (and against competition) or favorable to individual competitors (rather than to competition) or to yield easily to populist views that have a negative impact on the investment decisions of companies in the long term. But, in the case of ECTEL, it was not clear whether choosing either an autonomous regional body vested with executive power or a regional body with an advisory role in telecommunications combined with a national structure would make the difference between a good or a bad regulator.

The governments wanted to create a regulator that would draw its strength from regional unity and pooling of resources. But an all-powerful regional regulator might give rise to disagreements over policy that would drive the countries apart—the opposite of the intended effect. For countries to delegate executive power to a regional body, there has to be a clear mandate—otherwise who controls performance of the regional organization?

So they created an organization that was, de facto, a hybrid. "The prime ministers determined they wanted to have a strong regional body—but retain a certain degree of authority," said Williams. ECTEL would make regional decisions on an advisory basis, but power would still be formally vested at the national level.

ECTEL was established under a treaty signed on May 4, 2000. Its primary roles are to design a transparent, objective, competitive, and investor-friendly licensing and regulatory regime to be implemented at the national level, to manage numbers and frequency allocations in each of the member states, and to create a forum for coordination of OECS telecommunications policies and regulations. The organization was funded via spectrum and license fees, which were treated as a regional asset.

The governance of ECTEL is based on the Council of Ministers, the Board of Directors, and the ECTEL Secretariat (for details, see box 5.1).

At the same time, at the state level, National Telecommunications Regulatory Commissions (NTRCs) were created. The NTRCs are responsible for implementation of regulations and policies, with technical

---

Box 5.1

Governance Structure of ECTEL

- **The Council of Ministers** comprises the ministers responsible for telecommunications in the ECTEL states and the director general of the OECS as an ex officio member; responsibilities include
  - Giving directives to the board on matters arising out of the treaty, including the generation and disbursement of revenue;
  - Ensuring that the board is responsible to the needs of the member states in the conduct of the telecommunications policy;
  - Approving ECTEL's annual operating budget;
  - Determining, from time to time, the internal organizational structure of ECTEL; and
  - Determining the fees payable to ECTEL for the performance of its functions.
- **The Board of Directors** comprises one member or an alternate from each member state appointed by the minister for a term of one year, and the managing director as an ex officio member. Responsibilities include
  - Making recommendations to the council on matters relating to telecommunications;
  - Advising member states on the management of the Universal Service Fund; and
  - Establishing rules and procedures consistent with the treaty for the management and operation of ECTEL.
- **The Directorate of Secretariat** comprises a managing director, and professional, technical, and support staff. Responsibilities include
  - The general administration of the ECTEL treaty and the day-to-day management of ECTEL.

Source: http://www.oecs.org/ectel/new%20ectel.htm.

assistance from ECTEL. There is substantial overlap of responsibilities between ECTEL and the NTRCs (box 5.2).

This structure came about via negotiation. "We did this largely through trial and error," said Cato. "The truth is that ECTEL as it is today is not what the governments originally committed to. It really evolved from conceptualizing several different legal and functional models."

Box 5.2

Comparison of Responsibilities of ECTEL and the NTRCs

ECTEL's Responsibilities

- A harmonized approach to telecommunications regulation in its member states
- Management and regulation of the telecommunications or radio spectrum
- Ensuring a competitive environment for telecommunications in ECTEL states
- Promoting fair competition in telecommunications services
- Working toward the provision of affordable, modern, efficient, competitive, and universally available telecommunications services to the people of the five member states
- Advising NTRCs and governments on matters relating to telecommunications and the spectrum, including regional policy, types of telecommunications services, licensing, fees, pricing, and provision of universal service

NRTCs' Responsibilities

- Formulation of national policy on telecommunications matters, with a view to ensuring the efficient, economical, and harmonized development of the telecommunications and broadcasting services and radio communications in their respective states
- Planning, supervising, and managing the use of the radio frequency spectrum in conjunction with ECTEL, including the assignment and registration of radio frequencies to be used by all telecoms licensees operating in, or on any vessel registered in, their respective states
- Investigating and resolving disputes relating to interconnections or sharing of infrastructure between telecommunications providers, as well as complaints related to harmful electromagnetic interference
- Monitoring anticompetitive practices in the telecommunications sector and advising the national body responsible for the regulation of anticompetitive practices accordingly
- Management of the Universal Service Fund

Source: http://www.oecs.org/ectel/new%20ectel.htm.

A New Model: The Early Years and Evolution of ECTEL

The early years of ECTEL were crucial. "One thing was to create the organization, and thus break the monopoly," said Cato, "and another was to create and *sustain* ECTEL."

What Happened to C&W?

New telecommunications acts opening the sectors to competition were announced, beginning with St. Kitts and Nevis in June 2000. In 2001, ECTEL agreed with C&W on a deal that would terminate monopoly rights in the ECTEL region. The first competitors were issued licenses in 2002, and the first cellular competitor started offering services early in 2003.

The positive effects of deregulation were immediate. The biggest change in the short term would be the proliferation of the market for mobile telephones. From 2000 to 2004, the regional penetration of cellular phones increased sharply. Table 5.3 presents the percentage increase in several quantity indicators: in Dominica, for instance, the number of Internet users increased by 208.3 percent and the number of mobile-phone subscribers per 1,000 increased by 3,341.2 percent between 2000 and 2004.

Of course, it would be absurd to attribute all this increase to deregulation. As table 5.3 illustrates, a similar rapid increase happened everywhere in the world between 2000 and 2004. At the same time, it is

Table 5.3. Percentage Increase in Number of Phone Subscribers, 2000–04

Country	Fixed-line & mobile-phone subscribers per 1,000	Internet users per 1,000	Mobile-phone subscribers per 1,000
ECTEL			
Dominica	162.4	208.3	3,341.2
Grenada	104.3	85.4	876.2
St. Kitts & Nevis	42.7	n.a.	688.9
St. Lucia	n.a.	558.8	3,450.0
St. Vincent & the Grenadines	173.2	126.7	2,305.0
Other Caribbean			
Antigua & Barbuda	46.7	284.6	135.7
Jamaica	202.1	1,200.0	485.9
Small States	84.9	151.9	234.3
Larger States	73.4	122.4	127.9

Source: Based on information from annex 5A, table 5A.1.
n.a. = not available.

noticeable that the percentage increase in mobile-phone subscribers was much higher in ECTEL countries than in Antigua and Barbuda, Jamaica, the average of small states, or the average of large states elsewhere in the world. Technological change spread everywhere, but the rate of increase in the number of mobile-phone users was much higher in countries which also saw deregulation between 2000 and 2004 than in any other group of countries in the world.

The steep rise in numbers of mobile-phone subscribers in ECTEL countries suggests that the institutional and market structure in the sector before ECTEL implied a significant pent-up demand for telephone services. The breakup of the monopoly in telecommunications facilitated an immediate adjustment in the number of mobile-phone subscribers—the technical possibility was there. The results were equally impressive in the number of Internet users; even so, the increase in penetration was less radical because there is much less competition in this sector and changes in the number of users depend more on changes in fixed-line infrastructure.

In some markets, mobile-telephone penetration would soon top 100 percent as customers purchased more than one phone. The entry of new companies—particularly, Digicel—resulted in intense competition. In one member country, C&W went from a 100 percent share in mobile telephones to being a minority player in just two months, according to a source in the private sector.

The competition for the mobile-telephone market was the primary engine for a precipitous decline in fees for international calls. As of mid-2006, C&W was still the only company offering fixed-line international telephone service, but because of the intense competition in mobile phones, C&W was compelled to cut its fixed-line international rates in a bid to retain customers. The average price for a phone call from the region to the United States and the United Kingdom fell rapidly (table 5.1); tariffs for domestic phone calls also fell (in St. Vincent and the Grenadines, from EC$0.17 per minute to EC$0.09 per minute—a trend that is seen as widely uniform throughout the ECTEL member nations).

ECTEL: The Early Days
ECTEL's early days were marked by difficulties perhaps typical of an organization trying to get on its feet. Technical issues were tremendously complicated, and at first the organization had problems recruiting qualified staff. "Telecoms is tough to learn; it's a separate language, not intuitive," said Geoff Batstone, the legal counsel for Cable & Wireless.

"You need a body of specialized knowledge to regulate. I give them (ECTEL) tremendous praise because they've learned so much in a short time." Other problems arose at first when individual countries allowed companies to go into arrears on their licensing fees, so that ECTEL's funding during the early days was tenuous.

There is also a feeling at C&W that errors were committed and that some of the early rulings were "unfair"—a problem that plagues the functioning of regulators worldwide (Levy and Spiller 1994; Khan 1998). Some of the staff at ECTEL were drawn from former C&W employees. "It felt at the beginning that regulators were out to get C&W," says a source in the private sector. "We actually heard: 'You've ripped us off for a hundred years, and now it's our turn.'" In some cases, C&W felt that it lost market share because regulators took an undue amount of time to process its applications for licenses.

Early in the relationship, however, as Batstone put it, "there was a 'watershed.'" In 2004, following a study by the World Bank that suggested that prices were too high, discussions began about installing a price cap. During negotiations for the broader deal, ECTEL implemented a temporary price cap. C&W took the decision to court and won. As the decision went to the appeals level, however, the company decided to sit back down with ECTEL and negotiate. The regulator and the company reached an agreement without litigation, and the lawsuit was dropped. From that point on, the relationship with ECTEL improved. "There has been an evolution. At the beginning, C&W was the devil, and the new challenger was an angel. Over time, I think we're getting past that." "Generally, I like ECTEL to be involved, because I feel I'm less subject to an arbitrary decision," says a source in the private sector. As the relationship has been harmonized and time has gone by, benefits have come to both the company and customers. Customers have benefited tremendously, and "competition has made C&W a better company. We've been forced to address our services."

ECTEL Grows Up: The Maturing Process

Given the improvised manner in which ECTEL was set up, it was always clear that its real power would be determined by the way the organization evolved, rather than by the formal rules of its charter. Although power is, in principle, vested at the national level, in practice, ECTEL still seems to have ultimate decision-making authority. Officials agreed that the NTRCs always seem to abide by the recommendations made by ECTEL.

"We've disagreed and had to quarrel with them (ECTEL)," said Mathurin of the St. Lucia NTRC. "But, in practice, once the decision is made, we comply."

Is ECTEL autonomous, in practice? It is, inasmuch as its counsel concerns general issues regarding the use of spectrum, interconnections, pricing policies, and the harmonization of the regulatory system across the region. Daily issues, such as license applications or interference complaints, are more the domain of the NTRCs. The relationship between ECTEL and the NTRCs is still evolving, however. "There are still some areas where the role of ECTEL and that of the NTRC can be more clearly defined," said ECTEL's Senior Financial Analyst, Cheryl Hector. The different nature of the organizations sometimes generates different points of view; for example, there has been some discord over requirements for financial reporting for companies seeking licenses.

Indeed, some officials believe that ECTEL's hybrid structure has impeded its ability to make decisions from a truly regional point of view. "I think the regional nature of ECTEL has gone by the board. I think in practice it deals with five separate entities instead of one. . . . There should be in theory a sixth viewpoint, . . . which is the overall regional interest. I'm not sure that is being adequately addressed, because of the nature of the beast that was created," Mathurin said. Companies also sometimes find the power structure unwieldy and not cost-effective. To use a hypothetical example, C&W can't afford to have a dedicated staff member in St. Vincent and the Grenadines to deal with the subject of regulation. "But, because of [the NTRCs], there is still the very real need to deal on a national level," Batstone said.

Regulatory consistency has value for investors. Because of regulatory consistency, companies can treat the member nations as a single market when doing business. This makes investment easier, officials said. "If each country is isolated, it's not a very attractive market," said Williams. "But, as a region, it is attractive."

Despite the problems, most of those interviewed believe that ECTEL has developed into an effective regulator. By virtue of ECTEL's regional approach, the organization has been able to accumulate a relatively well-respected pool of engineers, lawyers, and economists that might have been impossible to duplicate on a national level. "ECTEL takes a more pragmatic view. The strength of the regime is there is some consistency," said Batstone. "ECTEL tends to be quite responsive and deal with issues. Sometimes it takes awhile, but you feel like they're dealing with it, at least."

Lessons for the Future, and for Other Countries

ECTEL's relative success has already been seized on as a potential model for other countries or for other sectors. ECTEL officials have visited island countries in the South Pacific, for example, to discuss their track record. But, among those interviewed, opinions differ on whether the ECTEL experience could be repeated.

"A lot of this came about due to particular circumstances," said Cato. "Whether this is a model to be used elsewhere, I don't know." In interviews, the protagonists repeatedly emphasized the importance of the cultural similarities among the five nations and how they had been essential to the integration process. "You can't just replicate something like this," said Williams, of ECTEL. "It *can* be done, but I think there has to be a cooperation mechanism in place. Countries must have a tradition of doing things together. It doesn't even have to be economic; it could be sports, education . . . but there needs to be a tradition."

The nations' tradition of working together through regional institutions also made officials more sensitive to the considerable differences from one island to another. "You'd be amazed," said Williams. "Outsiders see these islands in the Caribbean that are so alike. And it's true; we *are* very much alike. But you would also be amazed by the differences between us." Recognition of these differences helped officials calibrate their policies from one nation to another. For example, one official said, citizens in Grenada generally tend to want more participation in the political process; they want to feel that they approved any major regulatory change, debated it on radio talk shows, and so on. By contrast, the general public in St. Lucia sometimes expects less direct participation, preferring instead to redress grievances via elections of political officials.

Officials also emphasized the political compromise between regional and national power that led to ECTEL's unique hybrid structure. "You have to be careful about what political traffic can bear, recognize that, and not graft onto it a political structure that it cannot carry," said Cato.

There were also mixed feelings about whether an ECTEL-like structure could work in other sectors. "In my interaction with other sectors, I've seen issues that are similar," said Williams. The pooling of regional technical knowledge into one body is seen as a major advantage. But at a practical level, it is not clear whether a single organization responsible for regulating all public utilities would work.

Still, as the nations of the Eastern Caribbean seek to integrate their economies further, ECTEL is constantly mentioned as an example to be followed. "ECTEL is generally regarded around the region as a positive model," said Williams. Plans are being made for an OECS economic union. The current thinking among political leaders is that this organization would again be a kind of hybrid, like ECTEL, and that certain responsibilities would be placed at a central, more powerful regional level, while others would still result from a sovereign national structure.

ECTEL's Future

Ultimately, the success of ECTEL and the regulatory framework created by the countries in the Eastern Caribbean will be measured by the capacity to attract new investment and incentives to competitors to enter the region and continuously introduce new advances in technology.

As of August 2006, many officials felt that the spread of broadband access will be a true turning point in the telecommunications industry's development. Until now, there has been a bottleneck in the improvement of broadband services because of C&W's continued exclusive control of international connections. However, the arrival of new fiber-optic cable in coming months should cause fixed-line and broadband Internet service fees to fall further, officials said.

There were some suggestions that ECTEL—and the region's whole regulatory system—could do more to reach out to the general public. "The majority of God-fearing St. Lucians are not in a position to know anything about ECTEL. They are not part of the same world. This is also true of the NTRCs. There is no substantial interaction," said a spokesperson from a consumer association in St. Lucia. "One would have thought that C&W was responsible for the price cuts out of the goodness of their hearts." However, it is unclear how much better ECTEL could do with its limited public relations budget. Officials said the "town hall" format of public consultation has not proven effective or constructive beyond allowing people to express their general displeasure with the system. Also, it is difficult for officials to explain and justify the structure of costs, particularly that companies are making a fixed investment (in transmission towers, cable, fixed telephone lines, and so forth) that they have to pay off over time.

C&W expressed some concerns over the speed and scope of ECTEL's present and future actions. ECTEL may sometimes look at regulatory efforts in the United Kingdom, for example, and decide that it wants to institute similar policies that may not be feasible in such a small market. The issue of telephone number portability was cited as an example. In some cases, the regulatory process has not moved as quickly as the company might like. For example, in 2006, C&W wanted to introduce a new voice over Internet protocol (VoIP) service before Christmas. After a very intense lobbying effort, C&W scheduled a meeting with ECTEL officials and explained that it was in a hurry to have the new service approved. ECTEL ultimately consented, and the VoIP service was rolled out in time. "The concern is that next time, the lobbying effort won't work in time," says a source in the private sector.

C&W seems to be content with ECTEL's performance, but does not wish to see the regulator expand much beyond its current size in the near term. "You don't want them (ECTEL) to get too big, because you (C&W) are paying for it," Batstone said.

There do appear to be possibilities for ECTEL to expand. One potential future member could be Antigua and Barbuda. Here, the situation is a bit different: the local fixed-line system is controlled by a state-owned company, while all outgoing fixed-line and broadband traffic is controlled by C&W. But this will change with the near-term arrival of new fiber-optic cable, and officials don't see the state-run company as an obstacle to joining ECTEL. "There is a good skill set at ECTEL that we should avail ourselves of," said Edmond Mansoor, the Minister of Information, Broadcasting and Telecommunications for Antigua and Barbuda. "Do I think they do a good job? Yes. Could they do more? Yes. Are we missing out? Yes." Mansoor said that Antigua and Barbuda must "get our own house in order" and make internal reforms to bring it up to date with ECTEL members. But he saw membership as a strong possibility. "We will come to a juncture where we will join ECTEL," Mansoor said.

ECTEL seems likely to acquire more heft over time. Here again, the example of the Eastern Caribbean Central Bank may be instructive. The ECCB's clout seems to derive largely from its positive reputation, acquired through years of effective action. As ECTEL ages, the member nations may become more comfortable with its institutional integrity. Thus, ECTEL may develop more authority over time, even if there are no changes in the formal structure, with its roots in sovereign national power at the NTRC level.

Reflections: What Did It All Mean?

The creation of ECTEL has its origin in the independence of its member countries. The arrangement during colonial times worked: the responsibility of controlling the company (C&W) that then had a monopoly fell to the British colonial authorities; the capacity of these authorities to exercise control was based on a global relationship with C&W's worldwide network. Once independence came, a vacuum became obvious: the

OECS countries had to replace the old order and create a new institution reflective of new technology and the new political scenario.

History and tradition mattered when the time came to design the new regulatory institution. The tradition of cooperation among Eastern Caribbean countries in monetary and banking matters and in defense and security, justice administration, and civil aviation provided a model to base the design of a new regulatory institution. The final design of ECTEL was not the result of a master plan, but the organizational structure has similarities to that of the prestigious Eastern Caribbean Central Bank.

The radical transformation of the market and institutions in the telecommunications sector was facilitated by the parallel technological revolution, especially in mobile-phone technology. Preserving the monopoly in telecommunications services was almost impossible in the context of the worldwide revolution in information technology. Still, the governments of ECTEL member countries accelerated the breakup of the monopoly by maintaining a firm stand during the negotiation with the incumbent.

The importance of the telecommunications sector for small states cannot be overstated. In 2003, the median share of telecommunications revenue in GDP in small states was 4.7 percent; 1.3 percentage points above that for states with populations above 2 million (see figure 5A.1 in annex 5A). The larger share reflects market and cost conditions, but also the importance that telecommunications has as an input in every activity in these countries. This stylized fact augurs well for small states: if they reform regulation so that market competition improves, the impact in overall growth over the next decade will be noticeable.

ECTEL was conceived as a regional advisory rather than an independent body vested with executive power. While many in the region consider that an independent body vested with authority to enforce regulation would have been preferable, it is not obvious that such a model would have worked in practice. "I advocated a fully independent regional body at the beginning," Cato said. "However, I tend to believe that ECTEL has been effective because of the way it was structured. Had it been independent, there may have been a degree of alienation during its early days. As there is a sense of ownership, however, it has survived. There is not in practice a body that does things whether we like it or not. All the countries sit around a table and talk about matters. And on a practical and pragmatic basis, I think that has worked."

The concept of autonomy is nuanced. When thinking about this aspect of ECTEL, it might be instructive to look at the development of a completely different organization: the U.S. Federal Reserve ("the Fed").

The formal rules governing the relationship between the Fed and the U.S. government have not changed in the past 30 years; but most economists and observers would argue that, de facto, the relationship has deeply changed and that the Fed is much more autonomous today than it used to be before the Volker era. This change has been influenced by many factors, among them a consensus among academics on the importance of stable rules versus discretion in monetary policy. It has also been the result of personalities able to muddle through turbulent waters and create an image of technical expertise—think of the celebrity culture of Alan Greenspan—in front of the public.

A similar challenge, and perhaps evolution, faces ECTEL (albeit on a smaller, less public scale). Perhaps, over time, the organization will evolve into something more powerful and more respected—not by virtue of technical changes in its charter, but by virtue of a hard-earned reputation. Perhaps this sort of organic growth is more desirable than an organized attempt to make it a regional organization closer to the "pristine" model originally conceived.

"ECTEL is recognized by us as being an innovative arrangement. We do recognize it is not necessarily the final word on how to organize a regional body," Cato said.

Annex 5A. Statistics

Table 5A.1. Number of Phone Subscribers, 2004 and 2000

Country	Fixed-line & mobile-phone subscribers per 1,000	Internet users per 1,000	Mobile-phone subscribers per 1,000
2004			
ECTEL			
Dominica	879	259	585
Grenada	719	76	410
St. Kitts & Nevis	745	n.a.	213
St. Lucia	n.a.	336	568
St. Vincent & the Grenadines	642	68	481
Other Caribbean			
Antigua & Barbuda	1,149	250	674
Jamaica	1,021	403	832
Small States	712	204	478
Larger States	605	169	376
2000			
ECTEL			
Dominica	335	84	17
Grenada	352	41	42

(*continued*)

Table 5A.1. Number of Phone Subscribers, 2004 and 2000 (*continued*)

Country	Fixed-line & mobile-phone subscribers per 1,000	Internet users per 1,000	Mobile-phone subscribers per 1,000
St. Kitts & Nevis	522	61	27
St. Lucia	329	51	16
St. Vincent & the Grenadines	235	30	20
Other Caribbean			
Antigua & Barbuda	783	65	286
Jamaica	338	31	142
Small States	385	81	143
Larger States	349	76	165

Source: World Bank (2007).
n.a. = not available.

Figure 5A.1. Telecommunications Share in GDP

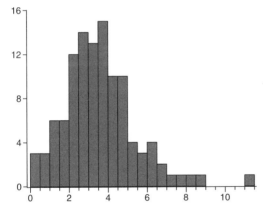

series: ST03	
sample 1 212 IF POP>2000000	
observations 110	
mean	3.581801
median	3.389252
maximum	11.01434
minimum	0.070257
std. dev.	1.835549
skewness	0.952914
kurtosis	4.991884
Jarque-Bera	34.83234
probability	0.000000

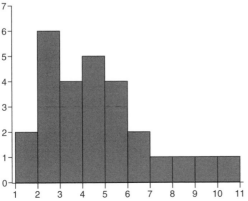

series: ST03	
sample 1 212 IF POP<2000000	
observations 27	
mean	4.642132
median	4.387048
maximum	10.45898
minimum	1.432810
std. dev.	2.368452
skewness	0.853145
kurtosis	3.090469
Jarque-Bera	3.284560
probability	0.193538

Source: Authors.

Annex 5B: Definition of Series Used in the Statistical Calculations

Series: FIXED: Fixed-line and mobile-phone subscribers (per 1,000 people)

"Fixed lines" are telephone mainlines connecting a customer's equipment to the public switched telephone network. "Mobile-phone subscribers" refer to users of portable telephones subscribing to an automatic public mobile-telephone service using cellular technology that provides access to the public switched telephone network.

Series: GDP: GDP per capita, PPP (current international $)

"GDP per capita based on purchasing power parity (PPP)" is gross domestic product converted to international dollars, using PPP rates. An international dollar has the same purchasing power over GDP as the U.S. dollar has in the United States. GDP at purchaser's prices is the sum of gross value added by all resident producers in the economy plus any product taxes and minus any subsidies not included in the value of the products. It is calculated without making deductions for depreciation of fabricated assets or for depletion and degradation of natural resources. Data are in current international dollars.

Series: INTER: Internet users (per 1,000 people)

"Internet users" are people with access to the worldwide network.

Series: MOBILE: Mobile-phone subscribers (per 1,000 people)

"Mobile-phone subscribers" are subscribers to a public mobile-telephone service using cellular technology.

Series: PFIXED: Price basket for residential fixed line (US$ per month)

"Price basket for residential fixed line" is calculated as one-fifth of the installation charge, the monthly subscription charge, and the cost of local calls (15 peak and 15 off-peak calls of three minutes each).

Series: STEL: Telecommunications revenue (percent of GDP)

"Telecommunications revenue" is the revenue from the provision of telecommunications services such as fixed-line, mobile, and data.

Annex 5C. List of Interviewees Cited in the Case Study

Name	Affiliations
Randolph Cato	Director of Economic Affairs, OECS
Geoff Batstone	Legal Counsel, Cable & Wireless
Eliud Williams	Managing Director, ECTEL
Eldon Mathurin	Chairman of the St. Lucia NTRC
Cheryl Hector	Senior Financial Analyst, ECTEL
Edmond Mansoor	Minister of Information, Broadcasting, and Telecommunications for Antigua and Barbuda

Notes

1. C&W Web site: www.cwhistory.com.

2. http://www.marpin.dm/who_we_are.htm.

3. Ibid.

4. OECS Web site: http://www.oecs.org/.

5. Prime Minister's Press Secretary. "The Week That Was." Web site. http://www.stlucia.gov.lc/pmpressec/TheWeekThatWas/should_cable_wireless_leave_st_lucia_pm_assures_smooth_transition_to_new_telecoms_entity_february_13_2001.htm.

6. With the exception of Antigua & Barbuda (A&B), all independent states members of OECS joined ECTEL. The main reason that A&B did not was differences in telecommunications market structure: in A&B, the local fixed-line system is controlled by a state-owned enterprise, and only outgoing fixed-line and broadband traffic is controlled by C&W. Therefore, the issue of renegotiation of an "exclusive license" and market deregulation was different from that of ECTEL member countries. Authorities in A&B anticipate that the island will probably join the regional regulator in the near future (see section on ECTEL's future).

References

C&W (Cable & Wireless). Web site: www.cwhistory.com.

ITU (International Telecommunications Union). 2006. *Telecommunications Indicators, 2006.* http://www.itu.int/ITU-D/ict/publications/world/world.html.

Khan, Alfred E. 1998. "Deregulation: Micromanaging the Entry and Survival of Competitors." *Electric Perspectives* (February). Edison Electric Institute, Washington, DC.

Levy, Brian, and Pablo T. Spiller. 1994. "The Institutional Foundations of Regulatory Commitment: A Comparative Analysis of Telecommunications Regulation." *Journal of Law, Economics, and Organization* 10 (2): 201–46.

OECS (Organization of Eastern Caribbean States). Web site: http://www.oecs. org/.

TeleGeography. 2006. *Global Traffic Statistics and Commentary.* http://www. telegeography.com/.

World Bank. 2007. *World Development Indicators.* Washington, DC: World Bank.

CHAPTER 6

E-Government in Cape Verde

Edgardo Favaro, Samia Melhem, and Brian Winter

Prologue

An Example of E-Government in Action

Some time ago, Hélio Varela, one of the leaders of Cape Verde's new organization for incorporating IT into the public sector, purchased a piece of land and went to a government office to obtain the corresponding land title. The clerk there used a computer to call up Varela's records. Because the e-government network in Cape Verde is able to integrate information across several departments, the clerk immediately saw that Varela owed past-due taxes. "I'm sorry, sir," the clerk said, "but I'm not allowed to give you the land title until you pay your taxes. Of course, if it was *my* decision, I'd just give you the title right now. But the system won't let me."

So Varela went to the tax bureau, where records also showed that he owed punitive interest payments on the late taxes. "I personally don't think you should have to pay these penalties," the tax official said, "and if I could, I would just make the charges disappear for you. But the computer doesn't allow that."

(continued)

Edgardo Favaro and Samia Melhem are, respectively, Lead Economist and Senior Operations Officer at the World Bank. Brian Winter is an employee of *USA Today*.

Of course, Varela paid the taxes—with the punitive interest—and soon acquired the land title.

"That little story shows exactly what we're trying to do here," Varela told us. "Using computers, we've been able to increase accountability. It's that simple. We've become much more efficient. Also, technology and integration have helped us keep people from getting around the system. It makes them follow the rules that are in place.... And that's what I'm most proud of. We have been able to completely change the culture in government."

At first glance, Cape Verde might seem like a surprising place to find an exemplary case of how governments can harness the Internet. For this nation of 10 windswept, arid islands, 280 miles (450 kilometers) off the western coast of sub-Saharan Africa, communicating with the outside world has always been an enormous challenge. International telephone rates are among the highest in the world. With 300 miles of ocean separating the extremes of this volcanic archipelago, the history of Cape Verde has largely been one of isolation and disconnection, even within its own borders.

Yet, the innovative use of "e-government" in Cape Verde would stir the admiration of authorities in even the world's most developed countries. This case study shows how a home-grown Cape Verdean organization—the Operational Information Society Nucleus (NOSI)—is leading an ambitious effort to overhaul the country's government using information and communications technology. The initiative has involved broad incorporation of ICT[1] into the public sector—integrating computer hardware and software into the production of services, the training of public servants in use of the new technology, the redefinition of services and their production processes, and the interaction between the government and the citizens.

NOSI has a unique internal structure and culture akin to a Silicon Valley start-up, even though it is under the umbrella of government. With a staff of just 50 employees, NOSI has led ambitious e-government reforms in the past eight years: it set up a network linking 3,000 computers in the public sector; designed and implemented an integrated financial management system that provides budget information in real time; set up a national identification database unifying information from several public registries; and developed domestic capacity to design software applications adapted to the needs of Cape Verde's public sector.

Moreover, technical savvy and strong political backing have opened the way to broad changes in the fundamental nature of government in Cape Verde. Some of the results are visible to the average citizen: the use of IT has increased transparency, enhanced tax collection, and reduced opportunities for fraud and corruption. Many more benefits are yet to be enjoyed, as different units in the public sector learn to exploit the information generated by the new systems and redefine the way they do business.

This story has ramifications far beyond the shores of Cape Verde and Africa, addressing questions such as: What is the role of the government in developing the IT sector in small states? What are the links between development of the IT sector and the cost of telecommunications? What are the pros and cons involved in developing an incipient IT sector in a small, isolated state? What challenges does IT pose to the reform of the state?

Cape Verde Before NOSI

Life in Cape Verde has always been difficult, despite its privileged position as a crossroads between Africa, Europe, and the Americas. Cape Verde became part of the Portuguese Crown in 1462, but large-scale settlement was very difficult because of the harsh climate and scarcity of fertile soil. Most of the islands are volcanic. The climate is volatile, prone to high winds and long periods without rain. Only about 10 percent of the land area is suitable for agriculture, and even today, 80 percent of the nation's food must be imported. Indeed, despite what the country's name suggests, most of the islands are visibly green for only about two months out of every year.

For centuries, the islands were an important commercial post for the slave trade out of West Africa. Frequent events such as famine, pirate attacks, and volcanic eruptions also disrupted the nation's development. The harsh conditions caused many Cape Verdeans to emigrate and settle in Portugal, Brazil, and the United States, and today the diaspora exceeds the local resident population. Cape Verde acquired its independence from Portugal in 1975 and then adopted a socialist dictatorship until 1991, when it switched to a multiparty, parliamentary democracy with free elections.

By the late 1990s, Cape Verde was a stable democracy with no conflict, a strong culture, and a national identity that seemed to transcend race and religion. Following the collapse of the Berlin Wall in 1989, the first wave of globalization was running its course: integration and trade had become the primary focus of policy makers worldwide, and the services industry was replacing agriculture and manufacturing as the main engine of economic growth. Officials and opinion makers in Cape Verde recognized that their own, local economic structure needed to change to keep pace. But the private sector was extremely weak, as a legacy of colonial and then socialist rule.

Authorities cast about, looking for an economic model to follow. Would Cape Verde be a tourism haven? A banking center? What would its identity be? "There was quite a debate going on," Varela said. "I love the beaches here, but I have to be honest—you go four hours away by plane, and Brazil's are better. So tourism didn't seem like the most obvious option. We have to import most of our food. We have no advantage in agriculture. However, we thought that, whatever we do, we have to use IT to link Cape Verdeans to the rest of the world."

Box 6.1

Cape Verde's Economy

According to the 2000 Census, Cape Verde had a resident population of 434,625, of which 55 percent lived in urban areas. Santiago is the most populated island, with 54 percent of the resident population, followed by São Vicente and São Antão, with 15 percent and 11 percent, respectively. Praia, the country's capital, is home to 23 percent of the resident population. During the past decade, the population growth rate averaged 2.4 percent per year, while the fertility rate was four children per woman. The population is young, with 68.7 percent under the age of 30. The labor force is made up of 166,000 people, of which 46 percent are female.

Real per capita GDP (PPP-adjusted) is estimated at US$5,834 (2005). At 3.2 percent, the average annual rate of growth of the GDP during the past decade was high in comparison with the rest of the region and worldwide. The strong increase in real per capita GDP was accompanied by a significant and continuous improvement of the Human Development Index (HDI), which measures life expectancy, income, and education. This index went from 0.587 in 1990 to 0.670 in 2002. At present, life expectancy is 72 for women and 66 for men.

The structure of the economy is dominated by the service sector, which represents 70 percent of the GDP. Exports are 34 percent and imports 62 percent of the GDP. Remittances amount to about 40 percent of imports.

Cape Verde has operated a fixed-exchange-rate system since 1998, with the escudo trading at a steady value to the euro. The rate of monetization of the economy (the ratio of the broadest monetary aggregate and the GDP) is 73 percent.

Source: World Bank 2007.

The History of NOSI

Clearly, information and communications technology offered Cape Verde a unique opportunity: IT could be used to help overcome the nation's geography, which had always been such an impediment to growth. Connecting the 10 islands with some kind of network could potentially solve problems of communication that had persisted for centuries. Yet as late as 1998, the domestic IT sector was practically nonexistent.

The main potential client for IT was the government, but as of 1998, computers had not been adequately integrated into everyday government activity. Until that point, the history of Cape Verde's efforts to incorporate computers into government had been checkered, at best. The budget was still put together using a typewriter. "If you made a single mistake, you had to start over," said Rosa Pinheiro, the current Treasury Commissioner, who has worked in the Finance Ministry since 1983. "Everything in Finance was like that. Some of us didn't even know what a computer was." Some officials had been trained to use programs like WordPerfect and Lotus 1-2-3, but in practice, few people used them. There was little organized structure in place for technical support or training. "If we wanted help, we had to scream as loud as we could, and others came running," said Pinheiro. Before 1998, access to the Internet was mostly limited to sporadic use of e-mail within some ministries.

The use of IT in the private sector was equally underdeveloped: the public utilities, the banks, and a handful of enterprises used computers, but they relied on foreign-based companies (mostly based in Lisbon) to support development of software applications; apart from a few computer hardware retailers, there was no domestic IT sector to speak of.

Before 1998, there had been some experience with bringing in foreign consultants to administer technology, but these projects were widely regarded as expensive and unsuccessful. The foreigners came and went, but did little to help build a lasting foundation for IT. In 1998, a Portuguese consultancy was hired by the government to help modernize the tax system. "When they finished, they went back to Portugal and took all the databases, all the software code back with them," said Jorge Lopes, today the general manager of NOSI. Later on, another consultancy came from Portugal to administer the elections. In terms of building local capacity and transferring knowledge and documentation, Lopes said, "Again, they left nothing. The government then understood that it was better to create a national capacity to develop systems."

Meanwhile, advances in technology meant that the Internet was becoming more accessible to developing countries. The question was how Cape Verde could seize the moment and use IT to its advantage.

Operational Information Society Nucleus (NOSI) evolved from a very specific need. In 1998, Jose Ulisses Correia e Silva, then Cape Verde's Minister of Finance and today leader of the opposition in Congress, saw that the information systems at his ministry were slow, costly, and incomplete. The data from the budget system, tax revenue collection, debt management, and the Treasury were in separate systems. Now, the government wanted to consolidate that information and be able to access it in real time. According to Correia, the idea of creating the unit that would become NOSI sprang from that necessity.

Correia was convinced that an IT project in Cape Verde was feasible, provided that there were adequate human and financial resources and that the design focused on building *local* knowledge. The previous, negative experience with foreign consultants, plus the legal and technical difficulties of having foreigners work with sensitive budget information, led the Cape Verde government to concentrate on developing a home-grown pool of talent—creating its own capacity, with a horizon of 5–10 years.

From the beginning, Correia opted to create one autonomous government unit in charge of implementing technology, rather than an individual IT structure in each department. This decision to centralize operations meant that the new organization would enjoy more direct, focused support from Correia to execute politically sensitive tasks. It would also allow for the concentration of the relatively limited pool of technical knowledge then available in Cape Verde.

The unit was created in 1998 and originally called "Administrative and Financial Reform (RAF)"—the predecessor to NOSI.[2] The personnel—remarkably, composed of just three engineers at the beginning—were from the private sector, with no experience working within government. This was seen as an asset: they could bring the values of the business world—efficiency, flexibility, and an emphasis on concrete results—to the public sector. Quite simply, the job of these three men was to effectively introduce computers and networks into government. But lack of experience in the public sector was also a liability: the NOSI engineers knew about information systems, but they were not known or trusted by most civil servants they had to interact with and they were not familiar with the working of government services.

There was no initial master plan or mandate for a broad overhaul of government; even so, the leaders of the project were fully aware from the beginning that introducing computers massively throughout the public sector would completely shake up the way business was conducted. The primary focus of NOSI would be on efficiency, integration, and transparency in government. "We believed in the power of technology to effect great change," said Hélio Varela, who was one of the original three staffers.

Some crucial decisions were made very early on:

First, inviting salary packages were put together to attract Cape Verde computer engineers trained overseas and mostly working in Portugal, Brazil, and the United States. NOSI was envisioned from the start as a kind of "super-agency" that was provided with the resources to pay salaries above the average of other government workers in Cape Verde. "Otherwise, we wouldn't be able to bring in people with such good qualifications as Hélio," said Correia.

Second, NOSI was set up as an entity outside of government, with staff working on annual renewable contracts. Funds from an existing World Bank project, plus grants from the United Nations Development Program and French Cooperation (the French aid agency), helped provide financing.

Third, no matter what the eventual scope of the project, all the systems installed would be able to *speak* to the others. NOSI believed that systems would only be effective if they were integrated in a way that expanded the quantity and the quality of information available to the administration. Therefore, the organization decided to design all software using a common platform, Oracle, which would help make this broad integration possible. Cape Verde's relative lack of technological development was a major asset in this drive: because there were few existing, or "legacy" systems, NOSI did not have to incorporate much old data or technology. In other words, it could start from scratch, using the latest technology.

This led to the fourth and perhaps most crucial point. Remarkably, NOSI was given carte blanche to make its own decisions and implement systems throughout the nation's government. Technological possibilities, rather than political considerations, would be the driving force. In cases where NOSI met resistance, it almost always had the political backing ultimately to get its way. "The Prime Minister basically told us: 'You may do as you wish,'" said Varela. "We could make a big change in a very short time" in NOSI's early days, said Angelo Barbosa, another original member of NOSI.

NOSI's staff knew from the very beginning that there would be two main tasks at hand: the technical development of government systems; and the reform of the state's processes, procedures, work flow, and legal framework to keep pace with technology. They knew that they would encounter significant resistance to their efforts. At the same time, they knew that the new technology would irrevocably cause the very nature of government to change. Without strong and unwavering political support, the whole endeavor might never have gotten off the ground.

The First Challenge: Getting People to Use Computers

In the early days, the main challenge for NOSI sounded simple: How could it convince government workers to use computers? This was more problematic than it sounded.

In fact, there had been many failures on this front, in Cape Verde and abroad. It was one thing to put computers in front of people; getting them to use them correctly was an entirely different matter. Persuading the public sector to take full advantage of computers has been a thorn in the side of many aid projects around the world. Even in Cape Verde, there had already been one false start with 80 computers that had been donated. Often, ministers and other managers took the new computers and put them in their own offices, NOSI officials recalled. Sometimes people simply refused to use new technology—to the point where, according to Treasurer Pinheiro: "Some people retired. Not just because of computers, . . . but they're used to doing things with calculators, with typewriters. There were other factors, but it pushed people out the door."

The answer to NOSI's dilemma proved to be, in short: Yes, computers themselves might be daunting. But the Internet is seductive.

NOSI discovered that, by giving officials basic Internet amenities—particularly e-mail and "chat" software—it could then over time induce them to use the computer for other, more complex applications. Programs like the Microsoft Network (MSN) Messenger were like a Trojan horse, getting computers onto officials' desks. "When you give people a computer and Internet access, at the beginning they chat and do everything but work," Varela said. "And then, over time, you find the motivation completely changes. People become much more involved with the technology. It is e-mail and chat that opens their minds. That was the most powerful instrument that we put in, even considering the software we made later." The rollout of a government-operated broadband Internet network also won many hearts and minds. "Where we really started to win was with the cable. Everybody wanted to be on the network," Varela said. "Once we had them integrated, we could offer other services."

Once the system was physically in place—once that battle to get computers on desks was won—many officials saw their previous prejudices disappear, and they quickly recognized the attractiveness and utility of the Internet. "Previously, with computers, there had been no instrument that made us all work together, that served as a base. But now, with e-mail and the Internet, I can see what's going on in accounting. I can see what's going on in the tax office. I can see what *everybody* is doing," said Pinheiro.

NOSI was given authority to make decisions about where to install computers in each ministry. That NOSI had power to do this was of tremendous strategic significance; systems needed to be deployed in the right spots, among both managers and lower-level officials inputting data, to arrive at a broader "tipping point" at which a particular branch of government would definitely come online. In retrospect, NOSI appears to have made very intelligent decisions in this respect.

Ultimately, the level of resistance to computers proved relatively low in Cape Verde, although some challenges remain (discussed in the section on problems and challenges below). Part of this comparative ease can be attributed to the youth and relatively high education of public sector workers in Cape Verde. The median age in Cape Verde is 19.8 years, and literacy is relatively high for the region at 76.6 percent, compared with literacy in Senegal, for example, at 40.2 percent (World Bank 2007). The combination of youth, relative literacy, and a large diaspora—plus a sufficiently large community of Cape Verdeans educated abroad in the ways of e-mail-based communications—helped to create an environment for success. But even in cases where education levels were low, NOSI staff learned that they could give computers to just about anybody, as long as some training was provided. "We find people with no education, or four years of education," Varela said. "People say they won't be able to use the computers. But no. It's not true. The computer is like magic. They can learn."

NOSI was also remarkably persistent. When they went to the Customs Office to propose a network, their overtures were met with indifference. Customs had its own internal system. A year passed. But, every Thursday, the NOSI team went down to the Customs Office and updated officials on their progress in developing a network. "Ultimately, they accepted us," Varela said.

Indeed, over time, the problems became completely different in nature. "People started threatening to resign if we *didn't* get them on the network," Varela said with a smile. "That was when we knew things had really changed."

Evolving Beyond the Original Charter

NOSI's work soon became well-known throughout Cape Verde's government. Virtually overnight, its staff was being summoned to install computers and networks well beyond the unit's original mandate at the Finance Ministry. This expansion was soon reflected at NOSI itself. By 2000, just two years after its inception, NOSI had expanded to 15 people from its original staff of 3. But the unit's rapid growth would raise new questions about NOSI's role in Cape Verde and create some new fronts of resistance.

Before the 2000 election, NOSI's staff had concerns about the future of the organization. If the opposition party won, would it continue with the IT agenda, or see NOSI as a pet project of the party in power and radically change it? The alternative of transforming NOSI into a private corporation was seriously considered: management explored the possibility with Portuguese and Brazilian IT firms of forming a new company in partnership with one or more international firms. The new government, however, put a halt to these plans. "The incoming Finance Minister grabbed the idea very well," said Correia, the former Finance Minister who had helped create NOSI. And, as Jorge Lopes put it, "This government understood that NOSI was indeed an institution that was very important for the financial management of the government. It was an institution that had great value, and I think it was the right decision to maintain it."

The transition for NOSI was nearly seamless. The new government continued to give the organization free rein to implement the IT program, and NOSI retained its status as a special organization within the umbrella of government. In the ensuing years, NOSI's reach continued to spread. Some ministries and departments still conducted their own IT programs, but NOSI seemed to have some kind of role almost every time a computer was installed in Cape Verde's public sector.

By 2003, NOSI was performing tasks for so many other sections of government that its old structure and charter were painfully obsolete. The new Prime Minister mandated an overhaul, naming Jorge Lopes (an electrical engineer trained in the Soviet Union, then the Minister of Infrastructure and Transport) as head of a committee to review NOSI's functions and propose a restructuring.

Lopes produced a report that recommended a moderate structural transformation of the organization. Within the structure of government, NOSI was moved from the Finance Ministry to the Prime Minister's office. "This was like a promotion," Varela said. This reorganization was also accompanied by a partial change in management. One of the original three staffers, Augusto Fernandes, left NOSI to continue his professional career in Portugal. Jorge Lopes became NOSI's Political Coordinator. Hélio Varela remained as Technical Coordinator.

Installing the Network

In building a nationwide computer network, once more NOSI essentially had to start from scratch. This mammoth task required its staff to perform pioneering, unique work in software and connectivity.

On the positive side, Cape Verde enjoyed ready access to international fiber-optic cable. Cape Verde is connected to the mainland by the Atlantis-2 submarine cable, which offers a top-notch gateway to the rest of the world. "The rest of Africa has a problem with the connection. They often have to set up a satellite to get good Internet service," Varela said. "Here in Cape Verde, the connection is already here. The main issue is cost."

Despite this advantage, the cost of non-fixed-line telecommunications services in Cape Verde is extremely high because of the monopoly in service provision. For instance, the average cost of a three-minute call to the United States was in 2004 US$6.08; the average cost of a similar phone call from 112 countries for which information is available was US$1.98, and the median cost was US$1.52 (figure 6.1).

Figure 6.1. Histogram: Cost in US$ of a Three-Minute Phone Call to the United States

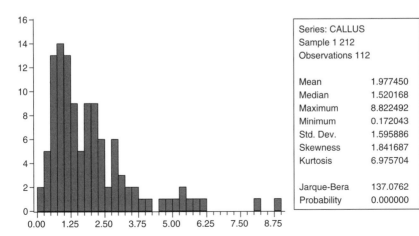

Series: CALLUS
Sample 1 212
Observations 112

Mean	1.977450
Median	1.520168
Maximum	8.822492
Minimum	0.172043
Std. Dev.	1.595886
Skewness	1.841687
Kurtosis	6.975704
Jarque-Bera	137.0762
Probability	0.000000

Source: Authors.

To address this problem, NOSI ended up building much of its own network infrastructure. In essence, NOSI became the de facto Internet service provider (ISP) for much of the government, particularly in the capital. It erected its own wireless network connecting government computers on the island of Santiago and started work on its own fiber-optic network, offering broadband Internet access on the *planalto*, the high plateau in Praia where there is a heavy concentration of government ministries and other public entities. The operation and maintenance of the government network (a WiMAX[3]-based intranet network, distributed in several buildings and islands, with around 3,000 workstations and a few dozen servers) is entirely manned by about 15 NOSI team members based in the central Praia office. In terms of total cost of ownership, the cost of the operation is on the very low end—current IT assets are very efficiently maintained.

For the users of the system, the setup was a dream come true: reliable, modern communication services connecting the citizens to e-mail, the Internet, world news, and reports—and free. This is almost unheard of, and helps explain the stunningly fast adoption of IT in public sector service—as opposed to its much slower adoption in other countries, where introduction of IT did not come with such a great incentive package.

Across the board, NOSI made a strong commitment to work with the latest technology. This was an interesting, perhaps controversial decision; often in lower-income countries, low-technology, cheap systems are deployed to cut costs. The disadvantage of that strategy, however, is that the equipment is often secondhand, having fully depreciated in Fortune 500 companies and then been sent to developing countries to be reused. As NOSI realized, the policy might have worked 10 years ago, but has no reason to be practiced today, given the very short life cycle of many of these refurbished machines, the high costs of transport/shipping, and the high environmental costs of disposing of all the unusable equipment. Very cheap computers are available now (for around US$300 per personal computer) that incorporate the latest in communication technologies (such as modems capable of wireless broadband communications) and that can be imported or even assembled in Cape Verde. To their credit, the NOSI team have been totally against using low-tech, cheap systems. "This is not a good idea," Varela said. "The system can fall apart or be vulnerable. As there was no legacy system here, we decided to do the opposite."

From the beginning, the NOSI team opted for proprietary software: the Microsoft Windows NT server platform, the Oracle database management system now in its 10 g version, the Microsoft Office platform for desktops, and so forth. This choice has been bitterly contested by some IT experts in the private sector who argue that an e-government system based on open-source tools would have been a better choice for the country (see annex 6A). For the time being, all we can say is that in the late 1990s and early in 2000, when the team was building its e-government systems, starting with the Financial Management Information System, open source existed, but was too risky for NOSI to implement. Its products were not mature enough, and its maintenance costs were quite high. In the future, NOSI can either stick to its current proprietary software or migrate to open source, provided that it plans the transition well and that it has enough qualified staff to run open-source systems. This of course assumes that the market for open-source software would afford a set of robust and world-class applications suitable for NOSI's needs.

NOSI software engineers relied on extensive feedback from their ultimate clients, the users, when designing the software that became the basis of Cape Verde's e-government system. Being "embedded" in the services made them act and feel like insiders and enormously increased their effectiveness. At Praia's public hospital, for example, many of the 78 doctors and approximately 200 nurses were consulted to see what exactly the software needed to incorporate to fit their needs. The same was true at the Ministry of Finance. Treasurer Pinheiro said, "Hélio [Varela] might not have known about public finance, but he understood technology. We could say, 'I want X, and I want it to work this way,' and he would do what I want—sometimes he went much further. All that has helped us function better."

Operating Principles and Corporate Culture
At the end of a hallway on the second floor of Cape Verde's Finance Ministry is an inconspicuous white door with a sign that says, "Please knock." Behind it lies NOSI's headquarters, which is dominated by one large, glass-enclosed room. Here, about a dozen programmers are typically seated at their computers, lined up at two long desks that run the length of the room on either side. The programmers stare straight ahead at their screens; they talk in low tones; a few of them have iPods. But the main sound is the clicking of keys, for of the 50 people on NOSI's staff, only 2 of them handle administrative duties full-time; the remaining 48 are engineers, all of them educated abroad, who are dedicated to developing software, maintaining equipment, or hatching strategy. Twelve-hour days and seven-day work weeks are hardly rare.

The internal structure and operating philosophy of NOSI could perhaps best be described as "informal." From the top down, the organization has always allowed technology to be its driving force; legal and structural changes are made after the fact. This approach has made NOSI tremendously flexible—and ultimately more effective.

In practice, NOSI is a hybrid, a mix between a government agency and a tech start-up. The operating budget is about US$1 million per year for its expenses, staff, and equipment. The entire staff serves on an annually renewable contract. As a result, NOSI has been able to retain professionals who would have been very difficult to attract to work for the government otherwise; deploy its employees in different programs and tasks with great flexibility; and terminate work contracts at short notice if productivity was below expectations.

NOSI's staff do not receive benefits equivalent to those for other civil servants—vacation, sick leave, and so on—but can get time off when necessary by requesting it from management. Most personnel earn a starting salary of about US$600 per month (compared with an equivalent of around US$400, with equal experience level, in other government agencies). Outstanding performers can easily see their salary double within a year. A programmer who has been in NOSI for three years makes around US$1,500 per month. NOSI staff have no written human-resources rules or career-planning procedures, but there are monthly meetings during which staff discuss their projects' status and management reinforces the agency's values. Any violation of those values is penalized. Several members of NOSI staff have been fired for reasons such as charging money to deliver services to a ministry, theft of computer equipment, or sending inappropriate material in mass e-mails.

A great deal of training takes place organically, on the job. Staff members bring a certain level of expertise from their university education and then augment it by observing and learning from other, more senior staff members. Even the physical layout of the office, with its glass-enclosed main room, encourages this atmosphere of camaraderie and shared knowledge. This more informal learning is augmented by rigorous training through more formal channels. Two years ago, nine NOSI staff took and passed the Microsoft certification test (a series of seven test modules)—this is an exceptionally high score, according to Microsoft accreditation results in the United States, and it reinforces NOSI's image of persistence and resilience.

The organization's informality goes beyond personnel and labor management rules. From the beginning, NOSI established procurement

Box 6.2

Who are NOSI's Managers?

NOSI's informal, spontaneous approach has always been evident, even when hiring its key leaders. Angelo Barbosa, one of the organization's first three staffers, had been living and working in the United States. In 1998, Barbosa came back to Cape Verde to visit his family on what was supposed to be just a two-week vacation. "All I had with me was a bag over my shoulder," Barbosa recalled. At a bar, he ran into Hélio Varela, who said: "Ah, you're Angelo. You're the guy I'm supposed to hire. We have a project for you." Barbosa ended up deciding to stay in Cape Verde for good. "And I never went back to the United States," Barbosa said. He added, with a laugh, "My old roommate still hasn't paid me back for my car!"

Varela himself came to NOSI in similar, improvised fashion. He had been working for Fujitsu in Portugal when Correia, the finance minister, called him to talk about plans for a new technological unit. The common thread between the men? Both had attended the same university and played basketball together. "I knew Hélio quite well, and knew that his philosophy would be suitable for NOSI," Correia said. Said Varela: "I brought the experience of the private sector."

People at NOSI seem to lead especially active and varied lives outside of work. Jorge Lopes is an accomplished guitarist; Angelo Barbosa has recorded his own CD that is sold in bars and music stores; Hélio Varela helps to coach Cape Verde's national basketball team. This trait also seems true of Cape Verde's public sector in general.

Source: Authors.

practices that would have been difficult to accept in operations financed by multilateral and bilateral development agencies in other parts of the world or, for that matter, in other projects in Cape Verde. For instance, before procuring hardware or software, NOSI's professionals search available alternatives, contact different suppliers, and assess the package the government will receive as a result of the transaction (emphasizing training to its employees, customer care, and openness of the contractor to sharing its source-code development process with NOSI). Following this stage, NOSI selects the supplier on a sole-source basis and normally keeps the same supplier in successive operations, justifying its decisions on the basis of the supplier's technical assistance and quality of services. As a result, NOSI can avoid the proliferation of hardware/software with different specifications, bought under multiple contracts from different suppliers, that is so common in other contexts and usually results in wasted or unused resources.

NOSI in Action: Examples of Implementation

Upon entering Cape Verde's Finance Ministry in 1998, a visitor would first pass the security guard at the front door. Then, he or she would find a group of 8–10 men loitering about, standing near the door, waiting to deliver letters and packages to recipients throughout the ministry. They were messengers; that was their only job.

Today, those messengers are gone. "It's all electronic now. There is no need for messengers anymore," Varela said. "That's just one example of how the way government works has changed dramatically."

That same simple experience has been repeated, with far more dramatic results, throughout Cape Verde.

The Public Hospital, Praia

The public hospital in Praia is a compelling example of how NOSI's technology has helped improve—sometimes even save—Cape Verdeans' lives.

Before NOSI arrived, the hospital did employ some computers, but they were not integrated into any kind of network. There was little communication between hospitals; this was, of course, particularly problematic in a country made up of 10 islands. Previously, if someone from the island of São Vicente got sick on Santiago, it was extremely difficult to access the patient's medical records quickly, according to A. Miguel, the lead hospital administrator. Often, the direct result was inferior medical treatment.

The new network, installed with the assistance of NOSI, will allow health officials to track medical cases more efficiently. Patient records will be shared from one hospital to another, a development that will improve care and, for example, inform authorities promptly if an epidemic is under way. The hospital also has acquired greater control over receipts and supply of medicine. Miguel said that technology has provided better information on pricing, which has reduced the hospital's costs of acquiring medicine by 25 percent.

The hospital in Praia is connected online on a consultation basis with a hospital in Coimbra, Portugal. In extreme cases of heart surgery, oncology, and neurology, patients are evacuated to Portugal. Now, thanks to connectivity, full medical case information can be transmitted to the relevant hospital in Portugal before the patient arrives—shortening the patient's stay in Portugal and improving the ability of the doctors there to diagnose and treat the patient's illness. "The patient leaves here ready to get treatment immediately upon arrival," said Miguel.

The Praia hospital also illustrates how NOSI's technology can single-handedly cut through decades of bureaucracy in a single stroke. Currently, each hospital in Cape Verde uses a completely different accounting system for patients—the database in Praia cannot "speak with" the database in São Vicente, for example. "With this new system, we'll be able to integrate the entire system for the first time," said Miguel. Conventional wisdom would suggest that this should be the purview of the Ministry of Health, but "only NOSI has the technological ability to do something like this," said Miguel.

Fully automating the hospital will take some time. The hospital expects to have computers soon for each of its nurses; next year, the hospital administration expects six computers with which to begin training them. Doctors are putting up some resistance: they still need some persuasion to get them "closer" to computers, to use PowerPoint and other applications, and initially they were "not too happy" with being charged with responsibility for data entry. Doctors were also concerned about nurses having access to all of patients' records, but are now getting used to the idea of an "open record" management system, said Miguel, adding: "Part of the challenge still is creating an Internet culture."

Miguel, who has no experience as a doctor, is an example of a government official who seems to have been selected primarily for his technological know-how and his "modern" administrative outlook. He studied hospital administration abroad, in Portugal. As people have come to recognize the value of technology, officials with this profile are increasingly being found in key positions throughout Cape Verde's government.

Interactive Map System
NOSI is working on an extraordinary system akin to Google Maps that incorporates much of its data in a visual presentation. NOSI even hired a plane to fly over all 10 islands to supply it with homegrown images. Soon, the organization plans to use the system to track progress on public-works programs in real time. For example, clients will be able to use the maps to see how much of a highway has been completed, using graphics (the image itself will not actually update in real time). Regular citizens of Cape Verde will also be able to use them to highlight a particular object or street corner and send an e-mail to the government with a complaint or a suggestion. The system will allow for an overlay of relevant statistical

data as well. "This way, we could cross-reference poverty statistics with the construction of a highway and ask: Does this project help serve the neediest citizens?" Varela said.

Municipality of São Vicente

The progress that NOSI has made on the island of São Vicente can be measured in books. Before, the municipality used 22 different books to store information on the city budget and other transactions. "We had to tell people to wait while we looked things up. It was very slow," said a municipal manager. "And now? Just one book. Everything else in this city is electronic."

The municipal government was not connected to the Internet at all until 2001. In just five years, it has made a dramatic transition, and now almost all of its budget operations are performed online. Through the greater control and supervision offered by a computerized system, the municipality has been able to *triple* its tax income since 2001. That increase is to the result of greater efficiency, rather than higher statutory rates. The system allows officials to see when people have not paid certain fees. A citizen in arrears on municipal taxes, for example, might not be allowed to obtain a permit for a car.

NOSI's clout and expertise, combined with strong political support, made this speedy computerization possible. Officials were able to overcome political resistance by focusing first on budget operations, where the benefits were most obvious and where a smaller, more specialized group were easier to convince. People were brought in from outside—in some cases, students on vacation—to help with input of data to replace the books. Now, 100 percent of accounting and treasury data are on computers.

Indeed, officials at NOSI consider the municipality a model case. São Vicente has also made good use of the greater efficiency afforded by the technology, which has allowed for a reallocation of government workers. The municipality has used its savings to create a special government department offering services to a tide of immigrants from West Africa.

The experience in São Vicente also shows how technological progress is usually spontaneous, rather than planned. At the beginning, NOSI took the initiative on technological improvements; the government let it work. Then, over time, municipal officials started providing input, based on things they could *see* rather than conceptual wishes. "We wanted to have servers, we wanted to link with the library," said a manager. It was a case of people standing on the street, pointing to a building, and saying, "Let's connect there," more than a technical concept of networking.

Casa do Cidadão ("House Of The Citizen")

This is the planned "front office" of the e-government program, organized through a Web site. It is envisioned as a simple, straightforward link between citizens and the government. Here, information from several different ministries is collected, simplified, and presented to the public. "We don't want to have areas that are in the shadows," said a senior public sector manager. There is a wide range of information, from instructions on how to register a business to a manual on teen sexuality. The Casa organizes the information, but it is the responsibility of each ministry to keep the content current. The Casa hopes to make the information accessible via three means: the Web portal, a call center (currently under construction), and a physical building.

The portal will operate with all the basic and advanced features of a transactional service portal, or a G2C (government to citizen) and G2B (government to business) portal, allowing dissemination of news and information, transactions with government line ministries, feedback, and, eventually, online payments for government services rendered or obligations (taxes and so on). This will help alleviate concern that the current NOSI system in Cape Verde is too inaccessible—that is, that there aren't enough links between common citizens and the technological advances the government has made.

Electoral Commission

This is one of the departments that has been most revolutionized by NOSI and technology in recent years. The voting is now electronic, and elections have been sped up. In 1999, definitive results of the presidential election were not available until three days after the vote. In the most recent election, 2001, near-total results were made available to the public in three *hours*.

Apart from speeding the process, significant advances have been made in the quality of information, particularly with regard to preventing fraud. The software is equipped with well-defined criteria to identify cases of suspicious activity. Anyone who tries to vote in more than one municipality—previously a common activity—is quickly identified. Duplicate names in the voter record are also weeded out much more efficiently than before. The system allows the controller to see the name of the election administrator who enters each record. "That way, if there's fraud, we can see who is responsible," said an electoral commission manager.

The system is remarkably flexible and is able to tolerate minor misspellings and still locate the correct record. The voting record also contains detailed information on each voter's background: the name of a voter's father, mother, previous places of residence, and so on, that come from the broadly integrated data base. "If I was a sociologist, I could find incredible information here," said an electoral commission manager. But only information that is in the public domain is freely available online; the rest is restricted to election officials only. The system cannot yet directly process votes from the large Cape Verdean community living abroad; those voters have to go to their local embassy with two forms of documentation; the tabulated votes are then faxed to electoral authorities in Cape Verde.

Again, the main impetus for all these advances was cost. "In a country like Cape Verde, these kinds of innovations were necessary to save money," said the electoral commission manager. "These last elections were the cheapest ones of all time."

Customs Office

Integration of the Customs Office is still largely a work in progress. Here, the country's geography is a particularly difficult nut to crack; all but two of the islands have their own Customs Offices. The goal is to integrate all the offices via the Internet and have them share real-time data. "That would enormously facilitate our operations," said a Customs manager. However, this is impractical right now because most of the offices have only dial-up connections, which are prohibitively expensive to keep online 24 hours a day, at current rates for telephone lines.

The Customs Office also wants to integrate its system so that an import/export business can pay duties at a bank, instead of going through Cape Verde's Treasury; that way, the transaction can take place before the cargo arrives, speeding the process. Successful implementation of the Customs management system will facilitate trade, reduce red tape, and possibly increase collections and compliances for the Internal Revenue Bureau.

Despite the numerous tasks at hand, officials realize that they have made enormous progress. "We have total satisfaction" with NOSI, said a Customs manager. The Customs Office has about 100 computers scattered throughout the country that are still interconnected through dial-up access. That compares with about 10 computers in 1999—or one for each island, on average—that were not integrated into any network at all.

The Public University

Technology has played an integral role in Cape Verde's quest to create the nation's first public university. Geography obviously could have been a problem in creating a university for 10 islands scattered over 300 miles of ocean, some with very small populations, and with a wide diaspora (see chapter 8 on the experience of the University of the South Pacific). "We asked ourselves, 'How could we make a public university in a country that is small and on the periphery?' The territory itself is very dispersed. We wanted to address the wide diaspora of Cape Verdeans. So we wanted to configure the project for the university to address that reality," said a member of the public university organization committee.

At the beginning of the process, the problems looked insurmountable. Some people wanted the university to have at least a small campus on each island. "You see this mentality a lot in Cape Verde," said the committee member. "People forget we don't have the critical mass for that. There is some redundancy in government. It's difficult to combat waste."

So the decision was made to create a university with a large presence online, with the help of NOSI. The university plans to build a central campus in Praia, but will offer a large portion of its curriculum via the Internet. Online-based universities such as the University of Phoenix are being used as a model. Not all material can be offered via the Internet, of course—"You can't educate a doctor via distance learning," said the same source—but many courses in accounting, social sciences, law, and economics can be offered online (see chapter 8 on the experience with ICT university education in the South Pacific). The idea is also to take advantage of preexisting professional schools on Cape Verde and integrate their material. The university also wants to sign agreements with universities abroad and broadcast some of their lectures and other material. The connectivity will allow for the development of outlying islands, but without spending money on a physical presence.

Part of the lesson here, said the same source, is that you can't be deterred by geographic barriers. Financing is coming from the Cape Verde government and cooperation with other universities. "This is a country of high costs of transport, communication. Things are not cheap." Officials hope the university campus will begin operations by circa 2010.

Budget Office

The jewel in NOSI's crown is the financial management system known as "SIGOF," which integrates tax revenue, the federal government budget, the Controller's Office, and the Treasury. SIGOF was developed using commercial off-the-shelf software such as Oracle (which handles all the database management back end) and Windows NT operating system on the servers and on the desktops; as well as Microsoft's office suite for office automation software and Adobe's suite for publishing. The system is being improved to incorporate monitoring and evaluation, increase security, and integrate with a Geographical Information System.

With NOSI, the Budget Office developed software that would track payments and expenditures throughout the archipelago. Bit by bit, municipalities are coming online—eight cities on the main island of Santiago now have the system. Further integration on the main island is being funded by the government of Austria. France is financing the integration of the islands of Fogo and Brava. The goal is to have all municipalities participating in the network by late 2008 or early 2009.

Of all the systems NOSI has installed, the Budget Office has reaped some of the most visible gains in efficiency. The process of auditing and approving budgets for each department, which used to take one to three months, has now been shortened to just four days. Previously, on any given day, there would be a long line of department directors at the Budget Office, "waiting, screaming, trying to find out the status of their disbursement," said a NOSI analyst. The government is also able to provide financial data more quickly and efficiently to foreign aid donors; if the IMF wants data presented a particular way, the software is able to present it in that fashion almost immediately.

Better than some other departments, the Budget Office has also been able to translate the technological improvement into a visible gain in productivity. The Office has been able to keep its staff frozen at 11 people; the director estimated that, without computers, the Office would have needed to expand in recent years to 15–20 staff members.

Problems and Challenges

Any organization that grows so quickly and achieves such quick and far-reaching results will struggle to adapt to new circumstances. NOSI's phenomenal growth since 1998 has resulted in a series of problems and challenges that it must face going forward.

Administrative Reform

One of the main challenges remaining for NOSI—and the Cape Verdean government at large—is getting the pace of administrative reform to match progress in technology. Put simply: Too many departments continue to do business in much the same way they did before computers were installed.

This phenomenon is also often observable in the private sector. In fact, in the private sector, "the greatest benefits of computers appear to be realized when computer investment is coupled with other complementary investments; new strategies, new business processes and new organizations all appear to be important in realizing the maximum benefit of IT" (Brynjolfsson and Hitt 1998). Conversely, when the complementary investments, changes in business processes, and training of employees are not in place, the impact of IT on productivity is low.

In many cases, computers have allowed for greater efficiency, but manpower has not been redeployed to reflect this. Some NOSI officials said that a second wave of modernization is needed in the public administration to match the progress in technology. One government official said, off the record, that new technology would probably allow him to cut 40 percent of his staff; yet, because of political pressure, he cannot. However, broad change throughout Cape Verde would not necessarily *have* to mean a reduction in public sector jobs; rather, it could take the shape of a reallocation of people to new tasks. As referenced earlier, the management of São Vicente has been able to use its great efficiency gains to create an entirely new department to look after immigration from West Africa. This experience may be repeated in other instances throughout Cape Verde's government.

In general, the necessary changes in government are much more complex than reshuffling personnel. The new technology provides a wealth of new information that potentially allows government to redefine the range of services it produces and to identify more precisely, in some cases, the beneficiaries. And the required innovations are likely to be "discovered" as the reform process goes along and different units of government redefine their objective and work methods.

Changes in government processes generally tend to be much slower than in the private sector; this is as true in Cape Verde as everywhere else in the world. This can lead to tension, especially when NOSI's operating philosophy, which is more akin to that of a private sector company, does not translate into rapid changes in government processes. For instance, Angelo Barbosa left NOSI to take a strategic position at the Finance Ministry, hoping that he could push more energetically for the next wave of reform from within the government bureaucracy. "The plane is taking off. The talk you hear is positive," said Barbosa. "But this is a country of words, and we're not very good at actions yet. You can sit down with a minister, propose something, and he says 'OK, that sounds good.' But then, in practice, three months later, nothing has changed. In the case of the Finance Ministry, they don't yet use the software to its fullest potential."

Aware of the challenge, in March 2006, the government created a new Cabinet position, Minister of Reform, directly under the Prime Minister's authority, to coordinate and advise all ministries on issues pertaining to the reform of the state (in particular, those made viable by the introduction of IT). Christina Fontes, the Minister of State Reform[4] and former Minister of Justice, has a more tempered view: "NOSI's staff is very competent. What happens is that NOSI was ahead of the different sectors (the 'business owners') in the public administration, including the civil servants responsible for the registries. Such sectors were not sufficiently integrated into the change process NOSI was leading. It is also often the case that NOSI pursues *quick wins* together with medium-term solutions, a strategy I share, while some sectors are more concerned about medium-term issues and plans."

For example, at the DGRNI (*Direcção Geral dos Registos, Notariado e Identificação*—the registry), officials were concerned that the rapid pace of NOSI-driven technological change might compromise the legal integrity of their system. "NOSI wants to do things with a lot of speed," said DGRNI director Jorge Pires. "We said: 'No, we need to create an underlying, strong, legal structure, and *then* come up with the software. You [NOSI] can work on the technical side and see things from that perspective. And I think that's fine. Fabulous. I love it. But my job is to make sure the judicial side of things is addressed. We need to meet in the middle.'" Minister Fontes is fully aware of these different views; perhaps that is why she refers to the change of mind-set necessary to push forward the reform of the state as "the work of an ant"—meaning that "it takes a lot of work to build confidence, guarantee full participation, and empower sectors involved in the different projects. Eventually, this proves to be critical for the successful implementation of a project. Still, we lose a lot of time in the process of inclusion and ownership reinforcement."

NOSI also faces some unanswered questions about privacy issues and the danger of security breaches. In general terms, the remarkable degree of integration in NOSI's system does pose the danger that a corruption of data in one place could infect records throughout the entire government with disturbing speed and ease. "There is a risk of people altering birth and death records," said Jorge Pires of the DGRNI. The general public has also shown some concern about confidentiality issues, given the transparency of NOSI's data—there was quite a stir in the 2001 election when the voter registries were "open" online for everyone to see.

"We didn't have strong laws on privacy at the beginning," Lopes said. "We're putting in some laws now that the system is already in place." But, at the same time, it is that seemingly liberal stance toward privacy issues that has been so influential in allowing the system to grow as quickly and comprehensively as it has.

Informality

As discussed earlier, the "informality" of NOSI's operations was initially an asset. The unit's willingness to allow change driven by technology, rather than political or structural concerns, resulted in more rapid modernization and a more agile and flexible organization. But, at the current stage, this emphasis on informality can be a two-way street, and it may be getting more and more problematic as NOSI matures.

NOSI's informal status as a special "super-agency" within government may be a particular obstacle to realizing NOSI's full value in the future, as it grows into a nationwide, and possibly international, entity. For instance, recently Guinea-Bissau asked for advice in developing its own information and technology systems. As a result of its organizational informality, NOSI can contract with Guinea-Bissau only through individual contracts to its engineers. In these circumstances, it would be difficult for NOSI to realize the value of intangibles such as knowledge and experience in the organization, and even to appropriate the value of software not protected by patents. This form of contracting may work initially to develop some experience in international consultancy, but is totally inappropriate if NOSI aims to develop international consultancy as a line of business in the future.

Informality also makes the government too dependent on a few managers at NOSI—and NOSI too dependent on the relationship between its management and the political system. Should these managers leave, the government would be extremely vulnerable. "This is a problem," acknowledged Jorge Lopes. Also, should a new government have a less harmonious relationship with the management of NOSI, both NOSI and Cape Verde would face serious problems.

NOSI's informal status has also postponed serious discussion about how the organization should reorganize its priorities. Should scarce engineering resources be allocated today to the development of applications in ministry X or in municipality Y? Should NOSI discontinue some activities and encourage private firms to develop them? Because NOSI has a very visible output, these questions are not asked today in Cape Verde. Even so, they remain extremely relevant, especially once NOSI has enough demands on its time that its clients (ministries and public sector agencies) have to wait in line before the organization can respond to their demands. The informal operational style affects NOSI's day-to-day operations, and there are some instances where the system may rely too much on personal contacts—where a ministry's relationship may be with a particular person, rather than with NOSI as an organization. This style of interaction, while potentially beneficial during the implementation phase, probably has the net effect of overstretching the staff in areas like technical support.

For example, there is a Web site akin to a message board where NOSI clients are able to post their technical problems. One such message said:

> "*Good afternoon Sofia* [a NOSI employee]—*The problem continues in the tribunal. The data is introduced in one field and when they save it appears altered in other fields.*"

The response, also visible on the message board, said:

> "*Sorry about the problem. It was only corrected for the MAA* [another government department]. *Laranjeiro* (another NOSI employee) *is going to correct it.*"

It is not difficult to imagine how this personalized kind of communication could result in staff becoming overstretched. In practice, individuals within NOSI are sometimes called away from more productive work to attend to matters that are of much lower priority.

If NOSI were a formal organization, it would have a bottom line, and priorities would be set so that results would be visible. NOSI's ambiguities in all these respects imply high costs.

Incentives for the Private IT Sector

In retrospect, we can see that NOSI developed the way it did because of the weakness of Cape Verde's private sector, particularly in technology. In part, this explains why the government did not opt to subcontract provision of IT to the private sector in 1998: there was nobody to contract with and there were too many unknowns.

This is undoubtedly true. But there are concerns that, today, NOSI may be crowding out Cape Verde's private sector. Small companies simply cannot compete with NOSI's technical expertise, its ready availability, and the simple fact that—for the public sector—its services are technically "free." It is possible that NOSI's expansion keeps private, Cape Verdean companies from taking over certain responsibilities. NOSI "is not very worried about the economics of things," said a senior public sector manager at the

Ministry of Finance. "They've got the government, and they have the World Bank to fall back on. If they want to go lay cable on the plateau, they go ask for the money. They don't worry about the cost. It's not fair. The private sector is at a disadvantage."

It is sensible to restructure incentives in government contracting so that private companies appear in the market. Conceivably, basic technical support to the government may be subcontracted; development of some applications can also be gradually delegated to private sector companies. The transition will not, however, be smooth: the private IT sector in Cape Verde is very underdeveloped. In fact, it is a catch-22 situation: the private sector cannot really expand until NOSI opens up space for companies to be competitive; yet, can companies compete without NOSI first using its privileged position to develop a core of local technical knowledge?

The medium-term prospects of Cape Verde's IT sector will be determined by the evolution of NOSI. Cape Verdeans may look back years from now and see that NOSI was an incubator of a robust, national technological competency; or it may continue to be an isolated (though positive) protagonist of technological progress. It all depends on which path forward NOSI chooses. "We are trying to discuss the right model for this adventure that would answer some of the concerns in our society," said Jorge Lopes. "I think we have to work with the private sector to create a space for them to participate." As to whether the way forward was to turn NOSI itself into a private company, Lopes responded: "We have to think this out very carefully because the state of Cape Verde has a strong dependency on NOSI."

The cost of telecommunications in Cape Verde is a far more important impediment than NOSI's role as a barrier to entry to the IT sector. Conceivably, a small IT company could establish itself as an Application Service Provider and offer software services such as security portals, databases, backup, and so on to dozens of small and medium-size local companies. However, to accomplish this, these companies would need a large capital investment in hardware (servers, routers, connectivity, and so on) and funding for the recurrent costs associated with a dedicated broadband connection. Such a connection is[5] around 20 times more expensive in Cape Verde than a much more powerful hookup in the United States.

A Bottleneck for Progress: The Case of CV Telecom

Cabo Verde Telecom (CVT) was a state-controlled entity until 1996, when it was privatized. Forty percent of stock, the maximum allowed by law, is held by "strategic partner" Portugal Telecom. The remaining shares were spread among the Institute of Social Security (INPS), with about 38 percent; Cape Verde/Senegal, a private company, with 5 percent; and another small portion held by CVT workers and the Cape Verde Post Office. In addition, the government of Cape Verde has a golden share, so the most important decisions influencing the sector must meet with approval of government. This shareholder structure appears to have the net effect of slowing change.

CVT has a legal monopoly on fixed lines and international telephone calls; the structure of prices reveals cross-subsidization. Local rates are kept artificially low, so international rates are used as a way of generating profit (table 6.1). Meanwhile, for political reasons, CVT cannot raise local rates significantly without provoking the ire of consumers.

The structure of prices poses a significant barrier to the development of private sector technology companies in Cape Verde and is an overall brake on the country's growth, some officials and companies say. "The high cost of telecoms is killing the private sector," said one of the managers of a private IT firm. A manager at the Ministry of Economy acknowledged that the status quo in the telecommunications sector was a "big obstacle" to private sector development. The indicators reported in table 6.1 support this view.

The last row of table 6.1 presents a "back-of-the-envelope" estimate of the cost of the telecommunications monopoly on consumers. At 1.4 percent, the cost estimated (under the scenario that liberalization will result in a fall in prices of 20 percent) is high (see chapter 9 on IT Sector Reform in Samoa).[6]

Table 6.1. Telecommunications Indicators

Indicator	Cape Verde	Median World	Median Small States
Mobile-phone lines per 1,000 people (MOBILE)	161.2	350.5	466.3
Price of mobile-phone basket (PMOB)	US$18.6	US$11.0	US$11.8
Price of mobile-phone basket, PPP-adjusted (PRMOB)	US$52.6	US$20.2	US$20.9
Telecom share in GDP (STEL)	6.9%	3.6%	4.7%
Price of Internet (PINTER)	US$40.3	US$22.1	US$23.9
Price of fixed line (PFIXED)	US$6.0	US$11.9	US$14.9
Welfare gain (as a percentage of GDP) if PRMOB falls by 20%	1.4%	n.a.	n.a.

Source: World Bank 2007.
Note: For definitions see Annex 6.C.
n.a. = not available.

The estimate is a lower bound of the cost to Cape Verde of the current telecommunications market situation. Even if the estimate is imprecise, it is conservative: first, a fall of the price of mobile services of 20 percent is extremely conservative, given what has been the experience of other countries: see chapter 6 on IT regulation in the Eastern Caribbean and chapter 9 on IT sector reform in Samoa. Second, the calculation did not take into account the impact of the reform on activities whose fixed costs were high enough to make them not profitable before the reform, but that become profitable afterward (Romer 1994; Goolsbee 2006). The importance of these activities may be much higher than is often anticipated, and hence the cost of the status quo is much higher than that reported in Table 6.1.

The World Trade Organization has spent three years seeking full liberalization of the telecommunications sector in Cape Verde because monopolies are not permitted. Despite internal and external pressure, change has been slow to come. The current contract allows CVT another 25 years of monopoly status on the fixed-line network and for international communications, although negotiations were under way in September 2006 to modify this.

Unfortunately, NOSI may also play a part in the government's decision to maintain the status quo. Over the past eight years, NOSI has been able to develop a privileged status as a client of telecommunications services in Cape Verde. It pays large telecommunications bills, but bills that are much lower than what a private company or an elementary school in São Vicente would pay to access broadband or make a phone call. This privileged status has made it possible to expand the public sector communications network. An unintended consequence, though, is that the de facto agreement has taken pressure off the government to get on with its reform of the current telecommunications regulatory regime.

Can NOSI Be Replicated in Other Countries?

"I think any country can do this. I think any country *should* do this," said Hélio Varela. "I do believe that for emerging countries, this is a solution—investing in IT to become more efficient."

Varela's optimism is in stark contrast with the experience of many countries who have tried to implement e-government projects (often much less ambitious than Cape Verde's) and have failed partially or totally (Heeks 2003). Does he portray too rosy a picture of what has been done in Cape Verde? Is IT a *solution* for emerging countries?

The unification of the public registries; the implementation of electronic integrated systems in administration and execution of the budget; and computerization of budget and tax collection systems in the central government and in some municipalities suggest that Varela's optimism is based on solid ground. At the same time, projects still to be implemented like the Casa do Cidadão (the planned "front office" of the e-government program); the still-limited access of the people of Cape Verde to e-government services; and pending reforms in administrative processes in the public sector suggest that much remains to be done.

For countries looking to learn from Cape Verde's initiative, the natural questions to ask are these: What aspects of the reform were critical to the results—and to what extent were these unique to Cape Verde? Are there pitfalls to be avoided—as well as solutions to be emulated—in this success story? What changes (if any) are necessary to consolidate pending aspects of the reform?

Of the many factors that contributed to the success of Cape Verde's reform, four stand out:

First, *strong political support*. If the Cape Verde experience is to be repeated elsewhere, the *political* conditions may be the most difficult to replicate. In Cape Verde, there was a clear convergence of political will in which leading officials—from the Prime Minister on down—gave NOSI the freedom to operate and a clear mandate to act in all sectors of government. There was a broad willingness to allow technological developments to lead the change, allowing the legal and political structure to "catch up" later. NOSI officials expressed some doubts as to whether this experience could occur elsewhere. "I think this is an experience that at the beginning can have strong barriers to implement," said Jorge Lopes. "Integration and sharing of data are very strong terms that make the hair stand up for men of law, human rights, jurists, and so forth." That said, if the political will is there, the technical aspect will follow with relative ease, NOSI officials said. "Countries should not be dissuaded by the task of creating a body of national technological knowledge," Varela said. "It takes months, not years. Technology itself is not *that* difficult."

Second, *insistence on building domestic engineering capacity*. Reliance on domestic engineering capacity, rather than on foreign experience, for the design and implementation of the IT reform has not been the result of a Cape Verdean nationalistic bent; the view was based on previous experiences with international consultants (see above) and conviction that a necessary condition for using external support efficiently is the capacity to identify precisely the problem to be addressed, to write the terms of reference for the task, and to assess the quality of the work. If such a capacity is not there, reform will proceed at a much slower pace.

Key to building this capacity were incentives to persuade the return of talented Cape Verdean engineers working or studying abroad: high salaries and an inviting workplace in Cape Verde in which they could interact with their peers and address interesting technical challenges (in many cases, at a very early stage of their careers).

Third, the creation of an *implementation agency controlled by the government, but operating under private sector rules*. Both aspects were important: NOSI's organizational location, first under the Ministry of Finance and then under the Prime Minister, facilitated interaction with authorities and with the rest of the civil service. Personnel and management rules akin to those of the private sector gave flexibility for hiring and firing personnel, prevented the development of bureaucratic practices, and helped develop a service-provider mentality among the personnel. Whether similar results can be achieved by a private firm operating under a government contract will depend on the country undertaking the reform. If the country has a well-developed IT sector, that option is available; if there is no private sector to speak of at the beginning of the program, the Cape Verde model is certainly attractive.

Fourth, *a service-provider culture* to weaken resistance to reform and create client ownership for the final product. NOSI has strict norms regarding the selection of hardware and software and insists that different systems should be developed with a capacity to speak to each other; nonetheless, its engineers develop IT products in response to clients' needs, rather than imposing on them products selected or developed on their behalf. Developing products instead of purchasing commercial off-the shelf packages is an arguable decision; in the case of Cape Verde, the practice helped defeat resistance and build ownership of the reform.

Among the changes necessary to consolidate the reform, two stand out.

First, *the transition of NOSI from informality to formality*. NOSI's informal organization facilitated operations in the first stage of the project, but will be a burden hereafter as the complexity of the tasks increases. Also, NOSI's sole-source procurement practices carry with them the risk of corruption. NOSI's managers are fully aware of this reality and are currently studying models to break up NOSI's functions into several firms and government agencies, with the view that they will gradually outsource part of the IT services currently provided by NOSI to the spin-offs.

Second, *the opening of the telecommunications market to competition*. The cost of telecommunications services in Cape Verde is a burden to the use of the admirable IT system developed in recent years. If services do not reach the people, political consensus in favor of the reform will be difficult to maintain. The extent to which the IT reform will be valuable to the people depends on the size of the network that uses the services, and the size is strongly determined by telecommunications costs. "Reform for the citizen must be something that he feels—it must touch the citizen, it must facilitate his life. Otherwise, it's simply not reform. Leaders should never forget that," said Jorge Lopes.

Annex 6A. Open-Source Versus Proprietary Software

This annex provides background relevant to assess the decision to build an e-government system based on proprietary software rather than open source. We thought we would investigate the issue a bit more deeply for the interested reader, because the issue of open-source versus proprietary software has been raging since the mid 90s.

Definitions: An open-source program is a program whose source code is made available for use or modification as users or other developers see fit. An open-source program is not necessarily free (a license fee is sometimes required), but its users are "free" to reuse, modify, and change the code. A proprietary program is one in which the code is not made available to users or developers. The open-source movement started in the 1980s under MIT's Free Software Foundation initiative, and it started to soar after a new operating system, Linux, was designed as an alternative to Windows NT, or IBM's UNIX, or Sun's Solaris, for server operating systems. To complement UNIX, a whole series of applications was created, such as Apache (Web server), MySQL (database), Mozilla (browser), and so forth, that compete with proprietary offerings from Microsoft, Novell, IBM (for application servers and operating systems), and Oracle (database). Today, Linux (whose most famous distributor is Red Hat) has grown to become a strong alternative to Windows. In the third quarter of 2006, US$1.5 billion of new servers were sold with Linux installed, against US$4.2 billion with Windows NT installed (*Financial Times*, November 3, 2006).

Open source can be mixed with proprietary software. Open source relies on a "buddy system" network to grow its products' features and to innovate in new products. It was started in universities and continues to develop its supporter base in universities, innovation labs, and research and development think tanks. It is much younger than most of the established proprietary software giants, all established in the 1970s or 1980s, and hence needs to catch up in terms of user base, skilled technicians, developers, documentation, packaged courses, accreditation process, quality assurance, and so on.

According to industry analysts, the enthusiasm for open source created a sort of passion and euphoria among software developers, especially in academia and among independent small software producers, all of whom tired of dependency on proprietary vendors. The application code, shifting from a jealously guarded trade secret to a publicly available good that one was free to modify, was a great paradigm shift for the software industry, for which this is as close as it gets to the concept of freedom.

Implementation has not been straightforward, though, because most analysis in Total Cost of Ownership (TCO), a measure developed by the Gartner Group, fails to prove that adoption of open source diminishes costs. In fact, some studies indicate that the total cost of ownership for open-source users can actually be higher than that of proprietary software.

TCO is a measure of (a) acquisition costs (license, transport, and so forth), (b) usage costs, (c) downtime and recovery costs, and (d) security breakage costs. While (a) and (b) are direct costs made available on any balance sheet, (c) and (d) are hidden costs that translate into productivity loss, with users suffering long downtimes, data loss, virus attacks, and so on.

Several studies have shown that (c) and (d) were higher for open-source users, because the open-source community suffers from lack of documentation, a dearth of qualified experts, lack of systematic marketing, and inadequate implementation of support and maintenance functions, along with some of the symptoms that young products typically experience, even if they turn out to be the "killer application."

In the past 12 years, many major vendors have started to provide support to open-source software: among them are HP, IBM, Novell, CA, Oracle, SAP, Sun, and recently even Microsoft. Microsoft has gradually revised its opposition to Linux, reflecting the fact that the rival system has now become a mainstream part of many companies' enterprise architecture. In November 2006, Microsoft signed a landmark agreement with Novell (whose SUSE Linux is one of the most used versions of the software) to make the rival technologies (Windows NT Server and SUSE Linux) work better together.

The story is far from being over, and time will tell how the market and the consumer experiences will affect the market shares of open source versus those of proprietary software in a few years.

Annex 6B

The standard economic approach to assessing the value of telecommunications reform (or lack thereof) is to measure the change in consumer surplus as a result of the opening of the market to competition. Consumer surplus is the excess between consumers' willingness to pay and market price.

A lower bound to the gain to consumers as a result of the reform is given by equation (6B.1):[7]

$$\Delta W = (p_b - p_a)Q_b + \frac{(p_b - p_a)(Q_a - Q_b)}{2},\tag{6B.1}$$

where
ΔW = the change in consumer surplus after the reform and
Q_i = telecom services consumed before (Q_b) and after (Q_a) the reform.

The gain has two components: the first component is the difference in price of services times the quantity consumed before the reform. The second component is a function of the change in prices (pre- and postreform) times the change in quantities (pre- and postreform).

Equation (6B.1) may be simplified further (after some algebra) to

$$\Delta W = \left[\frac{\Delta p}{p}\right]S_b + \left(\frac{1}{2}\right)\left[\frac{\Delta p}{p}\right]^2 \eta S_b,\tag{6B.2}$$

where

$$\frac{\Delta p}{p} = \frac{p_b - p_a}{p_b},$$

η = the price elasticity of demand for telecom services, and
S_b = the income share of telecom services.

The derivation of the consumers' loss presented in the main text was based on a Marshallian demand for telecom services. Consumer surplus is approximated as the area under the Marshallian demand curve in between the change in quantities and prices.[8]

The only nonobservable parameter in equation (6B.2) is the elasticity of demand for mobile-phone services. This parameter may be estimated using the methodology followed in annex 9B of chapter 9. A simpler alternative, followed here, is to use the elasticity of demand estimated for the Samoa case (−0.28) reported in chapter 9. While this procedure is a gross simplification, its overall effect in the calculation is innocuous once the elasticity is multiplied by the rest of the factors in the second term of equation (6B.2).

Annex 6C. Definition of Series Used in the Statistical Calculations

Series: **MOBILE**: Mobile-phone subscribers (per 1,000 people)

"Mobile-telephone subscribers" are subscribers to a public mobile-telephone service using cellular technology. *Source:* International Telecommunication Union, World Telecommunication Development Report and database, and World Bank estimates.

Series: **GDP**: GDP per capita at constant 2000 US$

"GDP per capita" is gross domestic product divided by midyear population. GDP is the sum of gross value added by all resident producers in the economy plus any product taxes and minus any subsidies not included in the value of the products. It is calculated without making deductions for depreciation of fabricated assets or for depletion and degradation of natural resources. Data are in constant U.S. dollars. *Source:* World Bank National Accounts data and OECD National Accounts data files.

Series: **PFIXED**: Price basket for residential fixed line (US$ per month)

"Price basket for residential fixed line" is calculated as one-fifth of the installation charge, the monthly subscription charge, and the cost of local calls (15 peak and 15 off-peak calls of three minutes each). *Source:* calculated by the World Bank, based on International Telecommunication Union data.

Series: **PINTER**: Price basket for the Internet (US$ per month)

"Price basket for the Internet" is calculated based on the cheapest available tariff for accessing the Internet 20 hours a month (10 hours peak and 10 hours off-peak). The basket does not include the telephone line rental, but does include telephone usage charges, if applicable. Data are compiled in the national currency and converted to U.S. dollars, using the annual average exchange rate. *Source:* International Telecommunication Union and World Telecommunication Development Report and database.

Series: **PMOB**: Price basket for a mobile phone (US$ per month)

"Price basket for a mobile phone" is calculated as the prepaid price for 25 calls per month spread over the same mobile network, other mobile networks, and mobile-to-fixed calls and during peak, off-peak, and weekend times. It also includes 30 text messages per month. *Source:* International

Telecommunication Union, World Telecommunication Development Report and database, and World Bank estimates.

Series PPP: Purchasing power parity conversion factor (Local Currency Units [LCUs] per international $)

"Purchasing power parity conversion factor" is the number of units of a country's currency required to buy the same amounts of goods and services in the domestic market as a U.S. dollar would buy in the United States. *Source:* World Bank and International Comparison Program database.

Series: PRMOB: The ratio of PMOB and PPP

PPP adjusted price basket for a mobile phone basket.

Series: STEL: Telecommunications revenue (% GDP)

"Telecommunications revenue" is the revenue from the provision of telecommunications services such as fixed-line, mobile, and data. *Source:* International Telecommunication Union, World Telecommunication Development Report and database, and World Bank estimates.

Annex 6D. List of Officials Cited in the Case Study

Name	Affiliations
Hélio Varela	Technical Coordinator, NOSI
Rosa Pinheiro	Treasury Commissioner
Jorge Lopes	General Manager, NOSI
Jose Ulisses Correia e Silva	Leader of the Opposition in Congress; Former Minister of Finance
Angelo Barbosa	IT Coordinator, Ministry of Finance
A. Neto	Hospital Administrator
Christina Fontes	Minister of Reform
Jorge Pires	DGRNI (Direcção Geral dos Registos, Notariado e Identificação)

Notes

1. "ICT" (information and communications technology) is generally referred to hereafter by its more commonly used acronym "IT."
2. To avoid confusion, the organization is referred to as "NOSI" in most instances in this text. RAF became NOSI in 2003; this transition is explained later in the case study.

3. WiMAX is a technology for wireless delivery of broadband.

4. The full title is "Ministra da PresidÍncia do Conselho de Ministros, da Reforma do Estado e da Defesa Nacional."

5. Statement based on information as of December 2006.

6. Annex 7B describes the steps followed to calculate the welfare gain.

7. The formula assumes the demand for telephones is linear in prices.

8. To simplify the calculation, we assume linear demand functions.

References

Brynjolfsson, Erik, and Lorin Hitt. 1998. "Beyond the Productivity Paradox." *Communications of the ACM* 41 (8, August): 49–55.

Goolsbee, Austan. 2006. "The Value of Broadband and the Deadweight Loss of Taxing New Technology." *Contributions to Economic Analysis & Policy* 5 (1): 1505. http://faculty.chicagogsb.edu/austan.goolsbee/research/broadb.pdf.

Heeks, Richard. 2003. "Most eGovernment-for-Development Projects Fail: How Can Risks be Reduced?" iGovernment Working Paper 14, Institute for Development Policy and Management, University of Manchester, United Kingdom. http://www.sed.manchester.ac.uk/idpm/research/publications/wp/igovernment/igov_wp14.htm.

Romer, Paul. 1994. "New Goods, Old Theory, and the Welfare Cost of Trade Restrictions." *Journal of Development Economics* 43 (1): 5–38.

World Bank. 2007. *World Development Indicators*. Washington, DC: World Bank.

CHAPTER 7

Impact of ICT on University Education in Small Island States: The Case of the University of the South Pacific

Ron Duncan and James McMaster

> ### Prologue
>
> Upoko Tupa, an ambitious young Pacific islands manager, was reflecting on his recent promotion to a senior management position as the chief executive officer (CEO) of a government business enterprise on the remote island of Rarotonga. Upoko is a science graduate from the University of the South Pacific (USP), with 10 years of work experience. His promotion from a technical operations manager into a CEO position demanded new competencies in strategic planning, finance, accounting, marketing, and human resources management.
>
> Sitting out on the oceanfront deck with a group of his friends, Upoko commented, "My new job is great, but I need training in management techniques. What I really need is an master of business administration (MBA)—but I can't take
>
> *(continued)*

Ron Duncan and James McMaster are professors at the University of the South Pacific.

time off to go to USP in Suva to take the course." His friend Tevia, a budding entre-
preneur who had just returned from a business trip to Samoa, said, "Last Saturday,
I met some guys in Samoa who were celebrating completing the MBA course they
had taken part-time at the USP Alafua campus there. They said the course made a
big difference to their performance as managers, and some have already taken up
CEO positions with big salary increases. I hear that the World Bank is helping to
upgrade the USP satellite communications system so that we will have access to
state-of-the-art distance learning." Upoko replied, "I know a dozen people who are
keen to do an MBA here in Raro. Why don't we lobby to get USP to deliver the
course here, using the new satellite technology and their new audiovisual studio?"

Rod Dixon, the USP campus director, was one step ahead of him. At the USP
council meeting held in May 2006 in the Cook Islands, he had lobbied the Dean
of the Faculty of Business and Economics to replicate the Samoa MBA program
delivery system in the Cooks and make full use of USPNet and a World Bank–
sponsored project that will considerably improve the speed and quality of videoconferencing and Internet communication among the 12 campuses that make
up this regional university.

The 2006 upgrade of USPNet is already making it feasible to deliver the MBA
more effectively in more Pacific island countries. Over the past 10 years, MBA
enrollments have grown rapidly, but until 2005, the course was only conducted
in Fiji, Suva, and Nadi. In 2005, with financial support from the European Union,
the MBA program began delivering the course on a face-to-face basis to 30
managers in Samoa, and in February 2007, a cohort of 35 executives started the
two-year program in the Cook Islands (again on a face-to-face basis) with financial support from the government. Planning and feasibility studies are now
being undertaken on delivering the MBA course in Tonga, Kiribati, Vanuatu, and
other member countries, depending on demand, cohort size, and financial support from donors. The recent USPNet upgrade will allow faster Internet speed
and better audio and video quality, thereby making blended-mode delivery of
the MBA more effective than at present.

Introduction

What's changed? This case study explores the complex story of how a
regional university is changing its delivery systems for teaching and
learning to serve the growing needs for tertiary education of students
living on thousands of small islands in the Pacific Ocean. It traces the
history of the foundation of the university by 12 island nations and its

use of communications technology. It examines the complex challenges the university faces in its quest to harness all the advantages of information technology to deliver first-class tertiary education.

Developing a regional university to serve 12 tiny countries spread out over the vast Pacific Ocean was a monumental task. The fact that USP has accomplished this feat and, moreover, "manages to punch well above its weight in teaching and research," in the words of its most recent vice chancellor, is a testament to perseverance and to taking advantage of developments in the field of international communications technology (ICT). At present, more than half of the university's more than 20,000 students are distance students; that is, in the modern jargon, they are distance and flexible learning (DFL) students who learn with the assistance of modern telecommunications media, comprising audioconferencing, videoconferencing, and the Internet, as well as paper-based materials.

This is the story of the development of USPNet of the University of the South Pacific. The case study describes how the university tapped into the initial stages of the development of satellite-based communication; how it has struggled to find the financing necessary to improve its crucial communications facility; how it has had to cope with the extremely high telecommunications charges and the regulatory obstacles resulting from the monopolized telecommunications facilities in the member countries; how it has contended with the enormous damage to infrastructure that can be inflicted by the physical environment; and how it has continually struggled to provide the most up-to-date multimedia learning to more than 10,000 distance students studying in some of the most remote places in the world.

The communication difficulties facing the small communities living on the small outlying islands and in the remote areas of the main islands have long been a concern for Pacific peoples. The advent of global satellite coverage and the rapidly declining costs of computers and VSAT (very small aperture terminals) equipment, together with the availability of solar power technology, have opened up the possibility for people in the remote communities to have immediate telecommunications contact with the rest of the world. This technology also opens up the opportunity for these communities to participate in the DFL offerings of USPNet. It is likely that the next big step for USPNet will be to develop its facilities to respond to this demand.

The case study suggests a number of strategic alternatives for the further development of DFL, including bandwidth expansion of the information highways to the 12 campuses and the extension of the information by ways to the small rural communities where many students would prefer to undertake their studies. The challenge is to develop a strategic plan based on the information presented that will lead to the achievement of the university's objective of making all its courses available by DFL by around 2010.

The Development of USPNet

The Establishment of the University of the South Pacific and USPNet

USP began in 1968 and was formally established by royal charter in 1970. It is a multicountry university with a membership of 12 Pacific island countries, comprising the Cook Islands, Fiji, Kiribati, the Marshall Islands, Nauru, Niue, Samoa, the Solomon Islands, Tonga, Tokelau, Tuvalu, and Vanuatu. The main campus is in Suva, the capital of Fiji. Currently, it has two other major campuses: the Alafua campus in Apia, Samoa, home to the School of Agriculture and Food Technology; and the Emalus campus in Port Vila, Vanuatu, home to the School of Law and the Pacific Language Unit.

The populations of these countries are very small, ranging from only around 1,500 people in Niue and Tokelau to 850,000 in Fiji. In addition, the countries are spread out over a huge area of the Pacific Ocean, estimated to be around 33 million square kilometers. Moreover, most of the countries are very dispersed, comprising many small volcanic islands or coral or atoll islands. The problems of providing tertiary education in such small, dispersed countries cannot be overstated.

USPNet is a satellite-communications network that was set up in 1973 as a means of distance education for those students who could not afford the high financial and personal costs of traveling to and living in Suva. USPNet used the PEACESAT satellite—a National Aeronautic and Space Administration experimental satellite—for voice broadcasts of educational material to the students studying by distance. USP was one of the early users of PEACESAT, and this early adoption of a new technology shows a surprising degree of enterprise on the part of the university. As an experimental activity, PEACESAT was not a commercial service, and its services were provided free. Furthermore, USP's participation was supported by the Carnegie Corporation and U.S. Agency for International Development (USAID). With terminals in each of the university's member countries, PEACESAT facilitated voice communication between the teachers and students.

In 1985, the PEACESAT satellite went off course, and the university's access to this facility was lost. An alternative was found in October 1986 in the form of space on the INTELSAT satellite, which normally provided communication channels on commercial terms, but provided access to USPNet initially free of charge for two years. In 1988, Cable & Wireless Public Ltd. (Hong Kong, China) agreed to meet the full cost of satellite space for USPNet for two years. This agreement was extended for two years in 1990—and for a further two years in 1992—on the expectation that the university would use that time to establish a more permanent, self-reliant system.

At this stage, the paper and voice-only communications between the main campus and the member-country centers of the university were very much a patchwork arrangement. The satellite links from the main campus to the university's other centers went via the earth stations of national telecommunications agencies in 5 of the other 11 countries: the Cook Islands (where the full costs of the space and ground links were paid by Telecom NZ International), Kiribati, the Solomon Islands, Tonga, and Vanuatu. Kiribati was disconnected by USP after extended discussions with its national telecommunications authority failed to persuade it to lower its high charges. The access provided by the national telecommunications authorities was said to be "highly subsidized," which likely reflects the high monopoly prices being charged in these countries—still a constraint to economic and other activity in many of the countries. But even though they claimed to be subsidizing this access, the national telecommunications authorities were, and remain, reluctant to allow USPNet to operate outside their jurisdiction. This reluctance stems, at least in part, from the concern that the university will offer communication channels in competition with the national monopoly. All licenses granted by the telecommunications authorities limit the use of telecommunication facilities to educational purposes.

In four of the six USP member countries where national telecom earth stations were not available (Nauru, Niue, Tuvalu, and Samoa), the university centers were linked to the main campus via a high-frequency (HF) radio system. The remaining two countries (Tokelau and the Marshall Islands), plus Kiribati after its earth station link was cut, had no connection to USPNet.

The system described above served reasonably well for some years. But there were persistent problems, and, with the development of telecommunications technology, no doubt people's expectations rose rapidly. The following ongoing problems were noted at the time:

- Only one-way voice communication
- Frequent faults, "outages" associated with within-country landlines and earth stations (outages often lasted for days)

- Total reliance on local goodwill for repairs
- Vulnerability to atmospheric conditions
- Insufficient HF power for the distances covered (where HF systems were in use)
- No computer communication or data transmission facilities
- Inequity in coverage between countries/students

Because of the frequent landline problems and with the availability of improved quality of landlines, the university, with the financial support of aid donors Australia, New Zealand, and the United Kingdom, undertook an upgrade of the system in the early 1990s. Through the national telecommunications authorities, which agreed to give "educational rates," 64-kilobit lines were leased to and from the five countries with earth stations. This upgrade allowed voice and data transmission.

In 1992, in the face of opposition from the national telecommunications authorities, the university council—consisting of the Education ministers from the member countries, and others—approved a USPNet proposal for the establishment of a network of USP satellite earth stations in all member countries. The council asked the university to seek approval to do so from the appropriate authority in each country. This proposal took five years—until 1997—to take effect.

The Upgrade of 2000

In June 1995, the university developed a "Project Proposal for the Upgrade of the University's Communications System: USPNet." The requirements in the proposal included earth stations and connections to the PBXs (private branch exchanges) at each university center so that telephone calls within the university throughout the member countries could be made at local rates. Also, it was proposed that Internet access be provided for all sites through a high-speed central connection at the main campus in Suva. These arrangements needed licenses for the satellite connections, Internet connections, and telephony.

No decisions resulted from this proposal, which was overtaken by events: developments in video transmission and the rapid reduction in bandwidth costs, which pushed for a decision for a stand-alone system. In July 1997, the government of Fiji, on behalf of USP, requested assistance from the government of Japan to upgrade USPNet to a stand-alone, private network. The 1995 proposal was for a satellite-based network providing 64 kilobits-per-second data and voice capability. The 1997 proposal for the building of a VSAT system included a video capability to allow videoed lectures to be broadcast from any of the three main campuses of the university (Suva, Port Vila in Vanuatu, and Apia in Samoa) and to be received by all locations. The remaining centers ("remotes") would have two-way voice and data capability and be able to receive video transmissions. Only the three main campuses would have two-way videoconference capacity.

The following problems faced in implementing the upgrade are typical of the problems that beset activities in these countries:

- The difficulty of finding a site for an earth station on islands barely above sea level and with limited land area
- Irregular power supplies (the frequent power outages made some form of alternative energy supply necessary)
- Extreme humidity and temperatures, which required finding reliable and inexpensive cooling systems
- High recurrent costs (which the university had to bear), for instance, for electricity, repairs and maintenance, satellite access, and IT
- Vulnerability to natural disasters, such as cyclones, earthquakes, and tsunamis for the damage inflicted on a USPNet satellite dish by the cyclone that hit Niue in January 2004

The proposal for the upgrade was eventually accepted by the Japanese government. Because of conditions applying to the Japanese Grant Aid Scheme, the government of Japan had difficulty in extending assistance to four of the member countries: the Cook Islands, Nauru, Niue, and Tokelau. New Zealand has close relationships with the Cook Islands, Niue, and Tokelau and agreed to fund the improvements to their facilities, as well as for Nauru. Australia agreed to fund the upgrade in Kiribati. USP was to bear all recurrent costs of the facilities.

The tendering process for the upgrade began in October 1998, with a completion date set for March 2000. The last earth station was duly installed in March 2000. The new configuration of USPNet was as follows: Suva was the hub earth station; Apia and Port Vila were minihub earth stations; and the Cook Islands, Kiribati, the Marshall Islands, Nauru, Niue, the Solomon Islands, Tokelau, Tonga, and Tuvalu were remote earth stations. Satellite space was leased from INTELSAT.

The timing of the completion of the upgrade was fortuitous, because there was a coup in Fiji in May 2000 and most regional students at the main campus returned home. The second semester was almost canceled, but through the medium of USPNet, 35 courses were delivered to the four regional centers with the largest concentrations of students (Kiribati, Samoa, the Solomon Islands, and Tonga). On several occasions of national disasters, such as Cyclone Heta in Samoa in January 2004, USPNet has provided the only link to the outside world.

The Upgrade of 2006

Almost immediately, driven by the rapid changes in telecommunications technology and continuing reductions in the cost of bandwidth and satellite space, there was demand for enhancement of the USPNet system. In 2000, thought was already being given to how USPNet might be developed to provide access to students beyond the centers. Provision of educational services to communities in the outlying islands of the Pacific countries has remained a concern of Pacific islanders.

A survey of the university centers in 2004 showed noticeable improvements in the services provided by USPNet following the 2000 upgrade. Audio conferences were much clearer, and more slots were available for delivering lectures and tutorials. The enhancement of the facility offered scope for audiographics and e-beam, and these had enhanced the interaction between lecturer and student. In those locations where videoconference (VC) facilities were available, they were much appreciated and were said to be the most useful aspect of the upgrade. Moreover, the capacity to videotape lectures and broadcast them at other times added flexibility to the system's use as a teaching medium. Still, the high bandwidth requirements and the inflexibility of the system meant that VC slots were very limited.

But already, partly because of heightened expectations from experience with telecommunication speeds in other environments, students were complaining about the slowness of data transmission via USPNet. In video broadcasts, voice was rated as reasonable, but picture quality was "poor." The Internet access was rated as "very slow." And physical space in the video and computer rooms at most of the centers had become very tight as the number of students continued to grow rapidly.

As early as September 2002, a joint report of the Japan International Cooperation Agency and USP had been prepared on further enhancement of USPNet. This report recommended an increase in the bandwidth, integration of USPNet with other educational communications systems, and expansion of USPNet services beyond the centers. There were difficulties in regard to connection to other educational communications systems (such as the Japanese government's J-Net and the World Bank's Global Development Learning Network) in the form of technical incompatibility, the high cost of the communications link, and the lack of common applications.

By March 2005, a USPNet Enhancement Project had been finalized. A proposal by Gilat, a communications company, was accepted to create an Internet-protocol (IP) platform at the Suva hub, with the 11 other centers having interactive data, broadband IP, and public and private telephony. This upgrade required at least a 128 kilobits-per-second data channel. Bandwidth could be shared between applications, however, so that spare capacity in one area could be shifted to others, improving the efficiency of the whole system.

The USPNet upgrade was launched at the end of 2006. It is now a stand-alone network with interactive videoconferencing possible between all campuses (the diagram at the end of this chapter illustrates the present configuration of USPNet, and gives an idea of the scale of the problem posed by the smallness of the countries and the vast distances between them). The quality of the picture and audio is excellent. Only time will tell, but the quality of communications that USPNet now offers has been greatly improved.

The Uses of USPNet

Tertiary Education by Distance

Distance education from USP commenced in 1970. The students were mainly in-service teachers taking courses for a diploma in Education. By 1976, 90 students were enrolled in 16 courses. Students could enroll through four of the university centers (the Cook Islands, Kiribati, the Solomon Islands, and Tonga) or through the departments of education in Samoa, Niue, Tuvalu, and Vanuatu. By 1996, there were about 5,400 students studying by distance out of a total student population of approximately 9,400 (that is, 58 percent of students were being taught through USPNet). The numbers have continued to grow: by 2004, there were nearly 10,000 distance students of a total in excess of 16,000 (that is, more than 60 percent of the university's students, with 150 courses offered over three semesters [including a summer semester]).

Courses are available for distance education at three levels: predegree, which is for preliminary and foundation studies; subdegree, which is vocational training; and degree courses. The university centers, now known as campuses, offer the distance student study space, study groups, a library, science laboratories, computers and Internet access, audio and video lecture playback facilities, real-time viewing of lectures, on-campus tutors, and summer lectures and tutorials by visiting lecturers. The audio and video lectures are now loaded onto servers at the campuses and can be viewed by the students at a time convenient to them.

The availability of the Internet has made it possible to deliver online courses using course-management software such as WebCT™, which provides online access to lecturers and tutors, sending and receiving assignments, and participation in student discussion groups. The Internet also allows the downloading of reading material and access to published databases. The campuses look after student enrollments, distribution of course material, handling of coursework, employment of local tutors, scheduling of tutorials, and scheduling of exams.

Initially, with the voice-only capacity of USPNet, students had instruction available only in the form of print, print with audioconferencing, and face-to-face instruction from visits by lecturers to the member countries (summer courses)—and later, face-to-face lectures and tutorials from academic staff located at the centers. By 2006, more than 200 courses were being offered by what is known now as Distance and Flexible Learning (DFL). The term "flexible" refers to the facts that distance education offers those who do not wish to leave their work or home the opportunity for tertiary studies and that instruction is offered in a multimedia format. All 100-level (that is, first-year) courses are offered by DFL, and the university council has asked that all courses, both undergraduate and postgraduate, be made available by DFL as soon as possible, hopefully by 2010. The design of DFL courses is giving priority to offering full degree programs. Until all degree programs are available through DFL, some students will have to attend the main campuses to complete their degrees.

The Pacific Ocean covers a large area and several time zones, which limits the real-time connectivity of the Pacific island countries. While this has benefits in the form of being able to undertake activities such as call-back centers for countries in different time zones, it does limit the amount of real-time connection for delivering lectures and using USPNet for other activities such as public education and university administration. Given the time zones of the member countries, lectures can be delivered only for five hours per day, for a total of 25 hours per week.

The difficulties that students experienced with instruction delivered through USPNet before the 2006 upgrade were reflected in their performance. Attrition rates during courses averaged 20.8 percent and were much higher in some countries (for example, Nauru, 53 percent; Niue, 36 percent; and Tuvalu, 36 percent). These are all very small countries that did not have an earth station; students were therefore suffering poor reception and frequent outages. In addition, the campus facilities were very limited. It is to be hoped that the 2006 upgrade will greatly improve the variety and quality of the instruction that the students can receive.

Other Uses of USPNet

The videoconference capability of USPNet between the main campus in Suva and the other two major campuses in Apia and Port Vila has meant that virtual face-to-face discussions can be held by the senior management of the university, thus saving considerably on travel costs. The videoconference facility between these points can also be used for activities such as interviews for university positions. The proposed integration of USPNet into the World Bank's Global Development Learning Network (GDLN) will allow all of the campuses to make such use of USPNet.

For the past three years, the annual Siwatibau Memorial Lecture on Good Governance has been broadcast to all campuses. This broadcast of a public lecture is an illustration of the usefulness of a communications facility such as USPNet for public education, which must be an important function for the university, particularly given the very high cost of communications among these countries.

Now that USP's campus has an optical-fiber link to Australia via the Southern Cross cable and is connected to the Australian Universities' Internet2 facility, the Suva campus is able to receive high-quality video-conference broadcasts from Australian universities. Through this medium, the Australian Agency for International Development (AusAID) has over the past two years funded videoconference discussions on important development topics, which have also been broadcast through the GDLN to groups in Port Moresby, Papua New Guinea, and in Dili, East Timor. These discussion groups have allowed interested staff and students at USP and in the wider community to engage in discussions of topics such as corporate governance, leadership, entrepreneurship, anticorruption, public-private partnerships, and telecommunications regulation and deregulation. Such discussion with peers is a very important means of learning. When the remainder of the university's campuses are linked into the GDLN—assuming that the telecommunications authorities in each country allow the reception of these broadcasts—all member countries of the university will be able to participate in these valuable discussions.

The videoconference discussion on entrepreneurship led the director of the MBA program at USP to establish a Web site on which considerable material has been placed from around the world to inform Pacific small business owners or potential small businesses about local business development assistance programs and agencies, financial and managerial practices, and even the pros and cons of entrepreneurial activity. A regional conference on entrepreneurship was also run by the MBA program. Another activity triggered by the videoconference discussions of entrepreneurship was the development of Web sites and business plans for ecotourism in villages in Fiji. These activities illustrate the multiplier effects of these discussions on important developmental topics.

The Operating Environment of USP

USP is widely regarded as the best example of cooperation between the Pacific island countries. Indeed, some would say that it is the only successful example of such cooperation. Other attempts at regional cooperation, such as the formation of a regional airline, have failed—largely as the result of unwillingness to give up on the idea of national carriers or to cede sovereignty. Unwillingness to cede sovereignty by countries that have been independent for a relatively short period is perhaps understandable. Attempts to integrate regional trade in the form of the Pacific Island Countries Trade Agreement (PICTA) and the Melanesian Spearhead Group have been basically unsuccessful. As the recent "beef war," "kava war," and "biscuit war" illustrate, as soon as a local enterprise is threatened by imports from another Pacific country, the barriers go up.

The success of USP as a form of regional cooperation is not to say that it has been entirely free of difficulties. The economic growth performance of most of the Pacific countries has been poor for many years, and in these circumstances, government budgets are always under strain. This has meant that some countries have not paid their dues to the university on time. However, although some dues may not be paid for several years, no country has refused to pay the assessed dues.

Participation in a regional university has also been subject to some stress from pressures for countries to have their own universities. Samoa has created the National University of Samoa, which must lead to tension with respect to funding and support between the regional and national activities. Ministers in the Solomon Islands government have also expressed interest in forming a national university.

Perhaps a source of greater difficulty for the university in the long term is the frequency of coups in Fiji and the resulting disruption in the university's operations. As noted earlier, the 2000 coup caused significant disruption to the delivery of courses, almost to the point of the cancellation of a semester. The coup also led to the loss of a significant number of staff. As a result of the coup, some of the students remaining in Fiji during the summer break were recalled by their governments. As luck would have it, the coup was at the start of the summer break; by the end of the break, conditions in Fiji were seen as nonthreatening, but the start of the academic year was delayed by two weeks.

Political instability and civil unrest, which are not uncommon in some of the Pacific countries, plus frequent very damaging natural disasters, raise questions about the flexibility with which the university—and particularly USPNet—can continue to operate. One issue that the university will have to address is the building of capacity to operate USPNet from alternative sites in the event that the Suva hub is restricted in some way.

Telecommunications monopolies in the member countries have been a persistent problem throughout the development of USPNet. It is difficult to reconcile the desire for regional collaboration in tertiary education with the unwillingness of governments to provide low-cost telecommunications services for USPNet. This is a problem that has affected economic development in all areas of these Pacific countries and illustrates the enormous power of such monopolies, reinforced by governments' myopic view of the attractiveness of profits from the monopolies. In a few member countries, there have been recent moves to liberalize the telecommunications sector, with quite dramatic results in terms of lower prices and wider coverage (for example, in Internet and mobile services in Samoa—see chapter 9). Hopefully, liberalization of telecommunications will become much more widespread, and the education sector will be able to benefit along with all other economic activities.

The Future of Distance Flexible Learning

The university's strategic plan states that all university courses should be designed for flexible delivery by 2010. This requires a quantum increase in the use of DFL and poses several challenges: first, the learning environment; second, the capacity of the network; and third, ensuring flexibility in the telecoms network.

First, what is the best DFL learning environment? What is the best mix of media from compact disks (CDs), the Internet, audioconference, videoconference, and paper? There is also strong support from the regional campuses for some face-to-face lectures and tutorials to supplement the

DFL materials. Part of the issue is: How much of its resources should USP continue to put into paper-based courses? Most of the course materials are booklets that guide students step-by-step through the course and have not required access to a computer or the Internet. Developing this material has proved to be time consuming, and in many cases, it is already available in the world's best textbooks. And even here, the university needs to consider the use of open-source electronic textbooks, rather than paper textbooks. Printed materials quickly become obsolete, and the cost of transporting printed course materials to all of the locations is increasingly expensive because of the high shipping and air transport costs. The paper-based approach limits severely the level of interactivity with faculty members.

On the other hand, preparing DFL materials is not without problems. The Centre for Educational Development and Technology (CEDT) has the prime responsibility for supporting the development of DFL through its Distance and Flexible Learning Support Centre. The staff of the center develop courses with the academic staff members of the faculties. The system that the university has been using is very labor intensive. An academic staff member is assigned to work with the DFL experts to prepare the learning material. The academics are given relief from face-to-face teaching for one semester so that they have time to develop a course for DFL delivery. But there is not a strong incentive for the faculties to move onto online learning. They cannot afford to have an academic staff member take leave from teaching duties for one semester.

The second challenge is a network with the capacity to deliver DFL. This involves problems of telecoms capacity (bandwidth), getting to remote areas, and equipping students with laptops.

In some of the locations, bandwidth remains insufficient. A way to make progress may be to identify where entire courses can be offered online, such as the MBA program and other graduate diplomas, and support these locations with a substantial upgrade of the bandwidth. If USPNet is not able to provide the bandwidth, an option would be to purchase the bandwidth from a local Internet provider.

What priority should USP place upon delivery of its courses to people located in the many remote locations throughout the Pacific island countries? The continuing high rate of migration from these outlying areas to the major towns ranks high on the list of concerns of Pacific governments. Many of the university's DFL students are studying in remote rural locations, sometimes where there is no electricity. The current challenge is to focus on cost-effective ways to link with these locations.

To build communication systems with rural areas, USP will need to partner with the local telecom monopolies in each country and the Internet service providers. The Pacific has some interesting projects to take Internet services to rural communities, including the People First project in the Solomon Islands. There is scope for the most remote locations to have Internet access (including audio and video services) through cheap laptops operating on solar power, small satellite terminals (VSATs), and the development of Pacific-wide satellite coverage to provide Internet service to airline passengers. More USP centers in the rural areas will also be needed.

DFL (and a more paper-free environment) would be facilitated by providing a laptop to every DSL student at USP, with all the course materials loaded onto it or distributed on CDs and flash disks. This might mean purchasing 8,000–9,000 laptops. The One Laptop per Child (OLPC) Pacific initiative suggests that this objective is feasible. This initiative is being implemented by the South Pacific Commission (SPC), which proposes to distribute 100,000 laptops to children in rural and remote areas over the next three years. A U.S. nonprofit organization created by faculty members from the MIT Media Lab will design, manufacture, and distribute the laptops. The cost of each OLPC laptop, including a comprehensive set of software, is expected to be only US$150. But getting laptops serviced in rural locations could prove a problem.

The third challenge is finding the optimal way to build into USPNet the flexibility to continue operation in the event of major disruptions arising from natural disasters, civil unrest, or political decisions. Presently, the Suva campus is the major hub for USPNet. Building flexibility into the system will mean some duplication of equipment at one or more of the other campuses.

But there are also some promising opportunities to move DFL forward. First, there are good signs that Pacific governments are willing to throw off the shackles of the public and private telecommunications monopolies that have plagued the region for so long. This may lower costs for the university, including the high costs of access to satellite space. Second, there are promising technological developments. The cost of international telephone calls has become extremely cheap using VoIP services from Skype and similar providers. Satellite space is also becoming more available and more affordable as new satellites with Pacific footprints are launched and satellite communications technology is improved. Additional Pacific countries are also looking to access the Southern Cross optical-fiber cable that Fiji is already using. This will provide faster and cheaper Internet facilities.

Further progress in DFL faces some complex challenges. The alternatives and trade-offs need to be evaluated. A number of projects need to be coordinated; for example, the World Bank—initiated project to increase bandwidth to the regional campuses and to construct audiovisual classrooms, and the Japan-funded project to build facilities on the Suva campus for IT teaching and research. The current approach to planning DFL appears to be fragmented, with responsibilities divided across the university's ICT and DFL Support Centre and the faculties. Given the ever-rising expectations and the rapidly changing technology, against the backdrop of budgetary pressures and regulatory constraints, what is the best path down which USPNet should advance? It would appear that the development of USPNet needs an explicit strategic plan.

Lessons from the USPNet Experience

Our review of the history of USPNet has identified six lessons from the experience relevant for the design of future capacity development projects in the Pacific islands.

- *Strong, consistent leadership at the top of the organization* is needed to drive the project over the long term. The USPNet project has greatly benefited from having vice chancellors who have given it high priority for resources. They have provided a clear vision for the project and have been champions who were able to convince aid donors to fund the various stages of development.
- *A highly participatory approach to project design and implementation* builds commitment and support for the project by the stakeholders. For the USPNet project, senior management from the outset adopted consultative decision-making processes on project design issues, especially those related to the priorities of the users, and put in place a system to gain regular feedback on USPNet performance from the clients located across the 12 campuses. The campus directors are major clients of the educational services delivered through USPNet. They know what aspects of USPNet are working well for the student and staff users and what services are slow or of poor quality. A system that ensures regular feedback and consultation on the needs of the clients and the extent to which USPNet is meeting those needs is necessary to gain the full support and ownership of the project.

- *Participatory approaches to project planning, monitoring, and evaluation* are equally valuable, in the form of an accessible project-planning system that provides information to all stakeholders on the project development path. A challenge in complex projects such as USPNet is to keep all the stakeholders informed of the annual project work program, the schedule for completing technical upgrades and equipment installation, and the dates when enhanced services are scheduled to come on stream. Related challenges are the coordination of the inputs of various parties and prioritization of the needs of the clients for new educational services. The USPNet project experience has demonstrated that in the absence of a comprehensive project plan accessible to all parties, the consequent difficulty that client groups experience in tracking the progress of project implementation can impede coordination among the parties involved and delay progress. Although high-quality plans have been prepared for this project, not all parties have had easy access to the plans. Our discussions with the stakeholders indicate that there would be substantial benefits, in terms of maximizing the capacity development potential of the project, from distributing regular USPNet progress reports widely across the university community.
- *Retention of staff in key positions* is critical, especially in technicalareas that are responsible for the ICT development aspects of the project. For the USPNet project, key positions are the director of Information Technology Services, the director of the Centre for Educational Development and Technology, and the head of the Distance and Flexible Learning Support Centre. The project has been adversely affected by the recent resignation of the highly experienced director of Information Technology Services, plus the loss of other key staff members who have undertaken extensive staff development and training programs to enhance their ICT technical skills for USPNet.
- Realizing the full potential of the project requires *clarity as to the roles and responsibilities of those persons responsible for implementation.* Reaping the educational benefits of the USPNet project has been somewhat delayed by lack of a unified organizational structure for project management that coordinated the roles of the main groups that make the project successful: the academic staff members in the faculties; the 12 USP campus directors; and the Information Technology Services Division, the Centre for Educational Development and Technology, and the Distance and Flexible Learning Support Centre.

- It is important to *promote the vision of the project as a capacity development tool to a broader range of potential users.* The leaders of the USP-Net project need to invest time in marketing the potential capacity development benefits to be gained from full use of the project to such potential users as public and private sector organizations for staff training programs, Pacific island public service commissions for online and videoconference professional development courses, and civil society organizations for educational needs.

Conclusions

USPNet has played an important role in the capacity development of the member countries through its provision of communication and education services to USP students. There is potential for widening its capacity development role through extending its educational services to civil society organizations, public service training academies, national governments, other regional institutions, and private sector development organizations.

Not many other regions in the world are faced with the combination of difficulties encountered by education in the Pacific—minute economies, limited resources, remoteness, the huge number of tiny inhabited islands that make up some of the countries, and the frequency of natural disasters. However, many developing countries have remote, poor, tiny communities that are desperate for education. Meeting that demand without the people having to migrate is a challenge. With the rapid developments in IT, including in its cost, its speed, and its availability, facilities similar in form to USPNet may well be an important means of meeting that challenge.

Annex 7A. List of Interviewees Cited in the Case Study

Name	Affiliations
Rod Dixon	USP Campus Director, the Cook Islands
John Bonato	Acting Director, Centre for Educational Development and Technology, 2005–06
Jeff Born	Dean of the Faculty of Business and Economics
Jennifer Evans	Head, Distance and Flexible Learning Support Centre, at the Centre for Educational Development and Technology (CEDT)

Feue Tipu	Fellow of the Pacific Institute of Advanced Studies in Development and Governance and the Graduate School of Business
Sam Fonua	Deputy Director of the University's Information Technology Services
Robert Hogan	Senior Lecturer, Centre for Excellence in Learning and Teaching
Dr. Esther Williams	Deputy Vice-Chancellor and Acting Vice-Chancellor
Kisione Finau	Former Director, Information Technology Services
Mark Lewis	Director, Planning and Development

References

McCawley, Peter, David Henry, and Matthew Zurstrassen. 2002. *The Virtual Colombo Plan: Addressing the ICT Revolution*. AusAid and World Bank. unpan1.un.org/intradoc/groups/public/documents/APCITY/UNPAN 007799.pdf.

Morris, Charles, ed. 1966. *Report of the Higher Education Mission to the South Pacific*. London: HMSO (Her Majesty's Stationery Office).

Open Universities Australia. Web site: www.open.edu.au/wps/portal. (This is an organization set up by several leading Australian universities to provide degree programs solely by distance learning).

PIFS (Pacific Islands Forum Secretariat). 2005. *The Pacific Plan for Strengthening Regional Cooperation and Integration*. PIFS, Madang, Papua New Guinea. http://www.pacificplan.org/tiki-page.php?pageName=Pacific+Plan+Documents.

USP (University of the South Pacific). 1970. *Charter, Statutes, and Ordinances; Standing Orders of the Council*. www.usp.ac.fj/fileadmin/files/academic/pdo/digitised/CHARTER.pdf.

———. 1998. *Strategic Plan: Planning for the 4th Decade*. http://www.usp.ac.fj/index.php?id=757.

———. 2004. *A Regional University of Excellence: Weaving Past and Present for the Future*. USP Review Subcommittee of the Council. http://www.usp.ac.fj/index.php?id=4140.

———. 2005. *USP Strategic Plan 2006–2010*. http://www.usp.ac.fj/index.php?id=4359.

CHAPTER 8

From Monopoly to Competition: Reform of Samoa's Telecommunications Sector

Edgardo Favaro, Naomi Halewood, and Carlo Maria Rossotto

An island with a population of about 185,000 (World Bank 2007), where the fishing industry and subsistence farming still largely provide for livelihoods, poverty has never been a major issue in Samoa. Samoa has seen rapid growth in the past decade, as its gross national income (GNI) per capita, purchasing power parity adjusted (PPP), increased from US$3,590 in 1995 to US$5,820 in 2005 (World Bank 2007). Despite this relatively steady economy, however, the availability of telecommunications services has been extremely limited. Until 1996, the Post and Telecommunications Department (PTD) of the government of Samoa (GOS) provided all communications services (fixed-line, international, and postal) as a monopoly. The functions of regulation and production had not been separated, nor even recognized as separable. Telephone mainlines were at five per 100 people in 1996, and the market was characterized by high international call rates that were

Edgardo Favaro, Naomi Halewood, and Carlo Maria Rossotto are respectively Lead Economist, Operations Analyst and Senior Regulatory Economist at the World Bank.

cross-subsidizing local call prices. Limited service and high prices have had large consequences for the Samoans, many of whom have family members who have migrated abroad.

In the 1980s, sweeping changes in digital and mobile technology revolutionized telecommunications services worldwide. But, because the scope of the sector was so limited, Samoans were not sharing the spoils. The changes in the technology and their benefits were especially noticeable in Australia, New Zealand, and the United States, where there is a significant Samoan diaspora. This awareness helped build up momentum for change.

Since 1996, the GOS has made some key decisions that have dramatically changed the telecommunications market. In 1997, the GOS granted a 10-year exclusivity license to Telecom Samoa Cellular Ltd. (TSC), a joint venture between the GOS and Telecommunications New Zealand (TCNZ). TSC started operations in 1998, bringing into Samoa mobile communications based on analog technology. But results did not meet expectations: for the following five years, market penetration remained low, quality of services poor, and international phone rates high.

In 2007, Samoa is well on the way toward a competitive telecommunications market: market penetration has greatly increased, the range and quality of telecommunications services has expanded, and prices have fallen. What happened? In 2005, the GOS passed a new telecommunications act, introducing the principle of competition into the sector and creating the Office of the Regulator. In 2006, the GOS issued two licenses to operate mobile-phone technology based on Global System for Mobile Communication[1] (GSM) technology. TSC left the Samoa market, and two firms—a state-owned enterprise, SamoaTel, and a multinational company, Digicel—fiercely competed to attract new customers.

This case study tells the story of the transition from public monopoly to open competition in the Samoa telecommunications sector and identifies the challenges faced by the GOS today. It addresses questions such as these: What are the dos and don'ts for improving quality of telecommunications services in a small state? What challenges does the change in the industry open up? How does a small state face the high cost of regulatory units? What are the benefits and costs of telecommunications reform? What political economy factors should be taken into account?

Background

Box 8.1

The Country and Its Economy

Samoa is in the South Pacific Ocean, located midway between Hawaii and New Zealand. New Zealand occupied the German protectorate of Western Samoa during World War I. It continued to administer the islands, as a mandate and then as a trust territory until 1962 when the islands became the first Polynesian nation to reestablish independence in the 20th century. The country dropped the "Western" from its name in 1997.

The economy of Samoa has traditionally been dependent on development aid, family remittances from overseas, agriculture, and fishing. The country is vulnerable to devastating storms. Agriculture employs two-thirds of the labor force and furnishes 90 percent of the exports, featuring coconut cream, coconut oil, and copra. The fish catch declined during the El Niño of 2002–03, but returned to normal by mid-2005. The manufacturing sector mainly processes agricultural products. One factory in the Foreign Trade Zone employs 3,000 people to make automobile electrical harnesses for an assembly plant in Australia. Tourism is an expanding sector: tourism receipts account for about 60 percent of total exports, as about 100,000 tourists visited the islands in 2005.

The Samoan government has called for deregulation of the financial sector, encouragement of investment, and continued fiscal discipline, while at the same time protecting the environment. Observers point to the flexibility of the labor market as a basic strength for future economic advances. Foreign reserves are in a relatively healthy state, the external debt is stable, and inflation is low.

Sources: World Bank, Samoa Data and Statistics (http://go.worldbank.org/PCWKJRTLD0); CIA World Factbook (http://www.cia.gov/library/publications/the-world-factbook/print/ws.html); WHO Country Context (http://www.wpro.who.int/countries/sma/).

Telecommunications Worldwide and in the Pacific

In the past two decades, the proliferation of mobile telephony and the beginning of the Internet era completely transformed business in the telecommunications sector. The revolution in technology had also begun changing the widely held view that telecommunications was a natural monopoly; the view that the sector could operate and thrive under competition started to dominate in policy circles. It was now economically feasible for more than one company to operate in telecommunications.

Mobile-telephone service—the network for which it is relatively easy for a new company to roll out—made small nations an attractive potential new market for both foreign and home-grown companies.

Many governments around the world overhauled their telecommunications sectors to reflect these changes. By the late 1990s, there had been a decade of experience with deregulation in Australia, Chile, Singapore, New Zealand, the United Kingdom, and the United States. The U.S. experience had begun with the agreement that forced the breakup of AT&T in 1982.

With the new technology, the role of a telecommunications regulator had drastically changed: it became a watchdog responsible for ensuring that business decisions by one company did not affect the capacity of other companies to enter the market or provide services. Deregulation had also spread to South and Central America, to Eastern Europe, and to the Caribbean region. As a result, many countries around the developing world saw their telephone sectors opened to competition and, in many cases, state-owned enterprises privatized. Many witnessed an improvement in service fees, quality, and breadth of services.

Meanwhile, in the South Pacific region, telecommunications deregulation lagged behind the rest of the world. Monopolies prevailed in most countries, preserving low penetration rates. For instance, as of 2004, the median of fixed-line and mobile-phone subscribers per 1,000 people in the South Pacific was 155, whereas at the time, the median for small states was 706 and the median for ECTEL[2] countries was 757 (see table 8.1) (World Bank 2007). Similar differences existed in Internet penetration and the number of mobile phones per 1,000 people. In most countries, international phone rates were set well above cost, and the extra revenue cross-subsidized below-cost domestic rates. For instance, the median price of a three-minute call from the South Pacific to the United States was US$5.80, 2.25 times the median for small states and 4.3 times the median for larger states.[3]

As of 2004, the median telecommunications income share for the South Pacific was 4.4 percent, about the same median as for small states and 0.9 percentage points of the GDP higher than the median for larger states.

The higher share of telecommunications revenue in GDP in the region may be consistent with higher prices, higher quantity of services consumed, or both. Lower penetration rates suggest that the likely culprit is higher price of telecommunications services. What part of this higher price is the result of higher cost of production, because of geographic isolation and low population density, and what part is the result of less

Table 8.1. Telecommunications Indicators for South Pacific Ocean Countries

Country	Fixed-line and mobile-phone subscribers (per 1,000 people)	Mobile-phone subscribers (per 1,000 people)	Telecommunications revenue (% of GDP)	Internet users (per 1000 people)
Fiji	254	229	—	77
Marshall Islands	86	11	5	35
Micronesia, Fed. States of	240	128	5	127
Samoa	21	130	5	32
Solomon Islands	28	13	4	8
Tonga	—	161	—	29
Vanuatu	83	60	—	38

Source: World Bank 2007.
Note: The data correspond to 2005.
— = Negligible.

competition? After all, it is reasonable to assume that the cost of producing telecommunications services in Samoa must be more expensive than in densely populated areas such as Delhi, India, or São Paolo, Brazil, or in small states, like Cyprus, whose proximity to continental Europe facilitates access to modern infrastructure (for instance, submarine cable connections) not available for many countries in the South Pacific. A definitive answer as to exactly how much of the higher price can be attributed to geography and how much to a less competitive regulatory framework is not possible; nonetheless, it seems highly probable that the latter played an important part in delaying the penetration of mobile-phone technology in the South Pacific during the 1990s.

From Monopoly to Competition

Modernizing the Telecommunications Sector: The First Steps

The PTD was the sole provider in all market segments (fixed-line, international data and voice, and postal services) until 1996, when the GOS took the first step toward modernizing its telecommunications sector by opening up the mobile service segment to include a mobile operator (table 8.2). (It is easier to introduce competition in the mobile service segment, where entry costs are significantly lower because technological solutions are cheaper; whereas provision of fixed-line services requires large upfront investments into backbone infrastructure.) The GOS entered into an agreement with TCNZ to form a joint venture, Telecom Samoa Cellular Ltd. (TSC), in which the GOS would hold 10 percent and

Table 8.2. Chronology of Events, 1996–2006

Year	Event
1996	An exclusive license to provide cellular services based on Advanced Mobile Phone System (AMPS) standard awarded to a joint venture between the PTD (10%) and TCNZ–TSC (90%).
1997	Postal and Telecommunications Internet Act 1997.
	The agreement on basic telecommunications negotiated under the auspices of the World Trade Organization (WTO).
1999	The Postal and Telecommunications Services Act 1999 (1999 Act) mandated (a) the separation of policy functions provided by the Ministry of Posts and Telecommunications (articles 5–7), from postal and telecommunications operations, offered by a "Licensed Provider of Services" (articles 8–10); and (b) established the Spectrum Management Agency (SMA) to regulate and monitor the allocation of radio spectrum (articles 11–22).
	Samoa Communications Limited (SCL) (later to be renamed SamoaTel) created following the 1999 Act, which included transfer of assets of PTD according to terms and conditions specified by a license awarded June 30, 1999 (amended April 6, 2000). According to this license, SCL is authorized to provide, exclusively, all services previously carried out by PTD until July 1, 2009 .
	Internet segment opened to three private Internet service providers (ISPs).
2003	New mandate for the Ministry of Communications and Information Technology (MCIT), previously PTD, expanded to include a broader area of communications and information technology. The converging ICT sectors cover telecommunications, postal and logistics services, IT services, and broadcasting.
	TSC starts offering D-AMPS services, using the same band initially allocated to it for AMPS. MCIT notes that new services include those that are not in the initial scope of the license awarded to TSC (that is, text messaging and prepaid cards) and prohibits TSC from offering new digital services.
	SamoaTel starts offering wireless local loop (WLL) services using global system for mobile (GSM) technology in the northern part of Savai'i, increasing the number of rural subscribers. MCIT notes that while such services contribute to the development of telecommunications access in rural areas, they fall outside the scope of services initially included in the license and should be subject to specific authorization or license.
	MCIT approves new ISP services based in Savai'i—helping to bridge the domestic digital divide.
2004	Draft law and regulations designed to update, simplify, and harmonize the entire telecommunications regulatory framework.
2004	Cabinet adopts a two-part decision: (a) formalizing the government's commitment to creating a regulatory body separate and independent from MCIT and (b) creating a legally separate postal subsidiary of SamoaTel.
	Telecommunications Act 2004 and Ministry of Communications and Information Technology Act 2004.
	Samoa ICT policy developed by MCIT.

(continued)

Table 8.2. Chronology of Events, 1996–2006 *(continued)*

Year	Event
	TSC launches a digital network, offers new services (text messaging), and successfully deploys a prepaid platform. Mobile subscribers increase from 4,000 in 2003 to 13,100 in 2004.
2005	An interconnection agreement is reached between SamoaTel and TSC, improving the environment for entry into the sector.
	A settlement between the GOS and TSC clears up commercial and technical issues before the award of a competitive digital cellular license. The government discusses a possible agreement with TSC by which TSC would waive all rights to object to the issuance of this license, including any claims of exclusivity under the JVA and TSC license of 1997. In exchange, the government would issue a license to TSC to own and operate a network and provide services based on the GSM standard. The licenses would be issued at the same time and have the same rollout expansion of GSM mobile services.
2006	Award of digital cellular license to Digicel Samoa Ltd., a consortium led by Digicel (51%) and including CSL as a local partner (49%). Digicel Samoa Ltd. plans to cover 80% of Samoa's population in the first year. Attorney general consulted to determine whether Digicel Samoa has conducted anticompetitive practices in expanding customer base.
	John Morgan selected as regulator in the newly created Office of the Independent Regulator.
	MCIT notes that SamoaTel's Internet pricing structure is unbalanced and discourages the development of the Internet infrastructure outside the greater Apia region.
2007	SamoaTel is preparing for the launch of its GSM service and the international gateway for the GSM segment.

Source: Authors.

TCNZ 90 percent. Soon afterward, in 1997, TSC was awarded a 10-year exclusive license to provide mobile service based on the Advanced Mobile Phone System (AMPS) standard—an analog transmission technology that had been dominant in the 1980s—to complement the services offered by PTD. Because PTD owned the only international gateway exchange[4] in Samoa, TSC relied on PTD for its international traffic. The interconnection arrangement between the two operators was based on the sender-keeps-all (SKA) principle, under which PTD billed the customer that originated the call and kept the full revenues billed to the client.

The details of the joint venture and exclusive license were based on two key assumptions: First, Telecom New Zealand was given a large share of ownership because, during negotiations with the GOS, TCNZ agreed to build a mobile network that would cover at least 90 percent of the population. The topography of the two islands did not pose much difficulty for mobile network expansion, and therefore the GOS was aiming for full mobile service coverage in Samoa, including in the more remote areas of Savai'i. Second, the logic behind the 10-year exclusive license was to allow TSC to recover initial entry costs or investments into the new mobile networks. Five- to 10-year exclusive licenses were the norm in telecommunications in the 1970s and 1980s; but, as competition became the norm in developed and developing countries, policy makers became aware of the real opportunity cost of exclusivity. Long-term exclusive agreements bind a government to a specific provider, who thus has little incentive to adopt new technologies. This was exactly the case in Samoa. The TSC license awarded in 1997 was based on norms of another era in telecommunications history and was later to be considered overly generous. Furthermore, TSC was given free access to various GOS facilities, such as direct access to fixed-line equipment owned by PTD, on which TSC built its networks.

The GOS took the second step toward modernizing the sector in July 1999, when it enacted the Postal and Telecommunications Services Act (PTSA), which mandated the separation of policy function from service provision. Policy and regulatory functions became the responsibility of the newly created Ministry of Posts and Telecommunications (MPT), to be renamed the Ministry of Communications and Information Technology (MCIT) in 2003, when the telecommunications sector was thought to require a ministry of its own to address the technological changes (table 8.2). The 1999 Act also established a Spectrum Management Agency (SMA) to regulate and monitor the allocation of the radio spectrum. SMA in fact was never established in that avatar, but a three-person spectrum management team was transferred from MCIT to the Office of the Regulator in 2006 (see discussion on Office of the Regulator, below).

The creation of Samoa Communications Limited (SCL) followed the 1999 Act.[5] This included the full transfer of assets of PTD according to the terms and conditions specified in the license issued in 1999, which authorized SCL to provide, on an exclusive basis, all services (excluding mobile until July 2009) previously carried by PTD. In addition, the GOS opened the Internet market segment[6] to three private ISPs. Computer Services Ltd. has the largest market share and was initially a state-owned information technology (IT) company. The other accounts were divided between iPasifika and Lesa Telephone Service. In sum, the GOS had introduced mobile telephony and the Internet to Samoa.

Growing Discontent

The general public was happy to see mobile phones in the market. The GOS, however, started to feel uncomfortable when it noticed that mobile technology in New Zealand and Australia was much more advanced and realized that the contract had locked the GOS for 10 years into the network built by TSC. As Brenda Heather, attorney general at the time, observed: "Early on, many inside the GOS felt that having awarded an exclusivity license to TSC had been a mistake. Over time, they started to look for ways to undo the agreement between GOS and Telecom New Zealand. But it took five years, 2001–06, of laborious and often rough negotiation to disentangle the agreement. Along the way, the views of GOS about the role of competition in the sector changed substantially."

Some of the discomfort stemmed from the lack of checks and balances when processing the license for TSC. For instance, the 10-year exclusivity agreement that awarded the mobile-phone license to TSC had been approved without prior request of an opinion from the attorney general's office—a request that would have been routine in most countries before a decision of this nature. To make matters worse, the GOS soon began to notice that TSC profits were flowing right out of Samoa. "There was a perception, inside GOS, that the arrangements between TSC and Telecom New Zealand allowed de facto transfer of profits without ever making TSC accountable for those profits, paying dividends to GOS, or providing a reasonable quality of services" (Brenda Heather).

But what worried the GOS most was the poor quality of the mobile network infrastructure rolled out by Telecom New Zealand on behalf of TSC. In 1998, Telecom New Zealand had started adding bits and pieces of secondhand equipment it had brought over from New Zealand to the existing infrastructure to which it had free access under the contract—for instance, placing microwaves on broadcasting towers that were state-owned. Furthermore, TSC put very little effort into expanding market share and increasing subscribers. Most saw this as an evident violation of TSC's license, which called on TSC to cover a large area of the population; for its part, TSC argued that the GOS had failed to provide interconnection facilities that it was required to supply under the license and for this reason it had not expanded the network.

Dissatisfaction mounted as Samoans became increasingly aware of what was happening overseas and began to realize that their technology, based on the AMPS standard, was very old and limited. Vodafone was offering digital service in Fiji, and the difference was very visible for Samoan business people and government officials who traveled there. By 2000, many in the GOS acknowledged that they had made a mistake and needed to reassess their strategy for modernizing the telecommunications sector.

The Ministry of Finance (MOF) approached the World Bank in this context with two main objectives: to get out of the exclusivity contract and to improve telecommunications services. Tuilaepa Lupesoli'ai Sa'ilele Malielegaoi, the then Deputy Minister of Finance and current prime minister, had clear views about the need to introduce competition into the telecommunications sector. He appointed Hinauri Petana, the Chief Executive Officer (CEO) at the MOF, as the main counterpart to the World Bank mission.

Bridging Differences in Visions for Reform

Both the GOS and World Bank agreed that there was a need to reassess Samoa's sector strategy, but the two bodies had different perceptions of the priorities. "The World Bank took a holistic sector approach, which included broad sector reforms, while the GOS needed to find a way out of the agreement that had created TSC and the limitations those imposed on the expansion of the mobile market and the existence of commercial competition. I did not believe that the GOS was ready for the wholesale reforms proposed by the World Bank. In fact, I believe it is still not ready for some aspects of these reforms" (Brenda Heather). Some of the disagreements centered on acceptable governance standards. World Bank projects would require high standards of transparency with all public tenders under the project (anything more than $500 tala) to be reviewed by the Statutory Tenders Board—which, although established in 1998, was not formalized until 2001. Other frictions originated in what were perceived to be unreasonable and onerous requirements for projects, such as cumbersome forms and reports, many of which did not apply to a small state like Samoa.

Not all inside the GOS agreed with the proreform views spearheaded by the MOF. "Some in Government were proreform; others were not. TSC was also very aggressive; it played GOS agencies against each other and cajoled ministers and politicians to delay the decision" (Brenda Heather). The World Bank project was to operate under an authority with two minds.

After examining the condition of the sector, the World Bank team recommended that Samoa initiate reform of the sector to create a policy and regulatory environment adequate to encourage robust development in telecommunications services. The team emphasized that a sound regulatory environment was critical if the sector was to continue to improve and to keep up with fast-changing technological developments. To this end, the project aimed to (a) promote competition and private sector participation in the provision of telecommunications services and (b) strengthen the existing regulatory framework for ICT.

To promote competition and update mobile service provision, the project provided technical assistance for awarding the second mobile license for digital cellular services. This meant that the newer GSM standard would be introduced. GSM, a cellular network to which mobile phones connect by searching for cells in the immediate vicinity, remains the most popular standard for mobile phones in the world. GSM differs significantly from its predecessors, such as the AMPS technology, in that both signaling and speech channels are digital call quality. Further, the ubiquity of the GSM standard makes international roaming common between mobile service operators, enabling subscribers to use their phones in many parts of the world.

To strengthen the regulatory framework, the project would help select a regulatory advisor and establish a regulatory unit to enhance spectrum management function. "Spectrum management" is defined as all activities associated with fixing the use of the radio spectrum, including the enforcement of such rules as may be applicable. Such management is critical in ensuring that market players operate in a fair regulatory environment. Other items included assistance in amending the existing 1999 Act and a new sector policy paper to alert investors to the intention to accelerate reform. First and foremost in the team's recommendations, however, was that GOS consider issuing a digital cellular license, according to an international, open, and competitive tender, allowing a new mobile operator to build and/or lease long-distance infrastructure. The team suggested that both SCL, the incumbent, and Telecom New Zealand, the holder of the first cellular license, be precluded from bidding to establish effective competition.

The Threat of Competition and Market Improvements

Until 2002, the mobile telephony market remained stagnant (table 8.3), but as imminent competition loomed, visible changes could be seen in the behavior of the two existing operators (one a fixed-line operator, the other a mobile operator). The most significant movement happened within the state-owned incumbent, SCL. In 2001, MCIT brought in a new CEO from New Zealand to ready SCL for further competition and future privatization. When Mark Yeoman came to SCL, he found that the books had not been kept properly: "Whole years of accounting were missing!" Further, SCL heavily relied on termination fees of international calls, which meant that the local fixed-line prices were being subsidized by the high international call prices. SCL was nonetheless losing profits because it had not worked out the interconnection regime properly.

Table 8.3. Number of Mobile-Phone Subscribers per 1,000 People in Samoa

	1997	1998	1999	2000	2001	2002	2003	2004	2005
Mobile phone subscribers (per 1,000 people)	4	9	14	14	14	15	58	87	130

Source: World Bank (2007).

For example, it had not negotiated the termination rates with the United States, so that the termination fees at both the United States and the Samoa ends were 30 cents. Yeoman immediately acted on this and brought the fee down to 4 cents. Furthermore, 60 percent of SCL consisted of bad debt, and the waiting list—said to be 5,000—was most likely grossly underestimated.

The second change in behavior triggered by the threat of further competition was the diversification of the mobile service product line. According to Tua'imalo Asamu Ah Sam, the CEO of MCIT, "In 2003–04, it was visible that new services were being offered. The threat of competition forced the incumbent to extend coverage; for instance, they introduced prepaid cards and doubled services." TSC started offering D-AMPS[7] services, using the same band initially allocated to it for AMPS services; SamoaTel started offering WLL[8] services using GSM technology in the northern part of Savai'i. The D-AMPS offered by TSC also included text messaging and prepaid card services. At this point, however, MCIT started to question whether TSC's license allowed it to provide these new services.

Risk of Litigation and Delayed Reform
The World Bank technical assistance (TA) loan to the GOS was negotiated in 2002 and became effective in April 2003. Kolone Vaai of KVAConsult describes the World Bank project as "very helpful at the beginning of the reform because it pooled expertise that was not there before and gave confidence to the government in the steps it was taking." However, Telecom New Zealand, recognizing the threat to its operations posed by reform and the introduction of competition in the mobile segment, expressed to the GOS its intention to sue on the grounds that the original license had unfairly restricted it from being able to provide services other than those based on the AMPS standard. TSC, for its part, lacking experience in operating GSM networks, was well aware that it would not be able to compete with an experienced foreign operator.

MCIT determined that the new services offered by TSC (that is, text messaging and prepaid cards) were not in the initial scope of the exclusivity license and prohibited TSC from offering new digital services. Because the exclusivity license was only for the AMPS technology, the GOS argued that it had the right to open up the market for GSM technology. In rebuttal, Telecom New Zealand argued that the exclusivity license extended to all mobile-phone technologies. Brenda Heather, who was attorney general at the time, says, "The matter of contention was how cellular services were defined. We [the GOS] took the view that the exclusivity of TSC was restricted to analog technology within the range of kilohertz specified in the license. However, there were threats of litigation. The problem with litigation was that it would have de facto delayed the opening of the market." Her opinion was that even if the GOS decided to go to court, it would be most likely a one-to-nothing scenario in which Telecom New Zealand would either win immediately, or in five years time, which would considerably slow sector reform and cost GOS a great deal in the resulting delay and uncertainty.

The GOS opted to negotiate. The World Bank team advised the GOS that regardless of the way the license had been awarded, it was a valid legal document that the GOS needed to honor. Eventually, the GOS reached an agreement (deed of settlement) in which TSC accepted the government's view and in return was awarded a license to provide mobile-phone services based on GSM technology. Granting a GSM license to TSC was an important concession. Without it, TSC's business in Samoa would have been considerably endangered by competition from a new mobile operator providing a superior and more consumer-friendly technology.

The Telecommunications Act of 2005

Under the World Bank TA project, consultants were hired to draft the Telecommunications Act of 2005 (hereafter, Act of 2005), which would provide a framework for sector reform. The Act of 2005 (box 8.2) is based on principles that have been used by many countries pursuing telecommunications sector reform; they include (a) relying as much as possible on market forces, such as competition and private sector investment; (b) establishing an independent regulator responsible for defining clear market rules; and (c) introducing a modern and procompetitive regulatory framework in all main areas of sector regulation (interconnection spectrum management, numbering, licensing, and others). The Telecommunications Act of 2005 establishes the objectives of the reform and the main principles of the new regime; for instance, the role of competition in promoting efficient provision of telecom services. In the opinion of John Morgan, Office of the Regulator, "Samoa has a good

Box 8.2

Objectives of the Telecommunications Act of 2005

- Facilitate the development of, and promote universal access to, telecommunications
- Promote efficient and reliable provision of telecom services, relying as much as possible on market forces such as competition and private sector investment
- Promote the introduction of advanced and innovative information communication technologies to meet the needs of the people
- Establish a framework for control of anticompetitive conduct in the telecom sector
- Promote efficient interconnection arrangements among service providers
- Promote the interest of consumers
- Define and clarify the institutional framework for policy development and regulation of the telecom sector, as well as separation of government policy and regulatory functions from those of providing services
- Promote efficient management and use of the radio spectrum and other scarce resources
- Establish a fair, objective, and transparent licensing regime for service providers
- Establish an efficient approval regime for telecom equipment
- Establish measures to enforce the implementation of the Act of 2005

Source: Telecommunications Act of 2005. http://www.parliament.gov.ws /documents/acts/
TELECOMMUNICATIONS_ACT_2005_-_Eng.pdf

Telecom Act on which to base liberalization of the telecom market. It is vitally important to clearly establish the legal guidelines and principles from the outset, or the Regulator would not have a firm basis on which to implement regulatory procedures."

In general, there is consensus that the Act of 2005 provided a good shell to promote competition in telecommunications, but there are some reservations about its scope, its suitability to local conditions, and the fact that it was rushed in the final stages, which did not allow adequate consultation. The current Attorney General's Office is of the opinion that the drafting of the law required more consultations with the GOS: the act provided a standard framework that did not take into account adequately the small size of the Samoan market and the local legal and parliamentary context. Several amendments have since been made to tailor the regulatory and policy framework to Samoa's context.

An Independent Regulator for a Small State

Establishing an independent regulatory authority is a major undertaking. It is an institution that is costly to run and requires a team with both legal and technical expertise. Currently, larger markets in the Pacific such as Fiji and Tonga are going about liberalization without an independent regulator. In the 1980s, the GOS was involved in discussions with other Pacific islands about setting up a regional or subregional regulator. There was little progress, because not all within the GOS were convinced that a small state like Samoa would be able to make full use of the functions of a regulatory authority. Also, the climate of opinion changed from a disposition toward regionalism among Pacific islanders in the 1980s to more nationalistic tendencies in the 1990s. According to interviewees, in comparison with the Organization of Eastern Caribbean States (OECS) experience (see the case study on the Eastern Caribbean Telecommunications Authority), it would be much harder to set up a regional regulatory authority in the Pacific, where the islands are further apart and there is greater diversity among its people: the Pacific islands include three different ethnic groups, multiple languages, and disparate colonial experiences.

The structure of the regulatory authority in the Samoan context, first discussed under the Asian Development Bank TA project, envisioned a regulatory authority that would cover all utilities. The GOS acknowledged that an independent body to manage the utilities market will become more and more essential for Samoa and decided that the telecommunications sector, entering the reform process, was ripe enough for the introduction of a regulator. The Act of 2005 established the Office of the Regulator (OR) as a separate entity within the GOS. Telecommunications was intentionally left out of the title of the institution in the expectation that the authority would eventually cover other utility markets. The OR is responsible for advising government on telecom policy matters and for the administration of the new regulatory regime: granting of licenses, enforcing the provisions of the Act of 2005, and so forth (box 8.3). The regulator is appointed by the head of state. The regulator may be removed from office only on the basis of conviction of an offense, bankruptcy, being deemed unfit to perform his or her duties by a medical practitioner, or breach of the code of conduct set forth in the Public Service Act of 2004. Appeals of an order of the regulator may be made only to the Supreme Court, which may declare the order to be lawful or unlawful and/or remit the order to the regulator for further determination, in accordance with any determination made by the court. During the current fiscal year, the OR is financed through the MCIT budget.

Box 8.3

Responsibilities, Functions, and Powers of the OR

- Advise the minister on policy for the telecom sector.
- Implement the legal and regulatory framework for the telecom sector.
- Issue individual and class licenses and monitor compliance of these licenses.
- Amend or revoke licenses, in accordance with the Act of 2005.
- Define network terminating points, if required, for the proper interpretation and administration of the Act of 2005, the regulations, and the rules.
- Prescribe procedures for the approval of telecom equipment for attachment to telecom networks of Samoa.
- Establish a radio spectrum plan and manage radio spectrum allocated to the telecom sector.
- Regulate interconnection among networks of different service providers.
- Establish and manage a number plan and assign numbers to service providers.
- Resolve disputes between service providers and between customers and service providers.
- Institute and maintain appropriate measures for the purpose of preventing dominant telecom service providers from engaging in anticompetitive practices.
- Maintain records of licenses and license applications, equipment approvals and applications, and interconnection agreements.
- Make rules for such matters as are contemplated by, or necessary for, giving full effect to the provisions of the Act of 2005 and for the due administration thereof of the regulator.
- Investigate complaints against licensees or other service providers, and conduct such other investigations as the Regulator deems necessary to ensure compliance with the Act of 2005, a regulation, rule, or order.
- In exercising the regulator's power and performing duties under the Act of 2005, a regulation, or a rule, determine any question of law or fact and despite any other law, the regulator's determination on a question of fact is binding and conclusive for all purposes, including, but not limited to, any proceedings in court, tribunal, or other adjudicative body.
- Take such other actions as are reasonably required to carry out the Act of 2005, the regulation, and the rules, and to perform such other responsibilities, functions, and power conferred on the regulator under any other law.

Source: Telecommunications Act of 2005. http://www.parliament.gov.ws/documents/acts/ TELECOM-MUNICATIONS_ACT_2005_-_Eng.pdf

Commencing from the 2007–08 fiscal year, the OR will be financed through telecom and radio spectrum license fees and operate under a separate budget.

Several factors influenced the decision to set up the office outside the ministry responsible for telecom policy (MCIT). MCIT is the descendent of PTD, a department responsible for policy making when the provision of services was separated from the sector policy function (table 8.2). The separation of policy and service delivery functions in 1999 had been a step into modernization, but MCIT's ability to implement policy was still very weak, especially in areas where new demands were being created as a result of rapid technological change. "The old Post Office Department did not translate well to the world of mobile phones, computers, and advanced technology, and there have been the inevitable struggles to 'catch up' with the advances. We had a typical old-style English bureaucracy able to support a provider of services; but at that time, we did not have any capacity to make policy in relation to the extent and the rapidity of the telephony and technology advances. Also, times had changed, and the consumer in Samoa was being increasingly exposed to what other countries were experiencing, through the media, films, and television" (Brenda Heather).

The decision to create an independent regulatory office outside MCIT met initial resistance—after all, it stripped MCIT of part of its power—but after a while, MCIT, recognizing that it lacked the requisite technical and financial analysis skills, fell in line with the strategy. Furthermore, the decision to make the OR independent of the ministry avoided the imputation that it might be biased in its policy stands.

The OR is largely independent of government, but does work closely with the minister of MCIT in relation to policy issues involving licensing requirements. The Rules on Licensing Telecommunication Services (established in March 2006) provide MCIT with the option of establishing policy in regard to the number of telecom licenses that may be issued and any restrictions that should be placed on those licenses. This practice plays an important part in maintaining a balance between policy and enforcement, with the minister of MCIT, as an elected official, being responsible for establishing general licensing and other policies that affect the public while the regulator must independently implement and enforce the provisions of the Act of 2005 and any rules or regulations made under the act.

This proximity often implies that the OR has to play a delicate balancing act to avoid losing independence in its decisions or being drawn into decisions that would be more appropriately kept under the jurisdiction of MCIT. For instance, SamoaTel has monopoly rights to carry all international traffic originated in fixed lines until 2009. "The Telecom Act is very clear about what is the road ahead, but the government has not yet agreed on what the policy will be. MCIT is currently reviewing validity of continuing these restrictions as part of the government policy process and is expected to establish firm policy in this area shortly" (John Morgan).

The OR lacks skilled human resources to staff its broad responsibilities. John Morgan, an experienced engineer from Canada with technical knowledge and vast experience in the field, has the respect of other government officials, especially at MCIT, and of the management of Digicel and SamoaTel. Even so, it is impossible to think that he can fulfill the responsibilities assigned to the OR by the Act of 2005 without help. As of March 2007, the OR is organized into two operation divisions: the Spectrum Management and Technical Services Division, with three staff who need additional training and experience, and the Regulatory and Consumer Service Division (currently unstaffed). The two operating divisions are supported by a Central Support Unit, which provides accounting and administrative support, and a legal analyst.

The GOS is fully aware that low capacity of the OR is the Achilles' heel of the reform. "I see difficulties to sustain a technically able Office of the Regulator. We will probably have to depend on an expatriate for several years," said Hinauri Petana, who is ready to consider other solutions, but realistic about their viability: "In the region, we have talked about sharing regulators and pooling scarce resources. But there is great diversity within the Pacific islands: we are three different ethnic groups; we have various colonial experiences and many languages. All these differences are an obstacle for this solution to crystallize now."[9]

Outsourcing regulatory advice may be another possibility. Under this solution, the GOS would maintain its executive capacity and rely on technical advice contracted from outside the public sector, and probably outside Samoa. "For us technicians, outsourcing would not be a problem, but for politicians, it is a problem for the time being. It is all a process of breaking down barriers" (Hinauri Petana). The current capacity weaknesses may be exacerbated or ameliorated, depending on the regulatory strategy followed in the future by the regulator. For instance, the regulator has currently contracted out a study that will provide a methodology to determine interconnection costs and set interconnection fees. Such a strategy to deal with interconnection fees may be complemented by a flexible policy regarding the building of infrastructure (so as to ensure that a disagreement between the incumbent and a new company may be solved, at worst, by the newcomer building parallel physical infrastructure, rather than paying an unreasonable right of passage).

Today, the limited capacity of the OR results in delays in adopting decisions. Last November, SamoaTel complained to the OR and to the Office of Commerce, Industry, and Labor that Digicel was practicing anticompetitive tactics. "Digicel phones could not be unlocked. Subscribers had to sign forms saying that Digicel would be their exclusive provider for 12 months. This was done so that Digicel could lock in TSC's 30,000 subscribers (both postpaid and prepaid), which it had acquired from TSC. A decision has not yet been made" (Brenda Heather). Another problem is interconnection fees, and still another problem is termination costs for international phone calls. Digicel has complained that SamoaTel keeps collecting all the termination costs for outgoing international calls. "Decisions to correct these regulatory issues must be timely and robust, or else the market will be stifled" (Brenda Heather).

Award of the Second Mobile License: Real Competition

In April 2006, the GOS authorized two GSM licenses. The first was awarded to Digicel through a tender process and then "unexpectedly for us, [Digicel] bought out TSC rather than exercise its right. The government was then advised to sell its minority holding in TSC. Also part of the settlement was that SamoaTel obtained a cellular license. As a result of this, we now have two providers" (Tua'imalo Asamu Ah Sam).

The results of just a few months of competition in mobile-phone services are already visible: an increase in the number of mobile-phone subscribers and improvements in coverage (table 8.4). "There are around 60,000 telephone subscribers [up from 27,000 six months ago], and coverage has greatly improved. It has become easier to communicate with rural areas, with coverage available in many remote areas of Upolu and Savai'i" (John Morgan).

Table 8.4. Telecommunications Indicators Pre- and Postreform

	March 2006	March 2007
Mobile-phone subscribers	22,000	60,000
Price of a 3-minute call to the United States	$4 tala per minute	$1.79 tala per minute

Source: Samoa: Office of the Regulator.

The benefits from competition are also visible in the international phone market. International phone rates have fallen rapidly following the opening of the market (table 8.4). "SamoaTel cut international phone rates by 50 percent one year before the advent of mobile competition. And simultaneously with the launch of Digicel, it cut international rates a further 20 percent" (Mike Johnstone, CEO, SamoaTel). Before the reform, the cost of an international three-minute call to the United States was around US$3.90, while the cost of a local call was US$0.04 per minute; as a result, around 40 percent of revenues from telephony services came from international outbound calls. After the reform, the importance of international phone rates in the revenue equation of telecom changed significantly. "It is still very high: 50 percent of our revenue comes from inbound and outbound international phone-call services, inclusive of voice and data. But we expect a 27 percent drop in revenue as Digicel uses its own gateway for its international mobile traffic" (Johnstone).

"The price of international phone calls will continue to fall with the advent of alternative technologies: voice over internet protocol (VoIP), SKYPE, and so forth. This change could be further exasperated if Digicel were to get the right in the short term to terminate fixed traffic because they would have access to all international inbound revenues without having to pay any local infrastructure costs to terminate calls on the fixed network, other than an interconnection fee" (Johnstone). This is especially so "if their [Digicel's] license is extended to voice and to carry the fixed-line traffic. Then Digicel would have dominance in the inbound international market for minimal additional cost, other than having to pay for an interconnect fee" (Johnstone).

For others, this view appears unrealistic: "Once you opened the international market to competition by awarding a license to Digicel and by introducing additional international operators, the importance of revenue originated in international phone was doomed. It was just a matter of time. Either SamoaTel continues cutting prices, or it will lose all its international phone traffic, which begs the question: Is it realistic for the company's strategy to be based on maintaining this revenue? What is killing them is not regulation, but technology," remarked a market observer.

There is clearly much room for improvement: "Short Message Service (SMS)[10] had not worked well, but we finally got it going last week. Although the two operators have said they would be activating General Packet Radio Service (GPRS)[11] in the first quarter of 2007, neither has done so yet. They may be having technical difficulties, including lack of technical staff" (John Morgan).

Changes in the quality and range of Internet services are less noticeable. There are three ISPs who buy an asymmetric digital subscriber line (ADSL)[12] connection from SamoaTel, and ISPs are not allowed to resell SamoaTel's broadband. These constraints keep costs high and limit growth and the range of services offered; they are also the root of critiques of SamoaTel, who: "should not be both the wholesaler and retailer. . . . ISPs can go under with the high prices SamoaTel is currently charging" (an ISP manager). "Businesses would like backup options to current services, but prices are high at about $2,500 tala per month, $1,000 tala for a leased line" (a business Internet client).

The main constraint to Internet services growth is poor physical infrastructure and limited bandwidth. In the absence of submarine cable connection, Samoa depends on satellite connection, which is more expensive and less reliable. "We have to physically bring in the last mile connection if we want to connect to the existing backbone infrastructure. Also, WiFi is insufficient for the demands that they are getting from some of their clients" (an ISP manager).

The opening of the telecom market has benefited those with sought-after telecom technical skills. "The new operator [Digicel] has been offering incentives for SamoaTel's executives to jump ship. So far, three executives from SamoaTel, including the CEO, have moved to SamoaTel" (a market observer).

Pending Issues

The privatization of SamoaTel—The government's privatization planning has been going on for a decade. According to the initial plan, some state-owned companies were scheduled to be privatized in the short term, and others in the medium and long terms. SamoaTel is projected to be sold in the long term (three to five years). In the interim, the GOS has contracted a study to assess obligations to the GOS arising from contingent liabilities and redundancy packages; study feasibility of introducing competition in fixed-line services; and assess different modes of privatization and options regarding postal operations.

The idea of privatizing SamoaTel "has been present since the beginning, but it has taken more speed now" (Kolone Vaai, KVAConsult). But there are doubts about the implications of privatizing the company, and there is resistance. In part, resistance is grounded in the perception that "if privatization happens, government will have no role in telecommunications service provision and will collect no dividends" (an MCIT manager). This opinion is shared by others in the Samoan civil service and in political circles, where SamoaTel is seen as a profitable government investment in spite of the fact that its contributions to the treasury were negligible over the past decade.

Hinauri Petana has no doubts about the importance of the privatization of SamoaTel for opening up competition in the telecom market. "It is very important to privatize SamoaTel. Having said that, I think we are not yet there. There is a need to establish the rules, such as whether we go about privatizing SamoaTel with or without the postal component or with or without the exclusivity to fixed lines. The issue is not how much money the GOS can get out of SamoaTel; it is about allowing time for SamoaTel to build itself so that it is a viable contender for competition. This will ensure competition in the sector." In this view, unless SamoaTel becomes a contender, the aggressive strategy of Digicel in the telecom market may lead to another monopoly situation.

The management of SamoaTel also thinks that privatization "needs to be thought through, as there are a number of options. I personally believe that the company should be privatized when the value is at its optimum. For this value to be attained, privatization should happen in the short term, as this would achieve the highest profitability for the government. The alternative of delaying the privatization date and simultaneously deregulating the market will leave SamoaTel with a steadily declining share that cannot be fully recovered from other revenue streams, such as mobile" (Mike Johnstone).

Deregulation—SamoaTel has a monopoly for fixed-line services and a partial monopoly in international phone traffic: it has the exclusive right to carry fixed-line-originated traffic and data until 2009. Digicel has its own international gateway for voice and data for its customers only. The government may accelerate the reform and open the market to competition faster, but so far it has been shy of adopting the decision.

Submarine cable infrastructure—The absence of a submarine cable connection is a major constraint. A submarine cable would provide access to high-speed backbone connectivity. It would also add redundancy, which is a major consideration in a small state like Samoa. Several solutions are under study: one possibility is to link Samoa to American Samoa and Hawaii, which would then provide access to the Southern Cross. Submarine cables are being discussed as a real option, and the government is looking at the possibility of using Telecom New Zealand's old fiber-optic cable to link Samoa to American Samoa (the U.S. territory) and New Zealand. A submarine cable to American Samoa will then link Samoa to Hawaii, giving Samoa access to the lowest rates in the world.

What Is the Value of the Reform?

The standard economic approach to assess the value of Samoa's telecom reform is to measure the change in consumer surplus as a result of the opening of the market to competition. Consumer surplus is the excess between consumer's willingness to pay and market price. A lower bound to the gain to consumers as a result of the reform is given by equation (8.1):[13]

$$\Delta W = (p_b - p_a) Q_b + \frac{(p_b - p_a)(Q_a - Q_b)}{2},$$
(8.1)

where
ΔW = the change in consumer surplus after the reform,
Q_i = telecom services consumed before (Q_b) and after (Q_a) the reform,
P_b = the prereform price, and
P_a = the postreform price.

The gain has two components: The first component is the difference in price of services times the quantity consumed before the reform. The second component is a function of the change in prices (pre- and post-reform) times the change in quantities (pre- and postreform).

Equation (8.1) may be simplified further (after some algebra) to

$$\Delta W = \left[\frac{\Delta p}{p} \right] S_b + \left(\frac{1}{2} \right) \left[\frac{\Delta p}{p} \right]^2 \eta S_b,$$
(8.2)

where

$$\frac{\Delta p}{p} = \frac{p_b - p_a}{p_b},$$

η = the price elasticity of demand for telecom services, and
S_b = the income share of telecom services.

Table 8.5 presents a back-of-the-envelope calculation of the gain in consumer surplus resulting from the reform. The first column presents a

Table 8.5. Value of the Reform

Assumptions	$[\Delta p/p]S_b$	Area F $(1/2)[\Delta p/p]^2 \eta S_b$	Total ΔW
$[\Delta p/p] = 0.2$ $\eta = 0.28$ $S_b = 0.0422$	0.8 percent of GDP	0.2 percent of GDP	0.9 percent of GDP
$[\Delta p/p] = 0.6$ $\eta = 0.50$ $S_b = 0.0422l$	2.5 percent of GDP	0.4 percent of GDP	2.9 percent of GDP

Sources: World Bank (2007); own estimations (see annex 8B).
Note: The parameters used were estimated in the demand equations presented in table 9B.1 and/or obtained from ITU (2007).

range for each of the parameters underlying the calculation. The last column presents a range for the welfare gain between 0.9 and 2.9 percent of GDP.

A consumer benefit in the range of 0.9 to 2.9 percent of GDP is not to be underestimated, especially if it is a gain that will accrue annually forever. Even if the estimate is imprecise, it is conservative: first, it was obtained using the lower values for each of the parameters. Second, the calculation ignored the gain in producer's surplus resulting from the reform. Finally, the calculation did not take into account the impact of the reform on activities whose fixed costs were high enough to make them not profitable before the reform, but that become profitable afterward (Goolsbee 2006). User comments such as, "Accessing the Internet through my mobile phone will help me set up a fund-raising Web site for a diabetes awareness program I am working on" (a yoga private trainer), suggest that the importance of these activities may be much higher than is often anticipated—and hence the benefits of reform much higher than assessed at the beginning of the reform.

Conclusions

The award of a 10-year monopoly on mobile-phone services to TSC was a mistake. The decision brought cellular phones to Samoa, but the quantity and quality of the services were always poor. Neither the incumbent nor TSC had incentives to innovate.

The cost of the mistake was a five- to six-year delay in the introduction of modern mobile services in the country. Using the estimates of the preceding section of the paper, the accumulated cost of the mistake was at a minimum in the range of 4–5 percent of GDP!

The main departure from earlier telecom policy adopted by the GOS was the gradual recognition of the importance of a competitive framework in improving the quality and quantity of the services. Had the government defined the problem of Samoa as a "bad contract" between the state-owned enterprise and TCNZ, it would have focused on ending the "bad contract," rather than on fostering competition. By adopting a competitive framework, the GOS created incentives to expand and improve the quality of services and, at the same time, got out of the "bad contract." In fact, just the threat of competition brought results: for instance, the introduction of D-AMPS and WLL services in 2003–04 and the fall in international phone rates that preceded the opening of a second international gateway in 2006.

The views of agencies within the GOS as to the telecom sector were not always homogeneous. While smoothing these differences sometimes resulted in exasperating delays, the process of reaching consensus was important for passing the Telecommunications Act of 2005.

The role of the World Bank in supporting the GOS and facilitating the learning process cannot be overstated. Along the way, the Bank also helped improve governance. Brenda Heather contends, "The influence of the Bank has been enormous: the Bank is responsible for encouraging the operation of a robust Tender Board and a transparent tender process to undertake all public procurement. . . . The changes resulting in the way the government has decided to do business are huge."

Building a regulatory office for a country of the size of Samoa takes time and is expensive. Alternatives such as the Eastern Caribbean Telecom Authority (the outsourcing of advisory services in telecom) may be options to consider in future stages of the reform process.

Annex 8A. List of Interviewees Cited in the Case Study

Name	Affiliations
Tua'imalo Asamu Ah Sam	CEO, MCIT
Brenda Heather	Former Attorney General
Mike Johnstone	CEO, SamoaTel
Kolone Vaai	KVAConsult
John Morgan	Office of the Regulator
Hinauri Petana	CEO, Ministry of Finance
Mark Yeoman	Former CEO, SamoaTel

Annex 8B. Value of the Telecom Reform

The derivation of the consumer's gain in the main text was based on the Marshallian demand for telecom services. Consumer surplus is approximated as the area under the Marshallian demand curve in between the change in quantities and prices: $\Delta Q \Delta p/2$ where ΔQ is the change in quantity consumed (Q_b to Q_a) when prices change Δp (from p_b to p_a).[14] $\Delta Q \Delta p/2$, may be written as $(1/2)[\Delta p/p]^2 \eta S_b$, where η is the price elasticity of demand and S_b is the income share of telecom. For a new good, the price p_b is the price at which the virtual demand for Q equals zero.

To proceed with the calculation, it is necessary to take several shortcuts. There is no time series or cross-section data to estimate a demand for mobile services based on Samoa telephone information. To bypass this problem, we estimated a demand for phone services based on a cross-section of 120 countries for which data are available.

Second, we used the number of fixed-line and mobile-phone subscribers per 1,000 inhabitants as the dependent variable, rather than the number of mobile-phone subscribers per 1,000. The reason is that the price elasticity of demand when we use mobile-phone subscribers as the dependent variable is –1 (standard deviation 0.19), which was considered too high.

Third, we used as a measure of price "the price of a three-minute phone call to the USA." The reason is that this is the only price variable for which there is a reasonable sample size to base the estimation on.

The statistical results are reported in table 8B.1. The price elasticity of demand (–0.28) is statistically significant. (All the data are from World Bank [2007].)

Table 8B.1. The Demand for Telecom Services

	Estimate	Standard deviation
Constant	–5.43	0.76
Price elasticity	–0.28	0.10
Income elasticity	1.24	0.07
Telecom revenue share	0.0422	n.a.
Change in price (in %)	0.2	n.a.
Annual consumer gain (as % of GDP	0.009	n.a.
R squared	0.86	n.a.

Source: Authors.
n.a. = not applicable.

Annex 8C. Definition of Series Used in the Statistical Calculations

Series: FIXED: Fixed-line and mobile-phone subscribers (per 1,000 people)

"Fixed lines" are telephone mainlines connecting a customer's equipment to the public switched telephone network. "Mobile-phone subscribers" refer to users of portable telephones subscribing to an automatic public mobile-telephone service using cellular technology that provides access to the public switched telephone network.

Series: GDP: GDP per capita, PPP (current international $)

"GDP per capita based on purchasing power parity (PPP)" is gross domestic product converted to international dollars, using purchasing power parity rates. An international dollar has the same purchasing power over GDP as the U.S. dollar has in the United States. GDP at purchaser's prices is the sum of gross value added by all resident producers in the economy plus any product taxes and minus any subsidies not included in the value of the products. It is calculated without making deductions for depreciation of fabricated assets or for depletion and degradation of natural resources. Data are in current international dollars.

Series: INTER: Internet users (per 1,000 people)

"Internet users" are people with access to the worldwide network.

Series: MOBILE: Mobile-phone subscribers (per 1,000 people)

"Mobile-phone subscribers" are subscribers to a public mobile-telephone service using cellular technology.

Series: PFIXED: Price basket for residential fixed line (US$ per month)

"Price basket for residential fixed line" is calculated as one-fifth of the installation charge, the monthly subscription charge, and the cost of local calls (15 peak and 15 off-peak calls of three minutes each).

Series: STEL: Telecommunications revenue (percent of GDP)

"Telecommunications revenue" is the revenue from the provision of telecommunications services such as fixed-line, mobile, and data.

Notes

1. For a technical definition, see http://www.mobiledia.com/glossary/page3.html.

2. "ECTEL" refers to countries under the Eastern Caribbean Telecom Authority: Dominica, Grenada, St. Lucia, St. Kitts and Nevis, and St. Vincent and the Grenadines.

3. Statements such as "the median price of . . . for the South Pacific" refer to the countries presented in the table, rather than to the region as a whole.

4. An international gateway exchange is a telephone switch that forms the gateway between a national telephone network and one or more other international gateway exchanges, thus providing cross-border connectivity.

5. At the time, the name of the state-owned company was Samoa Communications Ltd.; in 2003, the company changed its name to "SamoaTel." To avoid confusion, we always refer to the company by the latter name.

6. Most of the Internet services offered are currently dial-up services. There are some leased lines to the GOS and enterprises; however, customers have to physically bring in the last-mile connection themselves if they want to connect to the existing backbone infrastructure.

7. D-AMPS, or Digital AMPS, are second-generation (2G) mobile-phone systems.

8. WLL, or Wireless Local Loop, is the use of a wireless communication means as the last-mile connection for the delivery of telephone and broadband services.

9. See chapter 6 regarding the possibility of a regional agreement pooling resources from small countries into a regional office, in the style of the Eastern Caribbean Telecommunications Authority.

10. SMS, or Short Message Service, which permits sending short text messages between phones and computers.

11. GPRS, or General Packet Radio Service, provides moderate-speed data transfer. It is available to users of GSM and some mobile phones.

12. ADSL, is a technology that enables faster data transmission over copper telephone lines than previously achived by common models.

13. The formula assumes that the demand for telephones is linear in prices. (See annex 8B for a detailed explanation of the calculations.)

14. To simplify the calculation, we assume linear demand functions.

References

Goolsbee, Austan. 2006. "The Value of Broadband and the Deadweight Loss of Taxing New Technology." *Contributions to Economic Analysis & Policy* 5 (1): 1505. http://faculty.chicagogsb.edu/austan.goolsbee/research/broadb.pdf.

Samoa, Government of. 2005. "Telecommunications Act of 2005." http://www.parliament.gov.ws/documents/acts/TELECOMMUNICATIONS_ACT_2005_-_Eng.pdf.

ITU (International Telecommunication Union). 2007. Publications Web page. http://www.itu.int/publications/default.aspx.

World Bank. 2007. *World Development Indicators*. Washington, DC: World Bank.

CHAPTER 9

Exploiting Tender Processes for Budget Reform in Small Countries: The Case of Samoa

Geoff Dixon

Pacific island countries often suffer from stubbornly high levels of public sector employment and low value for money from public spending. This has tended to crowd out private sector activity, resulting in slow economic growth (World Bank 2005, paragraph 11).

Samoa has relatively high levels of public employment, with around 6,000 full-time and part-time staff servicing the country's population of 180,000 (see chapter 8, box 8.1, for a general account of the country and its economy). The government of Samoa (GOS) has tackled the problem by adopting "a wide-ranging economic reform program, which has transformed the economy into one of the better-performing in the Pacific. As part of the reform, the Ministry of Finance (MOF) introduced output-based (performance-based) budget preparation in 1995, assisted by Australian Agency for International Development (AusAID). Budget appropriations to spending ministries no longer comprise separate budget lines for numerous different classes of inputs, such as electricity or vehicle maintenance, but allocations for outputs and suboutputs defined in the budget" (government official[1]).

Geoff Dixon is an independent consultant.

This was a big step beyond traditional input-focused budget preparation (sometimes called "bid-and-review" budgeting) to budget preparation that focuses on performance. Many other countries have attempted the same transition by introducing program-based budget allocations that focus on achieving program targets (such as a target reduction in maternal mortality), rather than associated outputs (such as a target number of assisted births). This gives the line agency greater flexibility to choose outputs to attain a performance goal—for example, using a flexible combination of prenatal care and assisted births.[2]

Introducing performance-based budget *preparation* is normally associated with a parallel reform in budget *execution*. This involves giving spending ministries more freedom in how they use budget funds to meet their assigned levels of output—and must be achieved without loss of control over the spending of taxpayer money. This case study recounts the experience of one small country in reconciling increased financial flexibility for line ministries with the maintenance of high standards of financial control.

Financial Control

In the past, the "loosening up" of financial controls on line-ministry spending has been a major obstacle to budget reform. The classical approach to budgeting is for the MOF to transfer budget funds to ministries in the form of very detailed line items (separate allocations for postage, rent, workshops, and so forth) to ensure that taxpayer funds are not diverted to the "wrong" inputs (travel, office accommodations, or wage supplements) or spent on the right inputs, but without regard to cost-effectiveness (for example, through casual or corrupt procurement practices) (box 9.1).[3] Transactions by line ministries are then preaudited by MOF or the Treasury Department (hereafter referred to as "Treasury") to ensure that they conform to the detailed budget lines and the finance regulations. At least in theory, this ensures that each line ministry uses its budget allocation appropriately, economically, and transparently.

It is generally accepted, however, that ministries of finance cannot tightly control *both* the inputs *and* the outputs of a line ministry. If line ministries are to be held responsible for producing outputs that are responsive to government objectives (as under performance budgeting), rather than being driven by historical budget allocations, they must be given more flexibility in the way they use the allocations. This does not mean that central agencies should ignore the way line ministries use their inputs. But the focus of control shifts from detailed ex ante planning of inputs to be used to planning of outputs to be produced. This, when

Box 9.1

What Is Financial Control?

Before modern performance budgeting was introduced, procurement and payroll functions were centralized in national treasuries, rather than devolved to line ministries, to prevent misappropriation of taxpayer funds.

There have been many forms of misappropriation. One type involves collusion between government officials and private sector suppliers: for example, high-cost suppliers can be chosen in return for kickbacks, invoices can be paid twice, invoiced amount can exceed the approved amount on the original purchase order, quantity delivered can fall short of the invoiced amount, or progress payments can be made for project work not completed. A common problem is grossly inflated claims for supply of stationery, transport, freight, or security services.

Other fraudulent activities involve officials only, rather than collusion between officials and suppliers. Examples are the processing of fake invoices from fictitious companies with fictitious letterheads and addresses, or creation and then retention of refunds, or loss of checks that have to be reissued, but are cashed in any event. Frequently, the fraud involves the complicity of senior officials and accounting staff, with proceeds shared.

Another category involves inappropriate "in-kind" benefits to officials, such as diversion of supplies or the work of contractors to officials' personal gain, or overspending on travel or office accommodations through misposting of payments to inappropriate accounts.

In the case of payroll, payments can continue to be made to a name after the person has moved on, ineligible allowances can be paid, or associates can be recorded as fake contractors. In some Pacific island countries, these practices have reached epidemic proportions.

Before the current focus on performance-based budgeting, preventing such fraud was a core rationale of budget systems. Prevention relied heavily on separating the responsibility for initiating transactions from that for approving them. Frequently, line ministries were not trusted to enforce this separation, and treasuries preaudited each transaction, often at multiple stages of the transaction. This preaudit still exists in Samoa.

Source: Author.

combined with ex post transparency of inputs actually used, helps the MOF to negotiate the funding required next year to deliver the best possible outputs for achieving government objectives.

Consistent with this thinking, the Samoan MOF had, as part of its budget reform, long wanted to introduce a more devolved budget execution system.[4] "Fundamental to developing this new environment is the need for the MOF to 'set the rules' and then let ministries get on with the role of delivering efficient and effective outputs and being responsible for the results" (Samoa MOF 2004, section 7.2). Giving line ministries greater financial flexibility to achieve their target outputs *required line ministries to take over much more responsibility for financial control of budget spending.*

Nonetheless, for almost a decade after the 1995 introduction of output-based budget preparation, a highly centralized budget execution system persisted in Samoa. Budgetary control stubbornly continued to focus on managing the spending process, rather than the outputs that resulted. Procurement and payroll were centralized in Treasury, and line ministries were obliged to request Treasury to make purchases on their behalf. Each purchase was subjected to preaudit by Treasury and the Audit Office to ensure that funds were available under the relevant budget line and that the purpose of the transaction was consistent with the output to be funded by that budget line. To obtain a purchase order, a line ministry was obliged to physically take a requisition order to the Treasury office. Basic financial control reports needed by each line ministry to check the amount of unspent funds in each budget line also had to be requested and collected from Treasury, often with a delay.

The Costs of Centralized Budget Execution

Continued centralization of budget *execution*, despite the introduction of output-based budget *preparation*, meant that Samoa faced two problems. First, line ministries failed to take over responsibility for their own performance. The new system used output targets to determine the budget allocations for each ministry, but these allocations continued to be distributed according to detailed line items. This prevented the focus of budget control from shifting from inputs to results (outputs). An MOF official admitted that "for the first five years after output budgeting was introduced, there was little focus on tracking outputs ex post (even by MOF). Outputs were really only used to determine inputs, and the focus continued to be on whether the inputs were spent according to the line items, rather than whether the outputs were actually achieved."

The second problem that arose from the continued centralization of budget execution applied to the more progressive Samoan ministries, such as education and agriculture. With the passage of time, these ministries *were* beginning to focus on improving their internal management processes. But to manage their spending effectively under Treasury's centralized accounting system, they were forced to develop their own "shadow" accounting systems to provide "flash" (instant) reports on the progress of their spending against the budget allocations, and funds remaining. These shadow financial control systems in larger line ministries introduced problems of duplication of data entry and of inconsistency of data with the central Treasury system. As the 2004 *Business Case* for replacement of the government financial system put it: "To create these shadow systems, all transactions passed on to the MOF for entering into TCS [Treasury Corporate System] are first entered by the ministry into their own system, such as an Excel spreadsheet. This potentially leads to disparate data being available to different levels of government for decision-making purposes. . . . Currently to overcome deficiencies in data integration, the Ministry of Finance requires ministries to undertake reconciliations between shadow system financial data and TCS data. These reconciliations are nonautomated and extremely labour-intensive" (Samoa MOF 2004, paragraph 2.3).

The time was clearly approaching when line ministries needed a freer hand in managing their budget allocations so as to achieve their output targets.

Why Are Detailed Input Controls So Persistent?
Why did detailed input controls persist for so long after Samoa introduced output budgeting? "For a long time, we have wanted a more devolved budget execution system. But it has not been implemented because *we don't have confidence in the ability of our line ministries to take over responsibility for financial control of budget execution from Treasury*" (MOF official).

It is true that Samoa has in the past been less prone to poor financial control than many Pacific island countries, such as Papua New Guinea or the Solomon Islands. However, MOF was unsure that spending ministries as yet had the capacity to maintain accounts and records properly; restrict spending to authorized transactions; ensure that all spending was for the output appropriated in the budget; and avoid spending that was self-serving of officials rather than essential to produce the outputs.[5] (Recently, six Ministry of Health employees were prosecuted for fraudulent use of budget funds, even under the existing highly centralized budget execution system.)

Moreover, "some CEOs of line ministries have shown a lack of enthusiasm for taking over responsibility for financial control in their ministries from MOF. Under the centralized system, it was easier for them to blame Treasury for failure to deliver their budgeted outputs, delay in paying suppliers, or poor financial control, particularly when their minister is pushing them to explain complaints from the public about poor performance" (MOF official). For CEOs of line ministries that were not reform focused, there was little incentive to take over the responsibilities of the accountable officer for spending under the Public Financial Management Act.

MOF was aware that a more devolved system of budget execution was desirable and that this required line ministries to take over more responsibility for financial control from Treasury. But it saw this as a "chicken-and-egg" problem: "Existing financial control capacities in line ministries are poor because the ministries operate within a highly centralized Treasury system. However, the Treasury controls can't be devolved because of the lack of capacity at line ministries" (government official).

For these reasons, and although output-based budgeting had been introduced as far back as 1995, budgetary control stubbornly continued to focus on managing the spending process, rather than the product. As a result, Samoa's budget reform realized few of the benefits of a properly implemented, performance-focused budget.[6]

This chicken-and-egg problem is common to both large and small countries undertaking budget reform. Introduction of performance budgeting requires less central control over the allocations to line ministries, but this devolution of responsibility needs to be synchronized with improvement of financial-control and -reporting systems at the agency level. This is particularly difficult in a small country, where the knowledge and resources required to design and implement agency-level control systems are limited.

In the case of Samoa's budget reform, there were, in hindsight, two particular problems:

- Lack of knowledge in MOF of how a more devolved financial control system might operate (an informational constraint).
- Lack of funding for a major new financial control system (a financial constraint). Introducing a new financial management system involves

fixed costs that do not vary in line with country size—including the cost of acquiring the software and associated hardware, which is high on a per transaction basis when the number of transactions is small. Other fixed costs arise from data migration and training.

Finding a Solution

Centralized control of budget execution might have continued in Samoa for the indefinite future had there not been an unexpected development. The Australian company supporting the software for highly centralized budget execution (Treasury Corporate System, or TCS) that had been installed in 1996–97 announced in 2003 that it would be withdrawing support for the system in a year's time.[7]

This forced MOF to initiate a process for procuring a new Treasury budget execution system. The focus of this case study is the way in which Samoa turned an apparent misfortune into an opportunity for introducing a more devolved budget system consistent with real performance budgeting. This was accomplished by using the procurement process for replacing the soon-to-be-legacy software to identify a "multipurpose" solution.

Directions of Change

At the outset, MOF knew that it wanted a more devolved system for executing the budget, but was unsure how to resolve the chicken-and-egg problem mentioned above. The desired directions of change were summarized in the MOF *Business Case* (Samoa MOF 2004) for investing in a new system (table 9.1). This identified four *drivers* that were to guide the replacement of the existing centralized TCS:

1. Provide timely, consistent, and reliable information for management decisions
2. Achieve efficiencies and operate effectively
3. Improve accountability for financial management at a ministry level
4. Provide a fully supported financial system able to meet the current and future requirements of public sector accounting

These drivers were used to assess the best approach to replacing the system. Three *options* for replacing the system were identified:

1. Maintaining functionality of the current system in the existing technical environment

Table 9.1. Current State versus Future State

Current state	Future state
Cultural environment	
Centralized decision making	Distributed decision making
Information closely held	Distributed information
Resistant to change	Embraces change
Organization territoriality	Collaboration
Business environment	
Multiple transaction approvals	Online transaction approvals
Multiple shadow systems	One system to meet all needs
Reconciliation intensive	One source of data
Treasury driven	Distributed authority
Paper intensive	Reduced paper
Information scarcity	Distributed information
Focus on controls	Focus on outputs
Labor intensive	Automated wherever possible
Data collection	Information management
Technical environment	
Limited communication	Wide area network
Customized software	Off-the-shelf software
Batch processing	Online data entry
	Centralized processing
Stand-alone systems	Integrated systems
Unsecured data access	Secured data access

Source: Samoa MOF 2005, section 3.6.

2. Reviewing functionality of the current system in the existing technical environment
3. Reviewing functionality of the current system *and* the technical environment[8]

The relationship between business *drivers* and *options* is illustrated in table 9.2, taken from the *Business Case* prepared by MOF (2004). The table assesses the extent to which each option meets the requirements of the core financial functional drivers. The ability of each option is assessed against a scale of 0–5, in which 0 indicates that the driver is not achieved and 5 indicates that the driver is totally achieved.

Option 1 (maintaining current system functionality in the existing technical environment) provided the simplest approach to replacing the soon-to-be-legacy Treasury system. From the perspective of a small country, with limited capacity to fund and install a new system, this was the least-risk solution. But this option scored only 17 out of 55 against

Table 9.2. Analysis of Options

Business driver	Functional driver	Option 1	Option 2	Option 3
1. Provide timely, consistent, and reliable information for management decisions.	(a) Ensure one source of financial data for decision-making purposes.	The ministry databases are still separate from MOF. Score 0	While there are still different databases, they are linked and updated electronically. Score 3	There is one source of data. Score 5
	(b) Ensure consistent, timely, and reliable financial reports to Parliament and ministry management to support the decision-making process.	Ministries are responsible for the reports prepared for ministry management. MOF is responsible for reports for Parliament. Score 1	Ministries are responsible for the reports prepared for ministry management. MOF is responsible for reports for Parliament. Processes can be reviewed to ensure timeliness and reliability. Score 3	All reports are generated from one system, ensuring consistency. Processes can be reviewed to ensure timeliness and reliability. Score 5
	(c) Provide online access to financial data to ministries.	Only inquiry function available on MOF system, although ministries can access their own system. Score 3	Ministries can access their own systems, and MOF system can be set up to provide full access. Score 5	Financial system can be set up to provide full access. Score 4
2. Achieve efficiencies and operate effectively.	(a) Streamline and standardize financial business processes across whole of government to operate more efficiently and effectively.	No reengineering will take place. Score 0	Business reengineering can take place for the MOF system, but ministries are responsible for their own system processes. Score 2	Business reengineering can take place for the financial system. Score 3

(continued)

Table 9.2. Analysis of Options *(continued)*

Business driver	Functional driver	Option 1	Option 2	Option 3
	(b) Eliminate shadow systems within government.	Shadow systems will still exist.	Shadow systems will exist, but will be electronically linked to the MOF system.	No shadow systems.
		Score 0	Score 3	Score 5
	(c) Centralized processing where efficiencies of scale can be realized (for example, payroll and accounts payable).	Yes	Yes	Yes
		Score 5	Score 5	Score 5
3. Improve accountability for financial management at a ministry level.	(a) Devolve data entry to ministries.	No. Data still need to be entered manually in the MOF system.	Data are entered at ministries and uploaded into the MOF system.	Data are entered at ministries into the financial system.
		Score 0	Score 5	Score 5
	(b) Implement standardized performance reporting throughout government.	No	Can be implemented through reengineered processes.	Can be implemented through reengineered processes.
		Score 0	Score 3	Score 3

4. Provide a fully supported financial system able to meet the current and future requirements of public sector accounting.	(a) The financial system should be able to be upgraded with minimal effort and cost.	Separate systems so minimal effort to upgrade at each site. If all sites need upgrading, there may be significant cost. Score 4	The large number of interfaces would involve considerable effort and cost to upgrade. Score 1	One system should allow easy upgrades with least cost. Score 4
	(b) The financial system should be a proven product in use in other government environments.	Able to ensure that MOF system complies. Unable to confirm in other ministries. Score 2	Able to ensure that MOF system complies and can set guidelines for ministry systems. Score 4	Able to comply. Score 5
	(c) The system must manage both cash and accrual environments.	Able to ensure that MOF system complies. Unable to confirm in other ministries. Score 2	Able to ensure that MOF system complies and can set guidelines for ministry systems. Score 4	Able to comply. Score 5
Total Scores	Out of a possible 55	Score 17	Score 38	Score 49

Source: Samoa MOF (2004), section 4.2.

the four business drivers (table 9.2). In addition, option 1 did not meet the third business driver relating to financial devolution to complete Samoa's budget reform.

Option 3 (reviewing both current system functionality and the existing technical environment), on the other hand, showed a score of 49 out of 55. This option involved a much more radical change to existing business processes. And while devolved budget execution systems are common at the national level in large countries, they can be complex, and it remained to be seen whether they would fit the cost and scalability requirements of a country as small as Samoa.

Analyzing the Choices: Supply and Demand

In discussing MOF's choices among the three options, it is useful to examine its procurement task from the perspective first of the demand side (MOF's technical user requirements), and second of the supply side (the technical solutions available in the international market).

Central to the demand side were MOF's technical requirements for a common, output-based budget system for that would devolve financial control from Treasury to line ministries without jeopardizing that control, while at the same time minimizing opportunities for corruption.[9] On the supply side was a wide range of alternative financial management packages developed in larger countries. Many of these could have met MOF's user requirements, but failed in regard to supply-side requirements (the solutions are tailored to transaction volumes in larger countries, and are too expensive or too complex to install in such a small country). Similarly, solutions that did meet MOF's supply-side requirements in regard to acceptable cost and appropriate scale could be too limited on the demand side in regard to functionality and capacity to support MOF's leading edge (for small countries) shift to output budgeting.

MOF's procurement challenge was, from the information base of a very small country, to find the best mix of demand- and supply-side characteristics consistent with the funds available in a small country to purchase and install a new system.

Meeting Samoa's Needs

When the process for procuring a successor to the old Treasury system commenced, MOF itself did not have a clear idea of how existing standards of financial control could be sustained in a more devolved performance-budgeting environment. As one MOF official put it, "We were forced into a procurement by the withdrawal of support for our existing centralized system, not by a strategy for reforming budget execution."

Reflecting MOF's limited understanding of reform options, it resorted to the tender process itself to trawl for possible solutions. For the process to perform a dual role of solution identification and system procurement, MOF adopted a broad, nonprescriptive approach to the supply side of the request for tenders (in regard to the technical environment), but a much higher level of specificity on the demand side, in the form of a very detailed set of user requirements—236 in total (see annex 9A for a sample of the requirements). "This approach to designing the tender process gave maximum scope for potential suppliers with large-country knowledge to identify small-country solutions which, being a small country, we did not know about" (government official).

By opening up both system functionality and the technical environment to tender proposals (option 3 above), MOF was able to trawl in larger countries for possible technical solutions for its budget devolution that might be unfamiliar to a small country, yet suited to a small country's cost constraints and transaction volumes. Had the user requirements been based on either of the first two options, it is less likely that the online processing systems widely used at the municipal level in larger countries would have been identified as a solution by possible suppliers.

The Babushka (Russian) Doll effect
Samoa needed a low-cost financial management system suited to devolved performance-based budgeting, but one that would be handling transaction volumes far smaller than those of most national governments installing a treasury system with similar functionality.

The use of low-cost, small-scale, financial-control systems to devolve financial control to spending subunits is actually quite common in larger countries. It occurs in leading-edge municipal governments, universities, and government agencies such as large hospitals. Many of these agencies have transaction volumes and information technology budgets of the same order as the Samoan government. They also have similar user requirements for a budget management system, based on a central financing department dispersing funds to line departments that themselves undertake key financial control and reporting functions.

With such a large market for *municipal*-level financial-management systems in bigger countries, numerous software providers in these countries have developed accounting and financial control packages for municipal governments. These are based on electronic workflow, and online transactions and reporting. Such systems preserve financial control in a devolved budgeting environment by adopting online processing and by limiting access and ability to approve transactions to authorized officials. This ensures separation of functions, the breakdown of which encourages misuse of funds (see box 9.1 on financial control). The systems are designed to ensure tight financial control, and they are relatively low cost.

The capabilities of such systems were not, however, known to MOF before the tender process. MOF unwillingly continued with centralized financial controls because it was not aware of better solutions already developed for smaller agencies in larger countries. As with a babushka doll—a traditional Russian nesting doll made of wood, with each doll containing ever smaller dolls—smaller-scale solutions can be invisibly embedded in larger-scale ones. Small babushkas are invisible until revealed by opening bigger dolls, starting from the largest down. A babushka effect was achieved by MOF through a well-designed tender process aimed at large-country contractors who might be familiar with small-agency solutions that are embedded in the larger environments in which they operate and that are not obvious to the small country itself *because* it is small.[10] The effectiveness with which some of the solutions proposed by tenderers could solve the long-standing chicken-and-egg devolution dilemma came as a genuine surprise to MOF.

Why Is This a "Small-States Case"?

Small states can reduce the drawbacks of "smallness" in several ways. One is joint production: producing public goods (usually produced separately by sovereign governments) jointly with another state. Joint production reduces costs, particularly in the spreading of fixed costs.

The Samoa tender process is a variant of the joint production principle. In this case, Samoa was able to achieve two benefits:

- Overcoming an informational constraint by identifying a solution to its long-standing chicken-and-egg problem of how to reduce central financial controls when line ministries lack financial control skills
- Avoiding the cost of developing a bespoke financial-control system, suited to its very small volumes of transactions, through the "babushka" effect—by acquiring a system already developed for smaller agencies in larger countries, *for which development costs were already substantially written off*

Overcoming an Informational Constraint

Following receipt of tender proposals, MOF invited three companies to Apia to demonstrate the solutions they proposed. (One of the three, a U.S.-based company, declined to travel to Samoa to demonstrate its system.) Samoan line ministries were invited to the demonstrations, which were designed to show how each solution handled a number of predefined financial-management scenarios.

"The online workflow systems demonstrated by the tenderers were something of a revelation to MOF" (government official). These systems use online requests and approvals for day-to-day financial transactions, which limit discretion in the line ministry and enforce separation of responsibilities, ensuring that administrative control is maintained. The system itself determines who can raise requisitions, who can approve them, recording the day and time of each action, while ensuring that appropriation limits are met. This ensures tight financial control. The off-the-shelf workflow is fully customizable—responsibilities and access can easily be transferred between officials, and files can be attached to transactions as evidence (see box 9.2 on how financial packages achieve devolved financial control).

Normally, the ministry of finance in a small country like Samoa does not have easy access to information on the business processes operated by small entities in larger countries. The tender process devised by MOF allowed potential suppliers to fill this gap in local knowledge. Being highly prescriptive in the tender process about user requirements and less specific about possible solutions helped produce solutions that were not readily apparent from the vantage point of a small country. Potential suppliers that had been exposed to a variety of user requirements in large countries proved to be in a better position than MOF to identify the best compromise between the tight budget constraints and the desired functionality.

Minimizing the Costs of Developing a Suitable Bespoke System

One thing that large and small states have in common is a set of similar-size public-spending entities: municipal governments in larger states and national ministries in smaller states. Both types of agencies rely on transfers from a central department of finance to support their spending. Samoa found a solution based on the applicability of the leading-edge business processes used in municipal governments in larger states to its own national-level ministries, even though the range of services provided

Box 9.2

How Financial Packages Achieve Devolved Financial Control

Modern financial management information systems ensure financial control in devolved situations in four ways:

First, they reject actions (entries) lacking key data (for example, description or authorizing officer). Approval limits for purchases are linked to positions (consistent with the payroll module), and the system provides online approval of purchase orders in accordance with approval limits. Authority to approve purchases is limited to particular types of goods or suppliers, as well as particular ledger accounts. The user name for a data-entry session is automatically attached to the transaction. Journal entries can be made only by specified users and approval limits apply. User access is restricted to specified modules, the user's own ministry, ranges of accounts, and specified data-entry screens and reports. Audit trails are provided for all system-access and data-entry sessions, together with security reports on unsuccessful log-ins.

Second, such systems flag suspicious activity. For example, the previous MOF system's check that the same invoice number could not be paid twice could be circumvented by placing a period after the invoice number. The new system flags a warning if invoice numbers are suspiciously similar. Government officials worked with the supplier of the new system to ensure that known malpractices were flagged.

Third, systems have the capacity for electronically tracking individual transactions. This takes a fraction of the time needed to search for hard copies of vouchers, encouraging more thorough checking of transactions.

Fourth, user-defined reports can be produced, such as these examples:

- Providing historical data on transactions with a particular supplier to identify suspiciously high levels of servicing
- Analyzing usage patterns of particular government officials, using the system to check for odd patterns of behavior (for example, large numbers of short sessions).

These user-defined reports are in addition to the routine, system-defined reports comparing actual against budgeted expenditures (pro rata or historic profile). User-defined reports are a very powerful control on fraud, but they do require some knowledge on the part of the operator.

Reflecting the large size of the market for such systems among states, local governments, and government agencies, the various packages receive regular updates every couple of years. Moreover, the IT environment is one of rapid development, with regular improvements to both hardware and software. This has resulted in an enormous increase in user-friendliness as lessons from implementation are reflected into new versions. Dot NET (.NET) or Java-based systems offer further increases in ease of use, while Web-based systems overcome network and dial-up problems associated with poor communication networks such as those in developing countries.

Source: Author.

and funding sources differ between national- and municipal-level governments. Adopting and adapting solutions already used by smaller administrative entities in larger nation states allowed Samoa to avoid unaffordable development costs to achieve its desired level of functionality and circumvent its limited buying power.

The case study suggests that for a country like Samoa, the concept of "small" is not absolute. The level of transactions in the national budget of Samoa is certainly very small relative to that of most other national governments, with consequent limitations on Samoa's ability to fund the sophisticated national-level financial-control systems used by larger countries. However, as observed by a supplier representative, "The key feature of the desired business process architecture is not linked to size of the country. Municipal governments also face the financial-control challenges of transferring funds to spending departments, which need flexibility in the use of funds (ruling out detailed line-item budgeting), but must also meet the public sector's need for strong financial control and transparency." Even in a medium-size country such as Australia, there are scores of systems at local and state government levels with functionality for devolved financial control that meet Samoa's user requirements.

Managing the Tender Process

A successful tender process did not happen without considerable planning and effort on the part of the Samoan government. Even though the MOF itself had no clear understanding of the solutions needed to implement devolved budget execution, the ministry did have a very clear idea of the strategic directions in which it wanted to move, and it expressed these in a clearly laid out set of user requirements sent to possible tenderers. If the user requirements had been poorly thought through and too general, it would not have been possible for potential suppliers to identify the possible solutions.

To define user requirements in detail, a highly interactive process was required between the Samoan stakeholders in the procurement. Line ministries were closely involved in defining the requirements, selecting the successful contractor, and preparing the more devolved business processes to be reflected in the new Treasury system. Interdepartmental teams analyzed such issues as payroll, accounts payable, and accounts receivable, drawing relevant staff from each ministry. Each team picked its own leader and, once the contract was awarded, worked with an expert from the successful tenderer to further define user requirements in that area. The teams were made to feel responsible for their focus area. Staff of line ministries were motivated by the expectation of receiving new responsibilities. The process of defining user requirements fell short in the area of output tracking (see the postscript below), but the process was more than adequate to ensure a comprehensive statement of Samoa's user requirements and screening of the solutions proposed for compatibility against these requirements.

At a later stage of the tender process, an application implementation management (AIM) study was undertaken by the successful tenderer in close consultation with the line ministries. This study defined in country-specific detail the new business processes required in the more devolved financial-control environment, such as appropriate procurement thresholds for different levels of seniority of Samoan officials and devolved versus centralized options. Team leaders reported to a working group of six driving the project, which in turn reported to a steering committee chaired by the financial secretary, including several heads of line ministries and the chief auditor. *MOF used this study to define the detailed business-process architecture of the financial devolution, drawing on the experience of the successful contractor.*

Thus the tender process was effectively used to tap the technologies available for reconciling small-country budget constraints with the user requirements for solving the chicken-and-egg dilemma of how to devolve financial flexibility to line ministries without loss of financial control. This would not have been possible if the demand side of the process (the user requirements) had been poorly thought through and too general, or if the supply side (the approach to be adopted by potential suppliers) had been overly prescriptive.

Not Quite Perfect?

This case study concludes with one further insight into how effectively Samoa managed to access appropriate solutions through careful tender planning.

The rationale of an output-based budgeting system, such as that adopted by Samoa in 1995, is to create a link between budget outlays and the results (outputs) they generate. This enables decisions about better use of budget funds—decisions that tend not to be made under input-focused budgeting. However, this requires monitoring and reporting of *both* costs *and* outputs for each budget line. It is precisely the ability to relate costs to outputs that is the strength of output budgeting.

In the event, this need to integrate output and financial information was apparently omitted from the set of user requirements prepared by MOF. This resulted perhaps from the limited involvement by the Budget Division in the tender process and the slowness of MOF to focus on tracking of outputs (as well as costs) as a budget-control variable. The MOF's *Business Case* (2004) specified the need to ensure one source of *financial* data for decision-making purposes, but it did not specify one source of *budget* data (data relating to *both* costs *and* outputs).

As a consequence, the Budget Division of MOF is now separately providing spending ministries with a form to be filled out to track their output performance against their output budget targets. Output information must then be imported into the Treasury system report writer (in the new system) to produce reports that *combine* output and financial variables. This roundabout process represents a failure to use emerging technologies for electronic capture of both financial and nonfinancial data at its source.

In reality, the new financial package chosen by MOF does allow nonfinancial data to be stored alongside financial data within a single system. (More precisely, a statistics ledger can be built up based on output codes.) But this functionality, which lies at the heart of output budgeting, was not identified in the user requirements and is not currently being exploited by MOF. In fact, MOF is itself building a shadow system for tracking outputs that is similar in principle to the line ministry shadow systems that it was hoping to eliminate. This emphasizes the need for a clear understanding on the part of the small country of the implications of its strategies for its future business processes. Without this, the potential benefit from large-country solutions is unlikely to be fully realized.

Annex 9A. GoFAR System Requirements (SAMPLE PAGE)

No.	Description	Mandatory Y/N	Comply Y/N/P/A	Comments
			Supplier response	
A. General setup				
1	The system will be able to be set up using a cash, modified cash, or accrual basis of accounting	Y		
2	The system will support the tala currency denoted by $ sign. Comma separators should be used to denote thousands, millions, etc.	Y		
3	The system's user language will be English	Y		
4	The system shall support multicurrency	Y		
5	The system shall allow multiple levels of data rounding for data entry and running reports	Y		
6	The system will provide for both real-time update of data or batch updating	Y		
7	The system shall be set up with a minimum of 3 years of historical data	Y		
8	The system will support drill-down from any enquiry or on-screen report to source transactions	Y		
9	The system will allow scanned documents to be attached to transactions	N		
10	The system will allow memos to be appended to any transaction	N		
11	The system will allow modification of data input screens to delete unnecessary fields	N		
12	The system should allow upload and download of data with Microsoft Excel	Y		
13	The system must provide the option of periods being open or closed by module	Y		
14	There will be a comprehensive online help that will provide screen-sensitive help	Y		
15	All manuals will be available online	Y		
16	Online manuals will have the facility to edit for inclusion of policies and procedures	Y		
B. General ledger management				
Organisational structure and chart of accounts				
17	The system will be able to accommodate the structure of government (as shown in attachment A)	Y		

(continued)

Annex 9A. GoFAR System Requirements (SAMPLE PAGE) *(continued)*

| | | | Supplier response | |
| | | Mandatory | Comply | |
No.	Description	Y/N	Y/N/P/A	Comments
18	The system must be flexible to easily accommodate changes to government structures	Y		
19	The system should maintain historical organizational structure information	Y		
20	The system must enable self-accounting entities (ministries) to perform their daily operations either locally or at a centralized consolidation point	Y		
21	The system shall have the ability to uniquely structure ledgers to meet the needs of self-accounting entities (ministries)	Y		

Source: Ministry of Finance.
Note: The complete list includes 236 requirements.
Y = Yes; N = No; P = Partial; A = Alternative solution

Annex 9B. List of Persons Interviewed

Name	Affiliation
Hinauri Petana	Chief Executive Officer, Ministry of Finance
Lusia Sefo	Deputy Chief Executive Officer, Ministry of Finance
Rosita Mauai	Chief Executive Officer, Information Technology Division, Ministry of Finance
Maeva Betham	Chief Executive Officer, Budget Division, Ministry of Finance
Tamaseu Leni	Controller and Chief Auditor, Audit Office
Lillian Hytonsue	Deputy Controller, Audit Office
Rosemary Assera	Principal IT Officer, Ministry of Education
Brenton John	Senior Consultant, Technology One
Darren White	Marketing Manager, Technology One (telephone interview)

Notes

1. For a list of persons interviewed for this case study, see annex 9B.
2. A drawback, however, is that the use of program-based—rather than output-based—allocations makes it harder to separate the effect of the government program from other factors that might influence achievement of the target.
3. Key control figures include the ratio of wages to total operating costs, and the level of spending on travel, vehicles, workshops, and office accommodation. For all of these, there are incentives for ministry officials to allow spending to grow beyond the minimum needed.

4. In 2001, the Public Finance Management Act (PFMA 2001, part II) enacted the principle of devolution of financial management to the ministers and chief executive officers responsible for the performance of a ministry. The act also defines the responsibilities of chief executive officers to ensure that all accounts and records are properly maintained; all expenditure is properly authorized and applied to the purposes for which it is appropriated; and there is no overexpenditure or overcommitment of funds. The principle was affirmed by the MOF in 2004.

5. The previously cited World Bank (2005) report (paragraph 12) states, "In many PICs (Pacific Island countries), weakness in public expenditure management has led to a recurrence of unbudgeted spending and arrears to government employees, to suppliers, or to holders of government debt. More generally, budget management has been weak, with loose procedures for enforcing public accountability and oversight."

6. It should be emphasized that if Samoa's budget reform is benchmarked against contemporary budget reforms in other countries, this result was not unusual.

7. Because at that time only two or three countries were using the system.

8. The technical environment includes such issues as whether to move to a wide area network and to use online data entry rather than batch processing.

9. "Based on an ability to meet identified business drivers, the recommended approach is to replace TCS with a single financial system that will meet the needs of both the MOF and other ministries" (Samoa MOF 2004, paragraph 4.3).

10. In the case of Russian dolls, the head of each doll is removed to gain access its smaller version.

References

Samoa, MOF (Ministry of Finance) 2004. *Business Case: Replacement Financial System for Whole of Government.*

World Bank. 2005. *Regional Engagement Framework FY2006–2009 for Pacific Islands.* Washington, DC: World Bank. http://www-wds.worldbank.org/external/default/ WDSContentServer/WDSP/IB/2005/05/09/000012009_20050509112554/ Rendered/INDEX/32261.txt.

Overview of Studies of Economic Growth

Edgardo Favaro and David Peretz

Introduction

This is an overview of four in-depth regional studies on economic growth of small states in Africa, the Caribbean, Europe, and the Pacific during the past decade. It provides context for the reports in the case studies of institutional and regulatory strategies that some small states have developed for integrating into the world economy. Both sets of studies are part of the project Economic Growth and Integration of Small States into the World Economy, cosponsored by Australian Agency for International Development (AusAID) and the World Bank (2005).

The following four growth studies analyze the patterns underlying the wide range of performance of small states during the 1990s:

- Dorte Domeland and Frederico Gil Sander (2007), "Growth in African Small States"
- Ron Duncan and Haruo Nakagawa (2006), "Obstacles to Economic Growth in Six Pacific Island Countries"

Edgardo Favaro is a Lead Economist at the World Bank. David Peretz is a consultant at the World Bank.

- Mizuho Kida (2006), "Caribbean Small States: Growth Diagnostics"
- Mark Roland Thomas and Gaobo Pang (2006), "Lessons from Europe for Economic Policy in Small States"

Rate of Growth of Small States: 1986–2005

The median annual rate of growth of per capita GDP of small states slightly declined from 2 percent in 1986–1995 to 1.8 percent in 1996–2005.[1] Over the same period, the rate increased from 0.3 to 1.6 percent per year for low-income countries (LICs) and from 1 to 2.3 percent per year for middle-income countries (MICs). The contrast between the improvement in performance of LICs and MICs and the less dynamic performance of small states says more about improvements in economic management in LICs and MICs than about poor performance in small states. But the statistic for performance of small states overall obscures marked differences in economic performance of small states across regions and within regions.

The four regional growth studies seek to illuminate why some small states have performed significantly better than others and what general lessons can be drawn about approaches that work and those that do not.

Wide Differences in Economic Performance

The average per capita growth rate in the world economy jumped nearly a full point from 2.5 percent in 1989–1995 to 3.5 percent in 1995–2003. This average was driven by continuously strong performances in developing Asian countries. The impact of information technology (IT) investment in explaining this growth is visible, especially in industrialized countries and in Asia (Jorgenson and Vu 2005).

Against this background, after 1995:

- In Africa, median growth of small states slowed (from 3.1 to 2.2 percent), but was overall robust. The two strongest performers continue to be Botswana and Mauritius, although the latter suffered from the phasing out of the Multifiber Arrangement (MFA) quotas. At the other extreme, per capita GDP fell steadily in Guinea-Bissau and slowed dramatically in the Seychelles and Swaziland.

- In the Caribbean, growth slowed (from 3 to 2.5 percent), but was also robust. The weakest performers (among those countries for which information is available) are The Bahamas, the richest country in the region, and St. Lucia. With the exception of Belize and Trinidad and Tobago (an oil-exporting country), the rate of growth of exports of goods and services slowed considerably in 1996–2005 (Kida 2006).

- In Europe, growth accelerated from 2.6 to 3.4 percent. Estonia and Slovenia, which had had sharp contractions in the previous decade, benefited from membership in the European Union (EU). Joining the EU allowed these countries to leapfrog what otherwise would have been an arduous period of development of national institutions and regulations (Thomas and Pang 2006).

- Pacific island states, with the exception of Samoa, had a weak performance in 1996–2005. In the Marshall Islands, the Solomon Islands, and Vanuatu, per capita GDP fell steadily during the decade. Vanuatu started a comprehensive reform program in 1998; results are visible in lower inflation, but little has been done to restructure the large public-enterprise sector, and growth has not recovered (Duncan and Nakagawa 2006).

Some themes recur as having been significant in countries in more than one region:

- *Political instability and civil strife.* Comoros and Guinea-Bissau in Africa (Domeland and Sander 2007) and Fiji, the Solomon Islands, and Timor-Leste in the Pacific (Duncan and Nakagawa 2006) were all afflicted by civil strife.

- *Trade preferences.* The prospect of a phaseout of preferences on agricultural exports (bananas and sugar) to the European market had a negative impact on growth in many countries of Africa and the Caribbean. The phaseout of the MFA quotas contributed to the decline in the rate of growth of Mauritius at the end of the period. The African Growth and Opportunity Act (AGOA) boosted exports from the region to the United States after 2000. The European Union's Generalized System of Preferences has had similar effects (for instance, on countries like Mauritius and St. Kitts and Nevis).

- *Macroeconomic management.* Growth in the 1980s was driven by unsustainable increases in government spending in some small countries in Africa, the Caribbean, and the Pacific. This led to high and sustained fiscal deficits, real appreciation of exchange rates, and rapid increases in external debt (for instance, the external debt increased by between 170 percent and 220 percent in some Caribbean island states between 1980 and 1989 [Kida 2006]). As these policies proved unsustainable, government spending slowed, and so did growth (Duncan and Nakagawa 2006; Kida 2006).

- *Real exchange rates* appreciated in many countries in the Caribbean because their currencies were pegged to the dollar while their real wages rose. This may have contributed to slow export growth in the period. For instance, tourism exports, which had grown very strongly in the 1970s and 1980s, slowed in the 1990s (Kida 2006).

- *Participation of the state in the economy, and low competition.* Strong participation of the state in the economy as a producer of goods and services through state-owned enterprises, regulation, subsidized credit, and special tax policies has stifled growth in many countries in the Caribbean and the Pacific (Kida 2006; Duncan and Nakagawa 2006).

- *Reform.* Some countries moved from state-led into private sector–led growth policies in 1996–2005. In the Pacific, the Cook Islands and Samoa privatized some state-owned enterprises (Duncan and Nakagawa 2006); notably, Samoa opened telecommunications to private sector competition in 2005 (see chapter 9). In the Caribbean, five small states deregulated telecommunications and opened up the sector to competition (see chapter 6). In Estonia and Slovenia (Thomas and Pang 2006) and Cape Verde (Domeland and Sander 2007), reform led to vigorous growth.

- *AIDS.* In Africa, the spread of AIDS is having a strong impact in Botswana (the star performer in the region) and Swaziland (Domeland and Sander 2007).

Policies That Helped Small States Succeed
The studies illustrate the disadvantages that small states often suffer (for example, in transport, infrastructure, and governance costs [Winters 2005]) as a result of size and remote location. They also show that small

size can sometimes confer benefits (for example, in the relative social cohesion in African small states compared with that of their larger neighbors; in the advantages of remoteness for some types of tourism; and in opportunities to pursue some niche businesses). It is clear from all four regional studies that all small states can achieve economic success if they follow the right policies to offset their disadvantages and exploit their advantages, with appropriate international support where needed.

One clear conclusion from the studies is that economic policies and institutions that have proved successful in larger countries are also key to success in small states. In Africa, small states with sound policies and institutions (notably Botswana and Mauritius) have prospered, while those with weak governance and policies (Comoros and Guinea-Bissau) have remained poor (Domeland and Sander 2007). In the Caribbean, countries with sound policies and institutions have become prosperous, while others following public sector–led, inward-looking policies (such as Guyana) have been among the worst performers (Kida 2006).

Sound Monetary and Fiscal Policies

Countries that follow sound monetary and fiscal policies (such as contracting monetary policy out to regional institutions or through membership of currency unions) tend to be successful (see chapter 4 and van Beek et al. 2000). Those that follow unsustainable fiscal policies face problems.

Political Stability and Good Governance

In Africa, small states as a group have outperformed large ones for more than two decades. At the root of this is higher political stability and good governance in many small African states. In sub-Saharan Africa, the probability of state failure (through coups, civil wars, and genocides) is 3 percent in small states against 26 percent in larger states; and small states score better on average than large states in respect to voice and accountability, government effectiveness, regulatory quality, rule of law, and corruption (Kauffman, Kraay, and Mastruzzi 2006; Domeland and Sander 2007).

The studies highlight a particular governance issue evident in some small states: the "Big Man" or clientist syndrome, in which powerful elites control patronage networks and levers of economic power (Duncan and Nakagawa 2006). Policies that promote domestic competition have proven effective in counteracting this behavior.

Redefinition of the Role of the State in the Economy

Small market size and ideology have historically supported the direct participation of the state in production of goods and services in areas that are, elsewhere, normally assigned to the private sector. But in the 1990s, there were marked changes in thinking and policies regarding the role of the state in these countries. In public utilities, small states have initiated a transition from monopoly and state-dominated activity to competition. This transition is incomplete, but the direction is steady (as illustrated by these two examples):

- In telecommunications, Dominica, Grenada, St. Kitts and Nevis, St. Lucia, St. Vincent and the Grenadines, and Samoa introduced competition and moved away from direct participation in provision of services to become regulators of the sector.
- In aviation, relaxing the government monopoly in international airline services in some Pacific countries led to an increase in tourist flows (Duncan and Nakagawa 2006).

At the same time, there are also successful examples of governments acting as incubators of new activities. For instance, in Cape Verde, in the context of an undeveloped domestic sector for IT, the state successfully sponsored a public sector agency responsible for the development of IT systems for the government (see chapter 7).

Encouraging Competition in Telecommunications and Other Sectors

Many small states started to liberalize their telecommunications markets in 1996–2005. However, small states as a group lag behind larger states (table A.1).

The advantages that deregulation in telecommunications has brought to these countries cannot be overstated. Competition brings down prices, encourages the development of new businesses, and facilitates the incorporation of new technology (Jorgenson and Vu 2005). The resulting improved connectivity brings considerable economic benefits in its turn.

Table A.1. Telecommunications Regulation
(average)

Market	Small states	Larger states
Fixed phone lines	0.52	1.21
Mobile-phone market	0.97	1.49
International	0.48	1.08

Source: ITU 2007.
0 = monopoly; 1 = partial competition; 2 = competitive market.

Improving the Business Environment

Small market size inevitably means few suppliers. A good business environment both increases competition and attracts the investment needed for growth:

- Keeping entry open to new businesses entices new suppliers, encouraging the kind of competition that keeps supply prices down in economies with a large number of competitors. Cape Verde privatized its telephone company, but did not open the sector to competition. As a result, it has one of the highest telephone costs in the world, to the detriment of its otherwise exemplary IT program.

- Keeping regulation simple reduces the cost of doing business, especially for foreign companies, and is critical for attracting new investment. Red tape (reflected in the Doing Business indicators) adversely affects the business climate in many small states, especially in Africa and the Pacific.

- Regional integration can help reduce transaction costs and encourage new businesses (within and outside the region). In the Eastern Caribbean, governments have favored harmonization of legislation and regulation in banking and telecommunications; in Central and Western Africa, governments enacted harmonized banking legislation (see chapter 4), and the regional Organization for the Harmonization of Business Law in Africa (OHADA) Treaty of 1993 is a systematic plan to harmonize business legislation across countries. When regulations are consistent in a region, it becomes easier to contract administration of that regulation to a regional body.

- The land tenure system in many Pacific small states inhibits inward investment (for example, property registration takes 188 days in Vanuatu and 513 days in Kiribati, against just two in New Zealand [Duncan and Nakagawa 2007]).

Looking Ahead

Small states face some permanent challenges: maintaining a business environment that facilitates diversification of the economy, reducing cost of public goods and services, improving connectivity with the rest of the world, and exploiting their own special opportunities. For developed countries historically associated with small states, the challenge is to facilitate the movement of people and capital from and to small states.

Facilitating Diversification of the Economy

Most countries in Africa, the Caribbean, and the Pacific—small as well as large—get preferential access to the European Union. The United States is also negotiating regional trade agreements that include preferences. But preferences are now eroding, with the abolition of textile quotas, multilateral tariff cuts, stringent application of World Trade Organization (WTO) rules to items like bananas, and the reduction of European subsidies on sugar.

Trade preferences are a mixed blessing: they make terms of trade more favorable than otherwise, but they discourage diversification. Small states that depend heavily on trade preferences often face serious challenges as these preferences erode—especially if cross-border factor mobility is limited.

Trade preferences encourage specialization of the economy, which enhances efficiency, but also entails risks. Anticipating these risks, some countries have introduced policies to boost other sectors in the economy, as these examples show:

- Mauritius used the rents from trade in agricultural exports to create conditions favorable to new investment in manufacturing, achieving high and sustained rates of economic growth for many years as a result (Domeland and Sander 2007).
- Barbados created inviting conditions for the development of a strong service sector in the 1970s and 1980s (Kida 2006).
- Cape Verde has diversified its economy through the development of the service sector (see chapter 6).

Thus, when trade preferences were phased out, the size of the necessary adjustment was lower and the possibility of reallocating resources to other activities higher.

In general, the studies suggest that services need to be nurtured as the main driver of growth. Harnessing services requires appropriate infrastructure (including, critically, good connectivity, as discussed below) and human skills, along with supporting policies and institutions. Many small states have overcome the disadvantages attached to their location. Maldives was once classified as a "least developed country," but has harnessed tourism to become the richest country in South Asia. Mauritius, despite the considerable drawback of a location 600 miles off the African coast in the southern hemisphere, has overcome this disadvantage with imaginative policies and institutions: beginning with exporting sugar, then diversifying into textiles, and now diversifying further into tourism and financial services (Domeland and Sander 2007).

Reducing the Cost of Public Goods and Services

Improving public sector efficiency and effectiveness, a priority for all countries, is crucial for small states, where (on average) government final consumption as a proportion of GDP is high (at 20.6 percent, relative to 14.7 percent in middle-income countries and 11.9 percent in low-income countries).

The case studies illustrate considerable opportunities for improving quality and reducing costs by creating common regional approaches. The scope for reaping scale economies is substantial in three broad areas: government services, infrastructure, and human development. For example, the states of the East Caribbean have formed a multicountry central bank, a common court system, and a common telecom regulatory authority. In the Caribbean and in the Pacific, small states have created tertiary education institutions: the University of the West Indies and the University of the South Pacific. The West African states have created a telecom authority and an economic community (ECOWAS) to promote regional integration. Francophone states have created monetary unions in West Africa and Central Africa and use a common currency (the CFA franc).

In 1996–2005, there were important advances in contracting out services to regional institutions. In 1998, Eastern Caribbean small states founded the Eastern Caribbean Telecommunications Authority (ECTEL), responsible for advising governments in all matters related to telecommunications (see chapter 5); in 2001–03, 12 Caribbean states established the Caribbean Court of Justice (see chapter 4); in 2004, Estonia and Slovenia joined the European Union, thereby acquiring access to a body of regional regulatory arrangements (Thomas and Pang 2006).

Two visible effects from the action of these regional bodies are an improvement in the quality of the services, compared with what countries could afford if they opted out, and more stable rules of operation. Conceivably, the cost of providing these services may also have fallen as a result of contracting them out, but there is as yet no empirical evidence to substantiate this conjecture.

Improving Connectivity

In their review of growth in the world economy, Jorgenson and Vu (2005) point to the leading role played by investment in IT in contributing to this growth.

For small states competing in a global service economy, investing in appropriate information and communications technology and reducing connectivity costs with the rest of the world are critical. Continuing inefficient monopoly and public service provision in this sector is therefore particularly damaging. The damage goes beyond limited access to the citizens of these countries to telephone and Internet services; it also inhibits the development of new activities (like business outsourcing or call centers) and makes it unprofitable to introduce the technologies that are the engine of growth worldwide.

The studies show that high-quality, low-priced telecommunications can make business offshoring viable. Mauritius and some Caribbean islands have demonstrated that the telecom revolution enables jobs in computer software, call centers, and sundry business processes to shift to small, remote states. A key issue is to ensure that good regulation keeps telecom rates competitive; here, English-speaking small states have a special advantage, since the main language of global business is English.

Modern communications and the Internet can also improve the quality of education, health, and other services. Small states with limited access to medical and university facilities can import such services through telemedicine and distance education (Duncan and McMaster 2007). The Internet also makes possible e-governance, which can greatly improve the quality of governance (Cape Verde is an outstanding example of this, see chapter 6).

Exploiting Special Opportunities

Many small states have special opportunities that can be exploited.

The Law of the Sea, for instance, gives islands and coastal states an exclusive economic zone covering a radius of 200 miles, within which they have sovereign rights for marine life (mainly fish and shrimp) and minerals on the seabed or underneath (mainly oil and gas). The exclusive economic zone of island states can be several times larger than the islands themselves. Technical advances in deep-water drilling have increased the potential of exclusive economic zones. Such states need state-of-the-art geological and other scientific surveys to establish economic opportunities. They also need effective regulatory regimes to ensure that they gain maximum and sustainable advantage from exploiting the resource.

Another opportunity open to some landlocked small states comes from *exploiting nonconventional forms of integration with large neighbors.* Water and electricity are usually considered nontradables, but Bhutan has harnessed its hydroelectric potential to sell electricity to India, and Lesotho sells water to South Africa.

Remote and less developed areas hold particular promise for tourism. The desire of tourists for variety and unspoiled destinations benefits areas yet to be developed, and the desire of high-end tourists to "get away from it all" makes the remoteness of some islands an advantage. All the Pacific islands have experienced fast growth in tourism. Exploiting this advantage requires investments in infrastructure and services.

A fourth opportunity already taken by many small states is the *exploitation of economic niches that do not exist in large states*. In these, the disadvantages of high cost can be overcome by lighter regulation, such as flags of convenience, offshore financial centers, and tax havens. Although it is now recognized that such activities need effective regulation in the global interest, they are likely to remain important at least in those states that have already developed them.

Facilitating the Flow of Capital and Labor

Small size implies that flexibility to adapt to external shocks is limited. Programs that favor temporary and permanent migration to developed countries can offset this disadvantage. For instance, in the Pacific, people from the Cook Islands have a right to move to New Zealand, and those from the Marshall Islands and Federated States of Micronesia can move freely to the United States (Duncan and Nakagawa 2006). Fiji and Kiribati are focusing on training citizens for nursing and other occupations that have a demand abroad (Duncan and Nakagawa 2006). As small states become prosperous, job opportunities will increase, and they should be able to attract back earlier emigrants, even highly skilled ones (as India and China have done).

What the International Community Can Do

The international community has for decades sought to support small developing countries with aid and trade preferences.

Small states received almost 17 times as much aid per capita as all developing countries in 1993–2004 (US$210 against US$12, respectively). Official development assistance is almost 15 percent of gross national income (GNI) in small states against 1 percent for other developing countries (World Bank 2006). Some small states have used these substantial aid inflows successfully, others have not. The studies suggest the following conclusions:

- Aid to small countries (as to other countries) can be highly effective in support of the right policies and deployed in the right way. Two examples are successful external assistance for infrastructure projects in Bhutan and Lesotho, and EU assistance for new EU member states.

External support has frequently provided an anchor to strengthen fledgling national and regional institutions; this assistance (as long as it does not delay needed policy reforms) is effective in helping to finance adjustment to changed circumstances.

• Reducing the cost of transactions associated with multiple aid agencies is even more critical in small states with limited government capacity than it is in larger states.

The studies also suggest that small states will continue to benefit from membership in regional associations with developed countries that go beyond free trade areas, particularly where these provide opportunities for migration and—as in the EU—access to support from regional organizations, including financial support when small states are faced with shocks or need to upgrade critical infrastructure.

Annex A.1

Annex tables A.1 and A.2 present estimates of the rate of growth of GDP, the rate of growth of per capita GDP, and volatility of growth during the periods 1986–1995 and 1996–2005.

Table A.1 Growth and Volatility

		1986–1995			1996–2005		
		GDP growth	Per capita GDP growth	GDP growth volatility	GDP growth	Per capita GDP growth	GDP growth volatility
Small States	mean (%)	3.65	1.98	4.13	3.15	1.67	3.25
	median (%)	3.73	2.08	4.03	2.81	1.68	2.81
	n	39	39	43	35	34	47
of which islands	mean (%)	3.80	2.39	3.81	2.90	1.42	3.30
	median (%)	3.79	2.78	3.74	2.61	1.51	2.82
	n	25	25	27	21	20	30
MICs	mean (%)	3.21	1.56	4.55	3.67	2.58	3.24
	median (%)	3.41	1.24	4.17	3.67	2.37	2.78
	n	60	60	71	68	68	74
LICs	mean (%)	1.57	−0.74	4.76	4.16	2.07	3.57
	median (%)	2.80	0.27	4.36	4.05	1.72	2.94
	n	54	54	67	65	65	67
All countries	mean (%)	2.58	0.82	4.27	3.81	2.33	3.13
	median (%)	2.94	1.04	3.60	3.64	2.19	2.54
	n	154	154	181	168	167	187

Source: World Bank (2007).

Note: This table is based on all countries for which information is available in one of the periods.

Table A.2 Growth and Volatility

		1986–1995			1996–2005		
		GDP growth	Per capita GDP growth	GDP growth volatility	GDP growth	Per capita GDP growth	GDP growth volatility
Small States	mean (%)	3.61	1.77	4.39	3.27	1.75	2.93
	median (%)	3.71	1.96	4.38	2.81	1.80	2.80
	n	29	29	29	29	29	29
of which islands	mean (%)	3.69	1.97	4.06	2.97	1.45	3.14
	median (%)	3.79	1.96	4.38	2.61	1.56	2.80
	n	17	17	17	17	17	17
MICs	mean (%)	3.03	1.32	4.34	3.46	2.17	3.04
	median (%)	3.04	0.96	4.04	3.41	2.25	2.64
	n	54	54	54	54	54	54
LICs	mean (%)	1.52	−0.79	4.50	4.03	1.84	3.36
	median (%)	2.76	0.26	4.34	3.96	1.62	2.94
	n	53	53	53	53	53	53
All countries	mean (%)	2.47	0.67	4.09	3.67	2.07	2.93
	median (%)	2.84	1.02	3.51	3.53	2.02	2.46

Source: World Bank (2007).
Note: This table is based on all countries for which information is available in both periods.

Annex table A.1 shows the following:

- If estimates are based on the total number of small states for which information is available in each period, the median rate of growth of per capita GDP fell from 2.1 percent (based on 39 country observations) to 1.7 percent (based on 34 country observations) per year.
- If we restrict attention to small island states, the fall in the median rate of economic growth was more marked: from 2.8 percent (based on 25 observations) to 1.5 percent (based on 20 country observations) per year.
- At the same time, the median rate of growth of per capita GDP increased from
  - 0.3 to 1.7 percent per year for low-income countries,
  - 1.2 to 2.4 percent per year for middle-income countries, and
  - 1.0 to 2.2 percent per year for all countries in the world.

Annex table A.2 is based on all countries for which information is available during 1986–1995 and 1996–2005. It shows the following:

- The median rate of growth of per capita GDP in small states fell from 2.0 to 1.8 percent per year (based on 29 country observations).

- The median rate of growth of per capita GDP in small island states fell from 2.0 to 1.6 percent per year (based on 17 country observations);.
- At the same time, the median rate of growth of per capita GDP increased from
  - 0.3 to 1.6 percent per year for low-income countries,
  - 1 to 2.3 percent per year for middle-income countries, and
  - 1 to 2 percent per year for all countries in the world.

The tables show a clear decline in volatility of growth for small states and low- and middle-income states. Volatility is defined as the standard deviation of the rate of growth in each decade.

Note

1. This calculation is based on a sample of 29 small states for which there is information on per capita GDP during the period 1986–2005. See Tables A.1 and A.2 in Annex A for a detailed explanation of the data.

References

Domeland, Dorte, and Frederico Gil Sander. 2007. "Growth in African Small States." To be available on the Web site for this book.

Duncan, Ron, and Haruo Nakagawa. 2006. "Obstacles to Economic Growth in Six Pacific Island Countries." To be available on the Web site for this book.

ITU (International Telecommunications Union). 2007. *World Telecommunications Indicators*. http://www.itu.int/ITU-D/ict/publications/world/world.html.

Jorgenson, Dale W., and Khuong Vu. 2005. "Information Technology and the World Economy." *Scandinavian Journal of Economics* 107 (4): 631–50.

Kaufmann, Daniel, Aart Kraay, and Massimo Mastruzzi. 2006. "Governance Matters V: Aggregate and Individual Governance Indicators for 1996–2005." World Bank, Washington, DC. http://siteresources.worldbank.org/ INTWBIG OVANTCOR/Resources/1740479-1150402582357/2661829-1158008871 017/gov_matters_5_no_annex.pdf.

Kida, Mizuho. 2006. "Caribbean Small States: Growth Diagnostics." To be available on the Web site for this book.

Thomas, Mark Roland, and Gaobo Pang. 2006. "Lessons From Europe for Economic Policy in Small States." To be available on the Web site for this book.

van Beek, Frits, José Roberto Rosales, Mayra Zermeño, Ruby Randall, and Jorge Shepherd. 2000. "The Eastern Caribbean Currency Union: Performance, Progress, and Policy Issues." Occasional Paper 195, International Monetary Fund, Washington, DC.

Winters, Alan. 2005. "Policy Challenges for Small Economies in a Globalizing World." In *Pacific Islands Regional Integration and Governance*, ed. Satish Chand, 7–25. Canberra, Australia: Asia Pacific Press.

———. 2006. "Small States: Making the Most of Development Assistance: A Synthesis of World Bank Evaluation Findings." Operations Evaluation Studies, Independent Evaluation Group, World Bank, Washington, DC.

———. 2007. *World Development Indicators*. Washington, DC: World Bank.

World Bank. 2005. "Economic Growth and Integration of Small States into the World Economy." To be available on the Web site for this book.

———. 2006. *Small States: Making the Most of Development Assistance: A Synthesis of Evaluation Findings*. Washington, DC: World Bank.

Index